Economics For Dummies

P9-DNZ-202

Cheat Sheet

The Big Definitions

Economics studies how people allocate resources among alternative uses. The reason people have to make choices is *scarcity,* the fact that we don't have enough resources to satisfy all our wants.

Microeconomics studies the maximizing behavior of individual people and individual firms. Economists assume that people work toward maximizing their *utility,* or happiness, while firms act to maximize profits.

Macroeconomics studies national economies, concentrating on economic growth and how to prevent and ameliorate recessions.

Types of Industries

The industries in which firms interact can be grouped into these basic structures:

- *Perfect competition* happens when numerous small firms that all produce identical products compete against each other. Firms produce the socially optimal output level at the minimum possible cost per unit.

- A *monopoly* is a firm that has no competitors. It reduces output to drive up prices and increase profits. By doing so, it produces less than the socially optimal output level and produces at higher costs than competitive firms.

- An *oligopoly* is an industry with only a few firms. If they collude, they reduce output and drive up profits the way a monopoly does. However, oligopoly firms often end up competing against each other.

- *Monopolistic competition* happens when many firms with slightly different products compete. Production costs are above what could be achieved by perfectly competitive firms, but society benefits from the product differentiation.

Market Equilibrium

Buyers and sellers interact in markets. The market equilibrium price, p^*, and equilibrium quantity, q^*, are determined by where the demand curve of the buyers, *D,* crosses the supply curve of the sellers, *S.*

In the absence of *externalities* (costs or benefits that fall on persons not directly involved in an activity), the market equilibrium quantity, q^*, is also the socially optimal output level. For each unit from 0 up to q^*, the demand curve is above the supply curve, meaning that people are willing to pay more to buy those units than they cost to produce. There are gains from producing and then consuming those units.

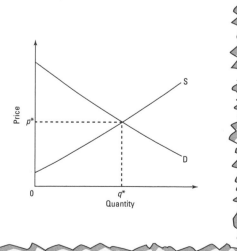

Economics For Dummies®

Cheat Sheet

Market Failures

Several prerequisites must be fulfilled before perfect competition and free markets can work properly and generate the socially optimal output level. Several common problems include:

- **Externalities caused by incomplete or nonexistent property rights:** Without full and complete property rights, markets are unable to take all the costs of production into account.

- **Asymmetric information:** If a buyer or seller has private information that gives her an edge when negotiating a deal, the opposite party may be too suspicious for them to reach a mutually agreeable price. The market may collapse, with no trades being made.

- **Public goods:** Some goods have to be provided by the government or philanthropists. Private firms can't make money producing them because there's no way to exclude non-payers from receiving the good.

Macroeconomics and Government Policy

Economists use *Gross Domestic Product* (GDP) to keep track of how an economy is doing. GDP measures the value of all final goods and services produced in an economy in a given period of time, usually a quarter or a year.

A *recession* occurs when a nation's output of goods and services is decreasing. An *expansion* occurs when output is increasing.

The *unemployment rate* measures what fraction of the labor force cannot find jobs. The unemployment rate rises during recessions and falls during expansions.

Anti-recessionary economic policies come in two flavors:

- *Monetary policy* uses an increase in the money supply to lower interest rates. Lower interest rates make loans for cars, homes, and investment goods cheaper, which means consumption spending by households and investment spending by businesses increase.

- *Fiscal policy* refers to using either an increase in government purchases of goods and services or a decrease in taxes to stimulate the economy. The government purchases increase economic activity directly, while the tax reductions are designed to increase household spending by leaving households more after-tax dollars to spend.

For Dummies: Bestselling Book Series for Beginners

Economics FOR DUMMIES®

By Sean Masaki Flynn, Ph.D.

WILEY

Wiley Publishing, Inc.

Economics For Dummies®

Published by
Wiley Publishing, Inc.
111 River St.
Hoboken, NJ 07030-5774
www.wiley.com

WILEY

About the Author

Sean Flynn earned his Ph.D. in Economics at the University of California, Berkeley, studying under Nobel Prize winners George Akerlof and Daniel McFadden.

He is a member of the American Economic Association, the American Finance Association, the Economic Science Association, and the Society for the Advancement of Behavioral Economics.

His research focuses on the often puzzling and seemingly irrational behavior of stock market investors, but he's also investigated topics as wide-ranging as the factors that affect customer tipping behavior at restaurants and why you see a lot of unionized workers only in certain industries. He's also a leading expert on closed-end mutual funds.

His great passion is the Japanese martial art of aikido, which he has taught for over a decade to thousands of students both in the United States and abroad. If you like the martial arts, you might enjoy reading his book, *Shodokan Aikido: Basics Through 6th Kyu,* which gives insight into both the mental and physical aspects of aikido.

Finally, he's gone out of his way to post extensive supplementary material for this book at www.learn-economics.com. Go check it out.

Dedication

To my dad, Thomas Ray Flynn, who always impressed upon me the importance of good economic policy both for improving our quality of life and as our last, best hope for lifting billions out of poverty and disease.

Author's Acknowledgments

I'd like to thank the many great economists who managed to get things into my head despite my very thick skull.

Among my teachers, I can't help but thank Caroline Betts, Tim Cason, Richard Ciccetti, Michael DePrano, Richard Easterlin, Robert Kalaba, Timur Kuran, Jeffrey Nugent, and Morton Shapiro for the excellent education I received as an undergraduate at the University of Southern California.

I was equally blessed at UC Berkeley, where I got to complete a doctorate under the tutelage of some true intellectual giants including George Akerlof, David Card, J. Bradford DeLong, Jan deVries, Barry Eichengreen, Richard Gilbert, Daniel McFadden, Maurey Obstfeld, Matthew Rabin, David Romer, Christina Romer, and Janet Yellen. It was especially fun when Professors McFadden and Akerlof won their respective Nobel Prizes during my last two years at Cal.

However, my fellow economics students often did more than my professors to explain things to me when I wasn't getting them. And they continue to educate me even now. So a very heartfelt thank you to Corinne Alexander, Lorenzo Blanco, Mark Carlson, Carlos Dobkin, Tim Doede, Mike Enriquez, Fabio Ghironi, Petra Geraats, Aaron Green, Galina Hale, Alan Marco, Carolina Marquez, Marcelo Moreira, Petra Moser, Marc Muendler, Stefan Palmqvist, Doug Park, Raj Patel, Steve Puller, Desiree Schaan, Doug Schwalm, Mark Stehr, Sam Thompson, Carla Tully, Jeff Weinstein, and Marta Wosinska.

I've also got to thank my students here at Vassar College. You're bright, diligent, and incredibly hardworking. By asking me so many challenging, insightful questions, you've made me a far better economist.

A big thank you to my literary agent Linda Roghaar and my old friend Mike Jones for getting me this book deal. They heard *Dummies* and immediately thought of me.

Alissa Schwipps, Joan Friedman, and the entire production team at Wiley also deserve huge praise. All their edits, suggestions, and formatting have turned out a book that's far better than anything I could have come up with on my own.

I also have to deeply thank Dr. Robert Harris, the technical editor of this book. His comments and suggestions have made it far better than it would have been otherwise.

Finally, I must thank Melissa Lape. She read every last bit of copy and made numerous suggestions that helped make *Economics For Dummies* both clear and concise.

If you've had the patience to read this far, you'll also likely have an inclination to go check out www.learn-economics.com, where I've posted lots of supplementary material to accompany *Economics For Dummies*. You just can't get enough, can you?

Publisher's Acknowledgments

We're proud of this book; please send us your comments through our Dummies online registration form located at www.dummies.com/register/.

Some of the people who helped bring this book to market include the following:

Acquisitions, Editorial, and Media Development

Project Editors: Joan Friedman, Alissa Schwipps

Acquisitions Editor: Tracy Boggier

Technical Editor: Robert Harris, Ph.D.

Editorial Manager: Michelle Hacker

Editorial Supervisor: Carmen Krikorian

Editorial Assistant: Courtney Allen, Nadine Bell

Cover Photos: © Annabelle Breakey/ Getty Images/Stone

Cartoons: Rich Tennant, www.the5thwave.com

Composition

Project Coordinator: Adrienne Martinez

Layout and Graphics: Lauren Goddard, Denny Hager Barry Offringa, Melanee Prendergast, Heather Ryan, Mary Gillot Virgin

Proofreaders: Leeann Harney, Jessica Kramer, Joe Niesen, Carl William Pierce, TECHBOOKS Production services

Indexer: TECHBOOKS Production Services

Publishing and Editorial for Consumer Dummies

    Diane Graves Steele, Vice President and Publisher, Consumer Dummies

    Joyce Pepple, Acquisitions Director, Consumer Dummies

    Kristin A. Cocks, Product Development Director, Consumer Dummies

    Michael Spring, Vice President and Publisher, Travel

    Kelly Regan, Editorial Director, Travel

Publishing for Technology Dummies

    Andy Cummings, Vice President and Publisher, Dummies Technology/General User

Composition Services

    Gerry Fahey, Vice President of Production Services

    Debbie Stailey, Director of Composition Services

Contents at a Glance

Table of Contents

Introduction

. . . .

*E*conomics is all about humanity's struggle to achieve happiness in a world full of constraints. There's never enough time or money to do everything people want. And things like curing cancer are still impossible because the necessary technologies haven't yet been developed.

But people are clever. They tinker and invent, ponder and innovate. They look at what they have and what they can do with it and take steps to make sure that if they can't have everything, they'll at least have as much as possible.

Making tradeoffs is key. Because you can't have everything, you have to make choices. For instance, you have to choose whether to save or spend, whether to stay in school or get a job, and whether the government should spend more money on elementary education or on cancer research.

Having to choose is a fundamental part of everyday life. The science that studies *how* people choose — economics — is indispensable if you really want to understand human beings both as individuals and as members of larger organizations.

Sadly, though, economics has typically been explained so badly that people either dismiss it as impenetrable gobbledygook or stand falsely in awe of it — after all, if it's hard to understand, it must be important, right?

I wrote this book so you can quickly and easily understand economics for what it is — a serious science that studies a serious subject and has developed some seriously good ways of explaining human behavior out in the (very serious) real world. If you read this book, you'll understand much more about people, the government, international relations, business, and even environmental issues like global warming and endangered species. Economics touches on nearly everything, so the returns on reading this book are huge.

About This Book

In this book, you find the most important economic theories, hypotheses, and discoveries without a zillion obscure details, outdated examples, or complicated mathematical "proofs." Among the topics covered are

- How the government fights recessions and unemployment using monetary and fiscal policy

- How and why international trade is good for us

- Why poorly designed property rights are responsible for environmental problems like global warming, pollution, and species extinctions

- How profits guide businesses to produce the goods and services we take for granted

- Why competitive firms are almost always better for society than monopolies

- How the Federal Reserve controls the money supply, interest rates, and inflation all at the same time

- Why government policies like price controls and subsidies typically cause much more harm than good

- How the simple supply and demand model can explain the prices of everything from comic books to open-heart surgeries

I do my best to explain these things, and much more, clearly and directly. I've also structured this book to put *you* in control. You can read the chapters in any order, and you can immediately jump to what you need to know without having to read a bunch of stuff that you couldn't care less about.

Economists like competition, so you shouldn't be surprised that there are a lot of competing views and paradigms among us. Indeed, it's only through vigorous debate and careful review of the evidence that the profession improves its understanding of how the world works.

In this book, I try to steer clear of fads or ideas that foster a lot of disagreement. This book contains core ideas and concepts that economists agree are true and important. (If you want to be subjected to my personal opinions and pet theories, you'll have to buy me a drink.)

However, economists have honest disagreements about how to present even the core concepts, so I've had to make some decisions about organization and structure. For example, I present macroeconomics using a Keynesian framework even when I explain some rather non-Keynesian concepts. (If you don't know who this Keynes fellow is or what makes him so *Keynesian,* don't worry — I introduce him to you later in the book.) Some people may quibble with this, but I think it makes for a succinct presentation.

Conventions Used in This Book

Economics is full of two things you may not find very appealing: jargon and algebra. To minimize confusion, whenever I introduce a new term, I put it in *italics* and follow it closely with an easy-to-understand definition. Also, whenever I bring algebra into the discussion, I use those handy *italics* again to let you know that I'm referring to an algebraic element. For instance, *I* indicates investment, so you may see a sentence like this one: I think that *I* is too big.

I try to keep equations to a minimum, but sometimes they actually help to make things clearer. In such instances, I sometimes have to use several equations one after another. To avoid confusion about which equation I'm referring to at any given time, I give each equation a number, which I put in parentheses. For example,

$$MTV = ESPN + CNN^2 \tag{1}$$

Finally, the following conventions are used throughout the text of all *For Dummies* books to make things consistent and easy to understand:

- ✔ All Web addresses appear in `this font`.
- ✔ **Bold** is used to highlight the action parts of numbered steps.

What You're Not to Read

The whole point of a *For Dummies* book is to give you quick access to the essentials so you don't have to wade through a bunch of stories, factoids, and anecdotes. On the other hand, sometimes stories, factoids, and anecdotes can be both fun and enlightening.

But even if they are, that doesn't mean you should be forced to read them. Consequently, I've clearly identified all the "skippable" material. This information is the stuff that, although interesting and related to the topic at hand, isn't essential for you to know:

- ✔ **Text in sidebars:** The sidebars are shaded boxes that share interesting stories and observations but aren't necessary reading.
- ✔ **Anything with a Technical Stuff icon attached:** This information is interesting but not critical to your understanding of what's being explained.
- ✔ **The stuff on the acknowledgements page:** Unless you're one of my friends who needs an ego stroke, there's nothing here for you.

Naturally, I'd like to believe that you'll choose to read *everything* I've written, but don't worry. I'll never know.

Foolish Assumptions

I wrote this book assuming some things about you:

- You're sharp, thoughtful, and interested in how the world works.

- You're a high school or college student trying to flesh out what you're learning in class, or you're a citizen of the world who realizes that a good grounding in economics will help you understand everything from business and politics to social issues like poverty and environmental degradation.

- You want to know some economics, but you're also busy leading a very full life. Consequently, while you want the crucial facts, you don't want to have to read through a bunch of minutia to find them.

- You're not totally intimidated by numbers, facts, and figures. Indeed, you welcome them because you like to have things proven to you rather than taking them on faith because some pinhead with a Ph.D. says so.

- You like learning *why* as well as *what*. That is, you want to know why things happen and how they work rather than just memorizing factoids.

- Finally, you're better-looking than average and have a good sense of style. In particular, you really love this book's snazzy yellow and black cover and feel almost hypnotically compelled to buy a copy.

How This Book Is Organized

This book is divided into four parts to make the material easier to understand and access. Part I covers the big concepts that motivate how economists look at the world. Parts II and III follow the traditional division of economics into two halves: *Macroeconomics* deals with big-picture issues like recessions and international trade, while *microeconomics* focuses on individual people, businesses, and industries. Part IV is The Part of Tens and contains a few fun but informative top-ten lists.

Part I: Economics — The Science of How People Deal with Scarcity

Economics is all about how people deal with scarcity. There's never enough time, and there's only a finite supply of natural resources like oil and iron. Consequently, people have to be clever about getting the most out of life — choosing wisely about what to do with the limited resources they're given.

Part I explains how people go about dealing with scarcity and the tradeoffs that it forces them to make. The rest of economics is just seeing how scarcity forces people to make tradeoffs in more specific situations.

Part II: Macroeconomics — The Science of Economic Growth and Stability

Macroeconomics views the economy from on high, at the national or international level. It deals with the choices countries face about economic growth and development and about how to best manage their economies to avoid recessions, and it deals with the misery caused by things like unemployment and inflation. In this part, you find out about monetary and fiscal policy, the Federal Reserve, the effects of taxation on the economy, and international trade and trade policy.

Part III: Microeconomics — The Science of Consumer and Firm Behavior

Microeconomics focuses on the behavior of individual people and individual firms. It studies what motivates them and how they act to achieve their goals given the constraints they face. In this part, you discover what motivates firms to produce output, how buyers and sellers interact in markets to allocate that output, and how markets can break down and do perverse things if not properly managed. You also find out about supply and demand, competition, monopolies, Adam Smith's Invisible Hand, and lots of nifty applications of economics to things like insurance markets and environmental issues. Economics really does get into everything.

Part IV: The Part of Tens

Every *For Dummies* book ends with top-ten lists that are both helpful and fun. In this part, I give you short bios of famous economists (explaining what they discovered and why it was so important), economic ideas to hold dear, and false economic assertions that you probably hear repeated all the time in the media and by self-serving politicians.

Icons Used in This Book

To make this book easier to read and simpler to use, I include a few icons that can help you find and fathom key ideas and information.

This icon alerts you that I'm explaining a really fundamental economic concept or fact. It saves you the time and effort of marking up the book with a highlighter.

Economics is chock full of theories, and sometimes it's helpful to kick those theories out into the real world and see how they actually work. This icon alerts you that a helpful example with real-world application is nearby.

This icon tells you that the ideas and information that it accompanies are a bit more technical or mathematical than other sections of the book. This information can be interesting and informative, but I've designed the book so that you don't need to understand it to get the big picture about what's going on. Feel free to skip this stuff.

This icon points out time and energy savers. I place this icon next to suggestions for ways to do or think about things that can save you some effort.

Where to Go from Here

This book is set up so that you can jump in anywhere and understand what you're reading. For example:

- Want to get the skinny on how the Federal Reserve changes interest rates to stimulate the economy and fight recessions? Jump right to Chapter 7.

- Want to know about environmental economics and how most environmental problems are caused by poorly designed property rights? Open the book to Chapter 14.

- Need to figure out why everyone talks about supply and demand? Hit Chapter 8.

The book is also divided into independent parts so that you can, for instance, read all about microeconomics without having to read anything about macroeconomics. And the table of contents and index can help you find specific topics easily.

But, hey, if you don't know where to begin, just do the old-fashioned thing and start at the beginning. As my favorite song from the movie *The Sound of Music* says, "Let's start at the very beginning! A very good place to start."

Part I

Economics — The Science of How People Deal with Scarcity

The 5th Wave   By Rich Tennant

"I think this is an economic strategy that everyone can get behind. It's high in unemployment, high in inflation, but low in carbohydrates."

In this part . . .

Economics studies how people deal with scarcity and the inescapable fact that our wants typically exceed the means available for satisfying them. The fact that life has limits may not at first seem like a good basis for an entire social science, but every government decision, every business decision, and a large chunk of your personal decisions all basically come down to deciding how to get the most out of limited resources. Consequently, as I explain in this part, economics is fundamental to nearly all aspects of life.

Chapter 1

What Does Economics Study?
And Why Should You Care?

- -

In This Chapter

▶ Taking a quick peek at economic history

▶ Observing how people cope with scarcity

▶ Separating macroeconomics and microeconomics

▶ Growing the economy and avoiding recessions

▶ Understanding individual and firm behavior

▶ Getting a grip on the graphs and models that economists love to use

- -

*E*conomics is the science that studies how people and societies make decisions that allow them to get the most out of their limited resources. And because every country, every business, and every person has to deal with constraints and limitations, economics is literally everywhere.

For instance, you could be doing something else right now besides reading this book. You could be exercising. Watching a movie. Talking with a friend. The only reason you should be reading this book is if it's the best possible use of your very limited time.

In the same way, you should hope that the paper and ink used to make this book have been put to their very best use and that every last tax dollar that your government spends is being used in the best possible way and isn't being dissipated on projects of secondary importance.

Economics gets to the heart of these issues, analyzing individual and firm behavior, as well as social and political institutions, to see how well they perform at converting humanity's limited resources into the goods and services that best satisfy human wants and needs.

Considering a Little Economic History

To better understand today's economic situation and what sort of policy and institutional changes may promote the greatest improvements, you have to look back on economic history to see how humanity got where it is now. Stick with me: I'll make this as painless as possible for you history haters.

Pondering just how nasty, brutish, and short life used to be

For most of human history, people didn't manage to squeeze much out of their limited resources. Standards of living were quite low, and people lived poor, short, and rather painful lives. Consider the following facts, which didn't change until just a few centuries ago:

- Life expectancy at birth was about 25 years.

- More than 30 percent of newborns never made it to their fifth birthdays.

- A woman had a one in ten chance of dying during childbirth.

- Most people had personal experience with horrible diseases and/or starvation.

- The standard of living for one generation was no higher than that for previous generations. Except for the nobles, everybody lived at or near subsistence level, century after century.

In the last 250 years or so, however, everything changed. For the first time in history, people figured out how to use electricity, engines, complicated machines, computers, radio, television, biotechnology, scientific agriculture, antibiotics, aviation, and a host of other technologies. Each has allowed us to do much more with the limited amounts of air, water, soil, and sea that people were given on planet Earth.

The result has been an explosion in living standards, with life expectancy at birth now well over 60 years worldwide and with many people able to afford much better housing, clothing, and food than was even imaginable a few hundred years ago.

Of course, not everything is perfect. Grinding poverty is still a fact in a large fraction of the world, and even the richest nations have to cope with pressing economic problems like unemployment and how to transition workers from dying industries to growing industries.

But the fact remains that the modern world is a much richer place than its predecessor, and we now have sustained economic growth in most nations, which means that living standards rise year after year.

Identifying the institutions that led to higher living standards

The obvious reason for higher living standards, which continue to rise, is that human beings have recently figured out lots of new technologies, and we keep inventing more. But if you dig a little deeper, you have to wonder why a technologically innovative society didn't happen earlier.

The ancient Greeks invented a simple steam engine and the coin-operated vending machine. They even developed the basic idea behind the programmable computer. But they never quite got around to having an industrial revolution and entering on a path of sustained economic growth.

And despite the fact that there have always been really smart people in every society on earth, it wasn't until the late 18th century, in England, that the Industrial Revolution actually got started and living standards in many nations rose substantially and kept on rising, year after year.

So what factors combined in the late 18th century to so radically accelerate economic growth? The short answer is that the following institutions were in place:

- **Democracy:** Because the common people outnumbered the nobles, the advent of democracy meant that for the first time governments reflected the interests of a society at large. A major result was the creation of government policy that favored merchants and manufacturers rather than the nobility.

- **The limited liability corporation:** Under this business structure, investors could lose only the amount of their investment and not be liable for any debts that the corporation couldn't pay. Limited liability greatly reduced the risks of investing in businesses and, consequently, led to much more investing.

- **Patent rights to protect inventors:** Before patents, inventors usually saw their ideas stolen before they could make any money. By giving inventors the exclusive right to market and sell their inventions, patents gave a financial incentive to produce lots of inventions. Indeed, after patents came into existence, the world saw its first full-time inventors — people who made a living inventing things.

- **Widespread literacy and education:** Without highly educated inventors, new technologies don't get invented. And without an educated workforce, they can't be mass-produced. Consequently, the decision that many nations made to make primary and then secondary education mandatory paved the way for rapid and sustained economic growth.

Institutions and policies like these have given us a world of growth and opportunity and an abundance so unprecedented in world history that the greatest public health problem in many countries today is obesity.

Looking toward the future

The challenge moving forward is to get even more of what people want out of the world's limited pool of resources. This challenge needs to be faced because a lot of problems still exist in the world that could be alleviated by higher living standards.

Some problems, like grinding poverty, can be cured by extending to poorer nations the institutions that have already been proven in richer nations to lead to rising living standards. But other problems, like the pollution and resource depletion that come with the institutional structures used in richer nations, will require new inventions and new institutions.

Consequently, there are two related and very good reasons for you to read this book and learn some economics:

- ✔ First, you'll discover how modern economies function. That'll give you an understanding not only of how they've so greatly raised living standards but also of where they need some improvement.

- ✔ Second, by getting a thorough handle on fundamental economic principles, you'll be able to judge for yourself the economic policy proposals that politicians and others run around promoting. After reading this book, you'll be much better able to sort the good from the bad.

Sending Macroeconomics and Microeconomics to Separate Corners

I've organized this book to try to get as much economics into you as quickly and effortlessly as possible. I've also done my best to keep it lively and fun. The English poet Thomas Carlyle called economics the "dismal science," but that ticks me off, and I'm going to do my best to make sure that you don't come to agree with him.

The main organizing principle I use in this book is to divide economics into two broad pieces, macroeconomics and microeconomics:

- *Macroeconomics* looks at the economy as an organic whole, concentrating on economy-wide factors like interest rates, inflation, and unemployment. It also encompasses the study of economic growth and how governments use monetary and fiscal policy to try to moderate the harm caused by recessions.

- *Microeconomics* focuses on individual people and individual businesses. For individuals, it explains how they behave when faced with decisions about where to spend their money or how to invest their savings. For businesses, it explains how profit-maximizing firms behave individually, as well as when competing against each other in markets.

Underlying both microeconomics and macroeconomics are some basic principles like scarcity and diminishing returns. Consequently, I spend the rest of Part I explaining these fundamentals before diving into macroeconomics in Part II and microeconomics in Part III.

Most of the rest of this chapter serves as a teaser for the rest of the book, so if you want to be surprised later on, you'd be better off flipping some pages right now. The exception is the last section, where I talk about how economists use charts and graphs. If you need some brushing up on how to read charts and graphs, read that section before jumping into other chapters.

Framing Economics As the Science of Scarcity

Scarcity is the fundamental and unavoidable phenomenon that creates a need for the science of economics. Without scarcity of time, scarcity of resources, scarcity of information, scarcity of consumable goods, and scarcity of peace and goodwill on Earth, human beings would lack for nothing.

Indeed, without scarcity, your life would be like that of the hard-partying couple in the Eagles' song "Life in the Fast Lane." That is, you'd have "everything, all the time."

Sadly, though, scarcity is a fact. There isn't nearly enough time or stuff to satisfy all desires, so people have to make hard choices about what to produce and consume so that if they can't have everything, they at least have the best that was possible under the circumstances. Chapter 2 gets deep into scarcity and the tradeoffs that it causes people to make.

Chapter 3 builds on Chapter 2 by showing you how economists analyze the decisions people make about how to best maximize human happiness in a world of scarcity. That process turns out to be intimately connected with a phenomenon known as *diminishing returns,* which describes the sad fact that each additional amount of a resource that's thrown at a production process brings forth successively smaller amounts of output.

Like scarcity, diminishing returns is unavoidable, and in Chapter 3, I explain how people very cleverly deal with this phenomenon in order to get the most out of humanity's limited pool of resources.

Zooming Out: Macroeconomics and the Big Picture

Part II of this book covers macroeconomics, which treats the economy as a unified whole. Studying macroeconomics is useful because certain factors, such as interest rates and tax policy, have economy-wide effects, and also because when the economy goes into a recession or a boom, every person and every business is affected.

Measuring the economy

In Chapter 4, I show you how economists measure *gross domestic product* (GDP), the value of all goods and services produced in the economy in a given period of time, usually a quarter or a year. Totaling up this number is absolutely vital because if you can't measure how the economy is doing, you can't tell whether government polices intended to improve the economy are helping or hurting.

Inflation measures how prices in the economy change over time. This topic, which is the focus of Chapter 5, is crucial because high rates of inflation usually accompany huge economic problems, including deep recessions and countries defaulting on their debts.

It's also important to study inflation because poor government policy is the sole culprit behind high rates of inflation — meaning that governments are totally responsible when big inflations happen.

Recognizing what causes recessions

Recessions linger only because institutional factors in the economy make it very hard for prices in the economy to fall. As I explain in Chapter 6, if prices *could* fall quickly and easily, recessions would quickly resolve themselves. But because prices can't quickly and easily fall, economists have had to develop antirecessionary policies to help get economies out of recessions as quickly as possible.

Fighting recessions with monetary and fiscal policies

The man most responsible for developing antirecessionary policies was the English economist John Maynard Keynes, who in 1936 wrote the first macro-economics book about fighting recessions. Chapter 6 introduces you to his model of the economy and how it explicitly takes account of the fact that prices can't quickly and easily fall to get you out of recessions. Because it takes that into account, it serves as the perfect vehicle for illustrating the two things that *can* help get you out of a recession.

These two things are monetary and fiscal policy, which are covered in-depth in Chapter 7:

✔ Monetary policy uses changes in the money supply to change interest rates in order to stimulate economic activity. For instance, if the government causes interest rates to fall, consumers borrow more money to buy things like houses and cars, thereby stimulating economic activity and helping to get the economy moving faster.

✔ Fiscal policy refers to using increased government spending or lower tax rates to help fight recessions. For instance, if the government buys more goods and services, economic activity increases. In a similar fashion, if the government cuts tax rates, consumers end up with higher after-tax incomes, which, when spent, increase economic activity.

In the first decades after Keynes's antirecessionary ideas were put into practice, they seemed to work really well. However, they didn't fare so well during the 1970s, and it became apparent that while monetary and fiscal policy were powerful antirecessionary tools, they had their limitations.

For this reason, Chapter 7 also covers how and why monetary and fiscal policy are constrained in their effectiveness. The key concept is called *rational expectations*. It explains how rational people very often change their behavior in response to policy changes in ways that limit the effectiveness of those changes. It's a concept that you need to understand if you're going to come up with informed opinions about current macroeconomic policy debates.

Getting Up Close and Personal: Microeconomics

While macroeconomics is concerned with government policies to improve the overall economy, microeconomics gets down to the nitty gritty, studying the most fundamental economic agents: individuals and firms.

Balancing supply and demand

In a modern economy, individuals and firms produce and consume everything that gets made. Consequently, Part III's coverage of microeconomics begins in Chapter 8 by focusing on how supply and demand determine prices and output levels in competitive markets. This is a logical place to begin because producers determine supply, consumers determine demand, and their interaction in markets determines what gets made and how much it costs.

Chapter 9 digs in deeper to see how individuals make economic decisions about how to get the most happiness out of their limited incomes. These decisions generate the demand curves that affect prices and output levels in markets.

In a similar way, the profit-maximizing decisions of firms generate the supply curves that affect markets. In Chapter 10, I explain how that happens, and I also explain how profit-maximizing firms actually go about maximizing their profits. If you've ever had some nasty thoughts about capitalism, this chapter will put you eyeball-to-eyeball with the enemy.

Considering why competition is so great

You may not feel warm and fuzzy about profit-maximizing firms, but economists love them — just as long as they're stuck in competitive industries. The reason, briefly, is that firms that are forced to compete end up satisfying two wonderful conditions:

- ✔ First, they're *allocatively efficient,* which simply means that they produce the goods and services that consumers most greatly desire to consume.

- ✔ Second, they're *productively efficient,* which means that they produce these goods and services at the lowest possible cost.

 These two great facts about competitive firms are the basis of Adam Smith's famous *invisible hand* — the idea that when constrained by competition, each firm's greed ends up causing it to act in a socially optimal way, as if guided to do the right thing by an invisible hand. I discuss this idea, and much more about the benefits of competition, in Chapter 11.

Examining problems caused by lack of competition

Unfortunately, not every firm is constrained by competition. And when that happens, firms don't end up acting in socially optimal ways.

The most extreme case is *monopoly,* a situation where there's only one firm in an industry — meaning that it has absolutely no competition. As I explain in Chapter 12, monopolies behave very badly, restricting output in order to drive up prices and inflate profits. These actions, which hurt consumers, go on indefinitely unless the government takes steps to regulate the firm's behavior.

A less extreme case of lack of competition is *oligopoly,* a situation where there are only a few firms in an industry. In such situations, firms often make deals to not compete against each other so that they can keep prices high and make bigger profits.

In Chapter 13, I examine oligopoly firms in-depth. I explain not only how they misbehave but also the fact that they often have a hard time keeping their agreements with each other to maintain high prices and high profits. This fact means that oligopoly firms often end up competing against each other despite their best efforts not to. Consequently, government regulation isn't always needed.

Reforming property rights

Markets and competition can only be relied upon to produce socially beneficial results if society sets up a good system of property rights. Almost all pollution issues, as well as all cases of species loss, are the direct result of poorly designed property rights generating perverse incentives to do bad things. Economists take this problem very seriously and have done their best to reform property rights in order to alleviate pollution and eliminate species loss. I discuss these issues in detail in Chapter 14.

Dealing with other common market failures

Monopolies, oligopolies, and poorly designed property rights all lead to what economists like to call *market failures* — situations where markets deliver socially nonoptimal outcomes. Two other common causes of market failure are asymmetric information and public goods:

✔ *Asymmetric information* refers to situations in which either the buyer or the seller knows more about the quality of the good that they're negotiating over than does the other party. Because of the uneven playing field and the suspicions it creates, a lot of potentially beneficial economic transactions never get completed.

> ✔ *Public goods* refer to goods or services that are impossible to provide to just one person; if you provide them to one person, you have to provide them to everybody. (Think of a fireworks display, for example.) The problem is that most people try to get the benefit without paying for it.

I discuss both these situations, and ways to deal with them, in Chapter 15.

Understanding How Economists Use Models and Graphs

Economists like to be logical and precise, which is why they use a lot of algebra and math. But they also like to present their ideas in easy-to-understand and highly intuitive ways, which is why they use so many graphs. To avoid a graph-induced panic as you flip through the pages of this book, I want to spend a few pages helping you get acquainted with what you're going to encounter in other chapters. Take a deep breath; I promise this won't hurt.

Abstracting from reality is a good thing

The graphs economists use are almost always visual representations of economic models. An *economic model* is a mathematical simplification of reality that allows you to focus on what's really important by ignoring lots of irrelevant details.

For instance, the economist's model of consumer demand focuses on how prices affect the amounts of goods and services that people want to buy. Obviously, other things, such as changing styles and tastes, affect consumer demand as well, but price is key. Let's consider orange juice, for example. The price of orange juice is the major thing that affects how much orange juice people are going to buy. (I don't care what dietary trend is in vogue — if orange juice cost $50 a gallon, you'd probably find another diet.) Therefore, it's helpful to abstract from those other things and concentrate solely on how the price of orange juice affects the quantity of orange juice that people want to buy.

Introducing your first model: The demand curve

Suppose that economists go out and survey consumers, asking them how many gallons of orange juice they would buy each month at three hypothetical prices: $10 per gallon, $5 per gallon, and $1 per gallon. The results are summarized in Table 1-1.

Table 1-1	Gallons of Orange Juice That Consumers Want to Buy
Price	*Gallons*
$10	1
$5	6
$1	10

Economists refer to the quantities that people would be willing to purchase at various prices as the *quantity demanded,* or *the demand,* at those prices. What you find if you look at the data in Table 1-1 is that the price of orange juice and the quantity demanded of orange juice have an *inverse relationship* with each other — meaning that when one goes up, the other goes down.

Because this inverse relationship between price and quantity demanded is so universal and holds true for nearly all goods and services, economists refer to it as the *Law of Demand.* But, quite frankly, the Law of Demand becomes much more immediate and interesting if you can *see* it rather than just think about it.

Creating the demand curve by plotting out data

The best way to *see* the data in Table 1-1 is to plot it out on a chart. In Figure 1-1, I've marked three points and labeled them *A, B,* and *C.* The horizontal axis of Figure 1-1 measures the number of gallons of orange juice that people demand each month at various prices per gallon. The vertical axis measures the prices.

Point *A* is the visual representation of the data in the top row of Table 1-1. It tells you that at a price of $10 per gallon, people want to purchase only 1 gallon per month of orange juice. Similarly, point *B* tells you that they demand 6 gallons per month at a price of $5, while point *C* tells you that they demand 10 gallons per month at a price of $1 per gallon.

Notice that I've connected the points *A, B,* and *C* with a line. I've done this to make up for the fact that the economists who conducted the survey asked about what people would do at only three prices. If they had had a big enough budget to ask consumers about every possible price ($8.46 per gallon, $2.23 per gallon, and so on), there would be an infinite number of dots on the graph. But since they didn't do that, I interpolate by drawing a straight line. The line should do a pretty good job of estimating what people's demands are for prices that the economists didn't survey.

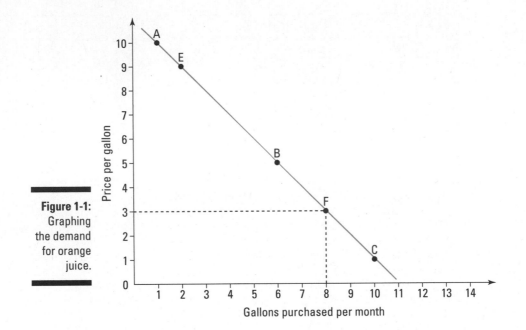

Figure 1-1:
Graphing
the demand
for orange
juice.

The straight line connecting the points in Figure 1-1 is called a *demand curve*. I know it doesn't curve at all, but for simplicity, economists use the term *demand curve* to refer to all plotted relationships between price and quantity demanded, regardless of whether they're straight lines or curvy lines. (This convention is consistent with the fact that economists are both eggheads *and* squares.)

Straight or curvy, you can now *visualize* the fact that price and quantity demanded have an inverse relationship. The inverse relationship implies that demand curves slope downward. You can now see that when price goes up, quantity demanded goes down.

Using the demand curve to make predictions

Graphing out the demand curve also allows for a much greater ability to make quick predictions. For instance, the straight line I've drawn in Figure 1-1 can be used to estimate that at a price of $9 per gallon, people would want to buy about 2 gallons per month of orange juice. I've labeled this point *E* on the graph.

Suppose that you could only see the data in Table 1-1 and couldn't look at Figure 1-1. Could you quickly estimate for me how many gallons per month people are likely to demand if the price of orange juice is $3 per gallon? Looking at the second and third rows of Table 1-1, you have to conclude that people will demand somewhere between 6 and 10 gallons per month. But figuring out exactly how many gallons will be demanded would take some time and require some annoying algebra.

If you look at Figure 1-1, it's easy to figure out how many gallons per month people would demand. You just start at the price $3 on the vertical axis, move sideways to the right until you hit the demand curve at point *F*, and drop down vertically until you get to the horizontal axis, where you discover that you're at 8 gallons per month. (To clarify what I mean, I've drawn in a dotted line that follows this path.)

As you can see, using a figure rather than a table makes coming up with model-based predictions much, much simpler.

Drawing your own demand curve

To make sure you're comfortable using graphs, I encourage you to do a simple exercise that involves plotting some points and drawing lines between them. That's not so hard, right?

Imagine that the government came out with a research report showing that people who drink orange juice have lower blood pressure, fewer strokes, and a better sex life than people who don't drink orange juice. What do you think will happen to the demand for orange juice? Obviously, it should increase.

To verify this, our intrepid team of survey economists goes out once again and asks people how much orange juice they would now like to buy each month at each of the three prices listed in Table 1-1: $10, $5, and $1. The new responses are given in Table 1-2.

Table 1-2	Gallons of Orange Juice That Consumers Want to Buy after Reading New Government Research
Price	*Gallons*
$10	4
$5	9
$1	13

Your assignment, should you choose to accept it, is to plot these three points on Figure 1-1. After you've done that, connect them with a straight line. (Yes, you can write in the book!)

What you've just created is a new demand curve that reflects people's new preferences for orange juice in light of the government survey. Their increased demand is reflected in the fact that at any given price, they now demand a larger quantity of juice than they did before. For instance, whereas before they wanted only 1 gallon per month at a price of $10, they now would be willing to buy 4 gallons per month at that price.

There is still, of course, an inverse relationship between price and quantity demanded, meaning that even though the health benefits of orange juice make people demand more orange juice, people are still sensitive to higher orange juice prices. Higher prices still mean lower quantities demanded, and your new demand curve still slopes downward.

Ready for one last exercise before you dive into the rest of the book? Use your new demand curve to figure out how many gallons per month people are now going to want to buy at a price of $7 and at a price of $2. Figuring these things out from the data in Table 1-2 would be hard, but figuring them out using your new demand curve should be easy.

Chapter 2

Cookies or Ice Cream? Tracking Consumer Choices

. . . .

In This Chapter

▶ Deciding what brings the most happiness

▶ Cataloguing the constraints that limit choice

▶ Modeling choice behavior like an economist

▶ Evaluating the limitations of the choice model

. . . .

*E*conomics is all about *how* groups and individuals make choices and *why* they choose the things that they do. Economists have spent a great deal of time analyzing how groups make choices, but because group choice behavior usually turns out to be very similar to individual choice behavior, my focus in this chapter is on individuals.

To keep things simple, my explanation of individual choice behavior focuses on *consumer behavior* because most of the choices people make on a day-to-day basis involve which goods and services to consume. But, of course, real life choices often encompass a lot of other things, some of them very weighty. For example, people must make choices about long-term things like whether to get a job or continue in school, as well as things of the greatest possible seriousness like whether to continue negotiating or declare war.

Human beings are constantly forced to choose because our wants almost always exceed our means. Limited resources, or *scarcity,* is at the heart not only of economics but also of ecology and biology. Darwinian evolution is all about animals and plants competing over limited resources to produce the greatest number of progeny. Economics is about human beings choosing among limited options to maximize happiness.

Considering a Model of Human Behavior

Human beings may be complicated creatures with sometimes mystifying behavior, but most people are usually fairly predictable and consistent, and they behave pretty much like other people. As a result, a lot can be gained by studying choice behavior because if we can understand the choices people made in the past, we stand a very good chance of understanding the choices they'll make in the future.

Understanding (and even predicting) future choice behavior is very important because major shifts in the economic environment are typically the result of millions of small individual decisions that add up to a major trend. For instance, the circumstances under which millions of individuals choose to pursue work or school cumulate to major effects on the unemployment rate. And the choices these individuals make about how much of their paychecks to save or spend affect whether interest rates will be high or low and also whether gross domestic product (GDP) and overall economic output will increase or decrease. (I discuss the GDP in Chapter 4.)

In order to predict how self-interested individuals make their choices, economists have created a model of human behavior that assumes rationality and the ability to calculate subtle tradeoffs between possible choices. This model is a three-stage process:

1. **Evaluate how happy each possible option can make you.**

2. **Look at the constraints and tradeoffs limiting your options.**

3. **Choose the option that maximizes your overall happiness.**

While not a fully complete description of human choice behavior, this model generally makes accurate predictions. However, many people question this explanation of human behavior. Here are three common objections:

✔ Are people really so self-interested? Aren't people often motivated by what's best for others?

✔ Are people really aware at all times of all their options? How are they supposed to rationally choose among new things that they have never tried before?

✔ Are people really free to make decisions? Aren't they constrained by legal, moral, and social standards?

I spend the next few sections of this chapter expanding on the three-step economic choice model and addressing the objections to it.

Maximizing Happiness Is the Objective

Economists like to think of human beings as free agents, with free wills. To economists, people are fully rational and capable of deciding things on their own. But that begs the question of what motivates people and, in turn, of what sorts of things people will choose to do given their free wills.

In a nutshell, economists assume that the basic motivation driving most people most of the time is a desire to be happy. This assumption implies that people make choices on the basis of whether or not those choices will make them as happy as they can be given their circumstances.

Using utility to measure happiness

If people make choices on the basis of which ones will bring them the most happiness, they need a way of comparing how much happiness each possible thing brings with it. Along these lines, economists assume that people get a sense of satisfaction or pleasure from the things life offers. Sunsets are nice. Eating ice cream is nice. Friendship is nice. And I happen to like driving fast.

Economists suppose that you can compare all possible things that you may experience with a common measure of happiness or satisfaction that they call *utility*. Things you like a lot have high utility, while things that you like only a little have low or even negative utility.

The concept of utility is very inclusive. For a hedonist, utility may be the physical pleasure gotten from experiencing various things. But for a morally conscientious person, utility may be something like a sense of moral satisfaction that he's doing the right thing in a given situation. The important thing for economists is that people are able to ascertain and compare the utilities of various possible activities. Utility acts as a common denominator that allows people to sensibly compare even radically different things.

Taking altruism and generosity into account

Economists take it as a given that people make their choices in life in order to maximize their personal happiness. This viewpoint immediately raises objections because people are often willing to endure great personal suffering in order to help others.

Yet, to an economist, you can view the desire to help others as being a personal preference. The mother who doesn't eat in order to give what little food she has to her infant may be pursuing a goal (helping her child) that maximizes the *mother's* own happiness. The same can be said about people who donate to charities. Most people consider such generosity "selfless," but it's also consistent with assuming that people do things to make themselves happy. If people give because doing so makes them feel good, their selfless action is motivated by selfish intention. Because economists see human motivation as selfish, economics is often accused of being immoral.

However, economics is concerned with how people achieve their goals, rather than with questioning the morality of those goals. For instance, some people like honey, but others do not. Economists make no distinction between these two groups regarding the rightness or wrongness of their preferences. Rather, what interests economists is how each group behaves given its preferences. Consequently, economics is amoral, rather than immoral.

Economists, however, are people, too, and they're very concerned with things like social justice, global warming, and poverty. They just tend to interpret the desire to pursue morality and equity as an individual goal that maximizes individual happiness, rather than as a group goal that should be pursued in order to achieve some sort of collective good.

Realizing that self-interest can promote the common good

Adam Smith, one of the fathers of modern economics, believed that if society was set up correctly, people chasing after their individual happiness would provide for other people's happiness as well. As he famously pointed out in *An Inquiry into the Nature and Causes of the Wealth of Nations,* published in 1776, "It is not from the benevolence of the butcher, the brewer, or the baker, that we can expect our dinner, but from their regard to their own interest."

Put differently, the butcher, the brewer, and the baker don't make stuff for you because they like you, but because they want your money. Yet because they want your money, they end up producing for you everything that you need to have a nice meal. When you trade them your money for their goods, everyone is happier. You think that not having to prepare all that food is worth more to you than keeping your money. And they think that getting your money is worth more to them than the toil involved in preparing all that food.

Adam Smith expanded on this notion by saying that a person pursing his own selfish interests may be "led by an invisible hand to promote an end which was no part of his intention." Because economists recognize this "invisible hand," they're less concerned with intent than with outcome, and less concerned with what makes people happy than with how they pursue the things that make them happy.

Red Light: Examining Your Limitations

Life is full of limitations. Time, for instance, is always in limited supply, as are natural resources. The second stage of the economic choice model looks at the constraints that force you to choose among your happy options.

For example, oil can be used to manufacture pharmaceuticals that can save many lives. But it can also be used to make gasoline, which can be used to drive ambulances, which also save lives. Both pharmaceuticals and gasoline are good uses for oil, so society has to come up with some way of deciding how much oil gets to each of these two good uses, knowing all the while that each gallon of oil that goes to one can't be used for the other.

This section outlines the various constraints, as well as the unavoidable cost — *opportunity cost* — of getting what you want. For more on how markets use supply and demand to allocate resources in the face of constraints, please see Chapter 8.

Resource constraints

The most obvious constraints on human happiness are the physical limitations of nature. Not only are the supplies of oil, water, and fish limited, but so are the radio frequencies on which to send signals and the hours of sunshine to drive solar-powered cars. There's simply not enough of most natural resources for everyone to have as much as they want.

The limited supply of natural resources is allocated in many different ways. In some cases, as with some endangered species, laws guarantee that nobody can have any of the resource. With the electromagnetic spectrum, national governments portion out the spectrum to broadcasters or mobile phone operators. But, for the most part, private property and prices control the allocation of natural resources.

Under such a system, the use of the resource goes to the highest bidder. Although this system can discriminate against the poor because they don't have much to bid with, it does ensure that the limited supply of the resource at least goes to people who value it highly — in other words, to those who have chosen this resource to maximize their happiness.

Technology constraints

There isn't any more oil or sunlight or timber right now than there was 1,000 years ago, but you have a much higher standard of living than your ancestors did. You have a cushier life because of improvements in the technology of converting raw resources into things we like to use.

In just the last 200 years, people have figured out how to immunize children against deadly diseases, how to use electricity to provide light and mechanical power, how to build a rocket capable of putting people on the moon, and how to dramatically increase farm yields so that we can feed many more people. In just the last 20 years, the Internet and cheap mobile phones have revolutionized everything from entertainment to how governments communicate with their citizens.

As technology improves over time, people are able to produce more from the limited supply of resources on our planet. Or, put slightly differently, as technology improves, we have more and better choices from which to choose.

Yet, because technology improves slowly, at any given moment our choices are limited by how advanced the technology is right then. So, it's natural to think of technology as being a constraint that limits choices. Fortunately, though, technology does improve over time — meaning that if we just wait a while, we'll have more and better choices from which to choose.

Time constraints

Time is a precious resource. Worse yet, time is a resource in fixed supply. So, the best that technology can do for people is to allow us to produce more in the limited amount of time that we have or to grant us a few more years of life through better medical technology.

But even with a longer life span, you can't be in two places at the same time. If you could, time really wouldn't be a limit because you could do double the work in the same amount of time. But because you can only be in one place at one time, you're constantly forced to choose, at each and every moment, to do the thing that makes the best possible use of that instant in time.

Opportunity cost: The unavoidable constraint

The economic idea of *opportunity cost* is closely related to the idea of time constraints. You can do only one thing at a time, which means that, inevitably, you're always giving up a bunch of other things.

The opportunity cost of any activity is the value of the next best alternative thing you could have done instead. For instance, this morning, I could have chatted on the phone with a friend, watched TV, or worked hard writing this chapter. I chose to chat with my friend because that made me happiest. (Don't tell my editor!) Of the two things that I didn't choose, I consider working on the chapter to be better than watching TV. So the opportunity cost of chatting on the phone was not getting to spend the time working on this chapter.

Opportunity cost depends only on the value of the next best alternative. It doesn't matter whether you have 3 alternatives or 3,000. The opportunity cost is simply the value of the next best alternative because you can always reduce a complicated choice with many options down to a simple choice between two things: Option X versus the best alternative out of all the other alternatives.

Opportunity costs can tell you when *not* to do something as well as when to do something. For example, I love ice cream. But I love chocolate chip cookies even more. If you offered me only ice cream, I would take it. But if you offered me ice cream or chocolate chip cookies, I would take the cookies. The opportunity cost of eating ice cream is to forego eating chocolate chip cookies. Because the cost of not eating the cookies is higher than the benefits of eating the ice cream, it makes no sense for me to choose ice cream.

Of course, if I choose chocolate chip cookies, I'm still faced with the opportunity cost of giving up having ice cream. But I'm willing to do that because the ice cream's opportunity cost is lower than the benefits of the chocolate chip cookies. Opportunity costs are unavoidable constraints on behavior because you always have to decide what's best and give up the next best alternative.

Making Your Final Choice

At its most basic, the third stage of the economic choice model is nothing more than cost–benefit analysis. In the first stage, you evaluate how happy each of your options would make you by measuring how much utility each would bring. In the second stage, you determine the constraints and opportunity costs of each option. In the third stage, you simply choose the option for which the benefits outweigh the costs by the largest margin.

The cost–benefit model of how people make decisions is very powerful in that it seems to correctly describe how most decisions are made. But this version of cost–benefit analysis can tell you only whether people choose a given option. In other words, it's only good at describing all-or-nothing decisions like whether or not to eat ice cream.

A much more powerful version of cost–benefit analysis uses a concept called *marginal utility* to tell you not just whether I'm going to eat ice cream, but also *how much* of it I will decide to eat.

To see how marginal utility works, recognize that the amount of utility that a given thing brings usually depends on how much of that given thing a person has already had. For instance, if you've been really hungry, the first slice of pizza that you eat brings you a lot of utility. The second slice is also pleasant, but not quite as good as the first because you're no longer starving. The third, in turn, brings less utility than the second. And if you keep forcing yourself to eat, you may find that the 12th or 13th slice of pizza actually makes you sick and brings you negative utility.

Economists refer to this phenomenon as *diminishing marginal utility*. Each additional, or *marginal,* piece of pizza brings less utility than the previous piece so that the extra utility, or *marginal utility,* brought by each successive slice diminishes as you eat more and more slices.

To see how diminishing marginal utility predicts how people make decisions about how much of something to consume, consider having $10 to spend on either slices of pizza or baskets of french fries. Suppose that slices of pizza cost $2 each, and baskets of fries also cost $2 each.

Economists presume that the goal of people faced with a limited budget is to adjust the quantities of each possible thing they can consume to maximize their *total utility*. In this example, because I know that the marginal utility of pizza diminishes quickly with each additional slice, I don't spend all $10 on pizza because the fifth slice of pizza just wouldn't bring me very much marginal utility. I'm better off allocating some of my spending to french fries.

If I buy only four slices of pizza, then I free up $2 to spend on a basket of fries. And because it's my first basket of fries, eating it probably brings me lots of marginal utility. Indeed, if the marginal utility gained from that first basket of fries exceeds the marginal utility lost by giving up that fifth slice of pizza, I'll definitely make the switch. I will keep adjusting the quantities of each food until I find the combination that maximizes how much total utility I can purchase using my $10.

Because different people have different preferences, the quantities of each good that will maximize each person's total utility are usually different. Someone who detests fries will spend all his $10 on pizza. A person who can't stand pizza will spend all her money on fries. And for people who choose to have some of each, the optimal quantities of each depend on their individual feelings about the two goods and how fast their marginal utilities decrease. Check out Chapter 9 for more detail on diminishing marginal utility and how it causes demand curves to slope downward.

Allowing for diminishing marginal utility makes this choice behavior model very powerful. It not only tells you what people will choose, but how much of each thing they will choose. It's not perfect, however. For example, it assumes that people have a clear sense of the utility of various things, a good idea of how fast marginal utilities diminish, and no trouble making comparisons. I discuss these substantial criticisms in the next section.

Marginal utility is for the birds!

Economists are very confident that cost–benefit analysis and diminishing marginal utility are good descriptions of decision-making because there's plenty of evidence that other species also behave in ways consistent with these concepts.

For instance, scientists can train birds to peck at one button in order to earn food and another button to earn time on a treadmill. If scientists increase the cost of one of the options by increasing the number or clicks required to get it, the birds respond rationally by not clicking so much on the button for that option. But even more interesting is that they also switch to clicking more on the button for the other option.

The birds seem to understand that they have only a limited number of clicks they can make before they get exhausted, and they allocate these clicks between the two options so as to maximize their total utility. Consequently, when the relative costs and benefits of the options change, they change their behavior quite rationally in response.

Most species also seem to be affected by diminishing marginal utility and become indifferent to marginal units of something that they've recently enjoyed a lot of. Even bacteria seem to display this behavior. So while economists' models of human behavior may seem to ignore some relevant factors, they do take into account some very fundamental and universal behaviors.

Exploring Limitations and Violations of the Economist's Choice Model

Economists assume that people are fully informed and totally rational when they make decisions. That's a strong assumption. The model of human behavior favored by economists works well most of the time, but it doesn't always make accurate predictions about what people will do. In the real world, people aren't always fully informed about the decisions they need to make, and they aren't always as rational or logical as economists assume.

Understanding uninformed decision-making

When economists apply the choice model, they assume a situation in which a person knows all the possible options, knows how much utility each will bring, and knows the opportunity costs of each one. But how do you evaluate whether it would be better to sit on top of Mount Everest for five minutes or hang-glide over the Amazon for ten minutes? Because you've never done either, you aren't well-informed about the constraints and costs of the choice and probably don't even know what the utilities of the two options are.

Politicians with novel new programs often ask us to make similarly uninformed choices. They make their proposals sound as good as possible, but in many cases nobody really knows what they may be getting into.

Things are similarly murky when making choices about random events. People buying lottery tickets in state lotteries have no idea about either the eventual possible gain or the eventual likelihood of winning because both the size of the prize and the likelihood of winning depend on how many tickets may or may not be sold before the drawing is made.

Economists account for this reality by assuming that when faced with uninformed decisions, people make their best guesses about not only random outcomes but also about how much they may like or dislike things with which they have no previous experience. Although this may seem like a fudge, because people in the real world are obviously making decisions in such situations (they do, in fact, buy a whole lot of lottery tickets), the people in those situations must be fudging a bit as well.

Whether people make good choices when they are uninformed is hard to say. Obviously, people would prefer to be better informed before choosing. And some people do shy away from less certain options. But, overall, the economist's model of choice behavior seems quite capable of dealing with situations of incomplete information and uncertainty about random outcomes.

Getting rational about irrationality

Even when people are fully informed about their options, they often make logical errors in evaluating the costs and benefits of each. I go through three of the most common choice errors in the following sections, but as you read them, don't be too alarmed. After people have these logical errors explained to them, they typically stop making the errors and start behaving in a manner consistent with rationally weighing marginal benefits against marginal costs.

Sunk costs are sunk!

Suppose that you just spent $15 to get into an all-you-can-eat sushi restaurant. How much should you eat? More specifically, when deciding how much to eat, should you care about how much you paid to get into the restaurant?

To an economist, the answer to the first question is: Eat exactly the amount of food that makes you most happy. And the answer to the second question is: How much it cost you to get in doesn't matter because whether you eat 1 piece of sushi or 80 pieces of sushi, the cost was the same. Put differently, because the cost of getting into the restaurant is now in the past, it should be completely unrelated to your current decision of how much to eat.

Economists refer to costs that have already been incurred and which should therefore not affect your current and future decision-making as *sunk costs.* Rationally speaking, you should consider only the future, potential marginal costs and benefits of your current options.

After all, if you were suddenly offered $1,000 to leave the sushi restaurant and eat next door at a competitor, would you refuse simply because you felt you had to eat a lot at the sushi restaurant in order to get your money's worth out of the $15 you spent? Of course not.

Unfortunately, most people tend to let sunk costs affect their decision-making until an economist points out to them that sunk costs are irrelevant, or, as economists never tire of saying, "Sunk costs are sunk!" (On the other hand, noneconomists quickly tire of hearing this phrase.)

Mistaking a big percentage for a big dollar amount

Suppose you decide to save 10 percent on a TV by making a one-hour round trip to a store in another town to buy the TV for only $90 rather than buying the TV at your local store for $100. Next, ask yourself whether you'd also be willing to drive one hour in order to buy a home theater system for $1,990 in the next town rather than for $2,000 at your local store. You do the math, and because you would save only 0.5 percent, you decide to buy the system for $2,000 at the local store.

You may think you're being smart, but you've just behaved in a colossally inconsistent and irrational way. In the first case, you were willing to drive one hour to save $10. In the second, you were not. Costs and benefits are absolute, but people make the mistake of thinking of the costs and benefits of driving to the next town in terms of percentages or proportions. Instead, compare the total costs against the total benefits because the benefit of driving to the next town is the absolute dollar amount you save, not the proportion you save.

Confusing marginal and average

Suppose that your local government has recently built three bridges at a total cost of $30 million. That's an average cost of $10 million per bridge. A local economist does a study and estimates that the total benefits of the three bridges to the local economy adds up to $36 million, or an average of $12 million per bridge.

A politician then starts trying to build a fourth bridge, arguing that because bridges on average cost $10 million but on average bring $12 million in benefits, it would be foolish not to build another bridge. Should you believe him? After all, if each bridge brings society a net gain of $2 million, you would want to keep building bridges forever.

However, what really matters to this decision are *marginal* costs and *marginal* benefits, not *average* ones (see the section "Making Your Final Choice" for more on marginal utility). Who cares what costs and benefits all the previous bridges brought with them? You have to compare the costs of that extra, marginal bridge with the benefits of that extra, marginal bridge. If the marginal benefits exceed the marginal costs, you should build the bridge. And if the marginal costs exceed the marginal benefits, you should not.

For example, suppose that an independent watchdog group hires an engineer to estimate the cost of building one more bridge and an economist to estimate the benefits of building one more bridge. The engineer finds that because the three shortest river crossings have already been taken by the first three bridges, the fourth bridge will have to be much longer. In fact, the extra length will raise the building cost to $15 million.

At the same time, the economist does a survey and finds that a fourth bridge isn't really all that necessary. At best, it will bring with it only $8 million per year in benefits. Consequently, this fourth bridge shouldn't be built because its marginal cost of $15 million exceeds its marginal benefit of $8 million. By telling voters only about the *average* costs and benefits of past bridges, the politician supporting the project is grossly misleading them. So watch out anytime somebody tries to sell you a bridge.

Chapter 3

Producing the Right Stuff the Right Way to Maximize Human Happiness

Although it's true that human beings face scarcity and can't have everything they want (as I discuss in Chapter 2), it's also true that they have a lot of options. Productive technology is now so advanced that people can convert the planet's limited supply of resources into an amazing variety of goods and services, including cars, computers, airplanes, cancer treatments, video games, and even totally awesome *For Dummies* books like this one.

In fact, thanks to advanced technologies, people are spoiled for choices. The huge variety of goods and services that can possibly be produced means that people must choose wisely if they want to convert the planet's limited resources into the goods and services that will provide the greatest possible happiness when consumed.

This chapter explains how economists analyze the process by which societies choose exactly what to produce in order to maximize human happiness. For every society, the process can be divided into two simple steps:

1. **The society must figure out all the possible combinations of goods and services that it could produce given its limited resources and the currently available technology.**

2. **The society must choose one of these output combinations — presumably, the combination that maximizes happiness.**

Economists view success in each of the two steps in terms of two particular types of efficiency:

- *Productive efficiency* means producing any given good or service using the fewest possible resources.

- *Allocative efficiency* means producing the kinds of goods and services that will make people most happy, and producing them in the correct amounts.

This chapter shows you how a society achieves both productive and allocative efficiency — that is, how a society determines what's possible to produce, as well as what's best to produce. I give you the lowdown on diminishing returns, Production Possibilities Frontier graphs (yeah, graphs!), and the interplay between markets and governments.

Reaching the Limit: Determining What's Possible to Produce

In determining what's possible to produce in an economy, economists list two major factors that affect both the maximum amounts and the types of output that will be produced:

- Limited resources
- Diminishing returns

The first factor is obvious: If resources were unlimited, goods and services would be as well. The second factor, despite affecting nearly every production process known, isn't understood by most people. Basically, *diminishing returns* means that the more you make of something, the more expensive it becomes to produce. Although the first few units may be produced at low cost, successive units cost more and more. Eventually, the costs exceed the benefits, which limits how much of it you want to produce, even if it's your favorite thing. Your resources should be devoted to producing units of other things for which the benefits still outweigh the costs.

A key result of diminishing returns is that societies are usually better off when they devote their limited resources to producing moderate amounts of many goods rather than producing a huge amount of just one thing.

This section gives you the lowdown on how limited resources and diminishing returns determine production possibilities. It also shows you how to represent these possibilities graphically.

Classifying resources used in production

You can't get output without inputs of resources. Economists traditionally divide inputs, or *factors of production,* into three classes:

- ✔ **Land:** Not just real estate, but all naturally occurring resources that can be used to produce things people want to consume. Land includes the weather, plant and animal life, geothermal energy, and the electromagnetic spectrum.

- ✔ **Labor:** The work that people must do in order to produce things. A tree doesn't become a house without human intervention.

- ✔ **Capital:** Man-made machines, tools, and structures that aren't directly consumed but are used to produce other things that people do directly consume. For instance, a car that you drive for pleasure is a consumption good, while an identical car that you use to haul around bricks for your construction business is capital. Capital includes factories, roads, sewers, electrical grids, the Internet, and so on.

In addition to these three traditional inputs, economists now often speak of *human capital,* which is the knowledge and skills that people use to help them produce output. For instance, I have a lot of human capital with regard to teaching economics, but I have extremely low human capital with regard to painting and singing. (Be very happy that you haven't heard me sing!)

If you put a person to work at a job for which she has high human capital, she will produce much better or much more output than a person with low human capital, even though they both supply the same amount of labor in terms of hours worked. An important consequence is that skilled workers (high human capital) get paid more than unskilled workers (low human capital). Therefore, a good way for societies to become richer is to improve the skills of their workers through education and training. If societies can raise workers' human capital levels, not only can they produce more with the same inputs of limited land, labor, and capital, but their workers will also be paid more and enjoy higher standards of living.

But building up human capital is costly, and at any given instant, you should think of the level of human capital in a society as being fixed. Combined with limitations on the amount of land, labor, and capital, the limitation on human capital means that the society will only be able to produce a limited amount of output. And along these same lines, the decisions about where to best allocate these limited resources become crucial because the resources must be used for production of the goods and services that will bring with them the greatest amount of happiness. (For more on limited resources and production possibilities, see the upcoming section "A little here, a little there: Allocating resources.")

Getting less of a good thing: Diminishing returns

Diminishing returns is probably the most important economic factor in determining exactly what to produce out of all the things that could possibly be produced given the limited supply of resources. It refers to the fact that for virtually everything people make, the amount of additional output you get from each additional unit of input decreases as you use more and more of the input.

Diminishing returns is sometimes referred to as the "low-hanging fruit principle." Imagine being sent into an apple orchard at harvest time to pick apples. During the first hour, you pick a lot of apples because you go for the low-hanging ones that are the easiest to reach. In the second hour, however, you can't pick as many because you have to start reaching awkwardly for fruit that is higher up. During the third hour you pick even fewer apples; you now have to jump off the ground every time you try to pick an apple because the only ones left are even farther away. Table 3-1 demonstrates how your productivity — your output for a given amount of input — diminishes with each additional hour you work.

Table 3-1	Diminishing Returns to Apple Picking	
Hour Worked	*Apples Picked*	*Labor Cost per Apple*
1st	300	2 cents
2nd	200	3 cents
3rd	120	5 cents

Another way to see the effect of diminishing returns is to note the increasing costs for producing output. If you pay workers $6 per hour to pick apples, your cost to have 300 apples picked in the first hour is two cents per apple, as shown in Table 3-1. The second hour yields only 200 apples, costing you three cents per apple (because you still have to pay the worker $6 for that hour's work). Only 120 get picked in the third hour, so the labor cost per apple rises to five cents.

Eventually, the effects of diminishing returns drive prices so high that you will stop devoting further labor resources to picking additional apples.

Virtually all production processes show diminishing returns, and not just for labor. Additional amounts of any particular input usually result in smaller and smaller increments of output, holding all other inputs constant.

A little here, a little there: Allocating resources

Because the diminishing returns factor assures that a production process will eventually become too costly, a society normally allocates its limited resources widely, to many different production processes.

To understand why this happens, imagine that you can allocate workers to either picking apples or picking oranges. You can sell both apples and oranges for $1 each, but the production of both fruits involves diminishing returns so that additional workers acting as fruit pickers yield successively smaller increments of output no matter which fruit they're picking.

Allocating all your workers to picking oranges, for example, is unproductive because the output you get from the last worker picking oranges will be much less than the output you get from the first worker picking oranges.

The smart thing to do is to take a worker away from picking oranges and reassign him to picking apples. As the last worker picking oranges, he didn't produce much. But as the first worker picking apples, he'll pick a lot of them. Because you pay him the same wage regardless of which fruit he's picking, you use your labor more intelligently by having him pick apples, because one apple sells for as much money as one orange.

You may also want to reassign a second worker, and perhaps a third or a fourth. But because diminishing returns applies just as much to picking apples as it does to picking oranges, you don't want to reassign all the workers. Each additional worker assigned to picking apples produces less than the previous worker picking apples. At some point, moving additional workers from picking oranges to picking apples no longer benefits you, and you've reached what economists refer to as an *optimal allocation* of your labor resource. As soon as you've found this sweet spot, you have no further incentive to move workers from picking one fruit to picking the other because no additional moving of workers will increase total fruit picking. At this point, you've maximized your fruit-picking potential.

Graphing your production possibilities

Economists have a handy graph called the *Production Possibilities Frontier* (PPF) that lets you visualize the effect of diminishing returns and view the tradeoffs you make when you reallocate inputs from producing one thing to producing another. The Production Possibilities Frontier, which is sometimes referred to as the *Production Possibilities Curve,* also shows how limited resources limit your ability to produce output. Figure 3-1 shows a PPF graph that corresponds to the data in Table 3-2.

Table 3-2 shows how the total output of apples and oranges changes as you make different allocations of five available workers to picking apples or oranges. For instance, if you put all five people to work picking only apples for one whole day, you get 700 apples picked and zero oranges picked. If you move one worker to oranges (so four workers are picking apples and one worker is picking oranges), you get 680 apples picked and 300 oranges picked. Because of diminishing returns, taking one worker away from apples reduces apple output by only 20. But moving that worker to oranges increases orange production by 300 because that worker is the first one picking oranges and can get the low-hanging fruit.

Table 3-2	Outputs of Apples and Oranges As the Allocation of Labor Changes					
	Combo 1	Combo 2	Combo 3	Combo 4	Combo 5	Combo 6
Workers picking oranges	0	1	2	3	4	5
Workers picking apples	5	4	3	2	1	0
Output of oranges	0	300	500	620	680	700
Output of apples	700	680	620	500	300	0

Figure 3-1 plots out the six output combinations that result from varying the allocation of workers in Table 3-2, thereby graphing all your production possibilities. Point *A* corresponds to putting all your workers to work picking apples. Point *B* corresponds to the output you get from four workers picking apples and one worker picking oranges, and so on.

Note that each of the six points is *attainable* in the sense that you can actually produce the corresponding quantities of each fruit through some allocation of the five workers' labor. On the other hand, a point like *C* is not attainable. You can't allocate your five workers in any way to produce that many apples and oranges. Perhaps if you had more workers you could produce such an output combination, but you're limited with only five workers.

Imagine that instead of allocating labor by worker, you allocate it by time. The five workers each work for one day, so you have 5 *worker-days* of labor to allocate. You can now allocate, for instance, 3.2 worker-days to apple picking and 1.8 worker-days to orange picking. This arrangement allows you to fill in the graph and draw a line connecting the six points that correspond to the output combinations that you get when allocating labor by worker.

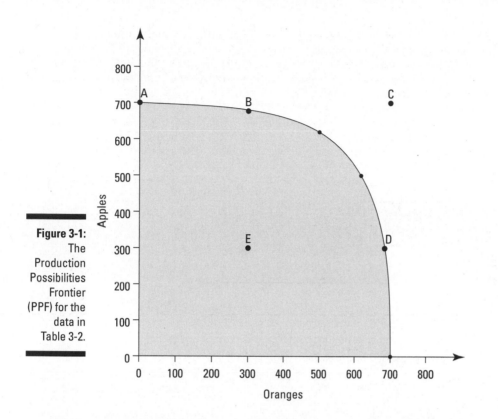

Figure 3-1:
The
Production
Possibilities
Frontier
(PPF) for the
data in
Table 3-2.

This line is called the *Production Possibilities Frontier,* or PPF, because it divides the area of the graph into two parts: The combinations of output that are possible to produce given your limited supply of labor are under the line, and those that are not possible to produce are above it. In this way, the PPF graph captures the effect of scarce resources on production. Some output combinations are just not producible given the limited supply of labor.

The bowed-out curvature of the PPF graph illustrates the effects of diminishing returns. The changing slope as you move along the frontier shows that the tradeoff between apple production and orange production depends on where you start. If you're at point *A,* where you're allocating all your resources to the production of apples, then you can, by reallocating resources, produce a lot more oranges at the cost of giving up only a few apples. But if you start at point *D,* where you're already producing a lot of oranges, then you have to give up a lot of apples to get just a few more oranges.

In economic jargon, the changing slope of the PPF in the face of diminishing returns is due to the fact that the *opportunity costs* of production vary depending on your current allocation of resources. (Check out Chapter 2 for more on opportunity costs.) If you're already producing a lot of apples, the opportunity costs of devoting even more labor to more apple production are very high because you're giving up a lot of potential orange production. On the other hand, the opportunity costs of devoting that labor to orange production are very low because you have to give up producing only a few apples. Clearly, you should devote the labor to picking the fruit that has the lower opportunity costs because, in this example, both fruits bring the same benefit: $1 per fruit sold.

The PPF is also very handy because any points that lie on the PPF itself (on the frontier) clearly show the output combinations you get when you're *productively efficient,* or wasting none of your resources. You can't increase the production of apples without reducing the production of oranges, and vice versa. For instance, if you start at point *B,* the only way to increase apple production is to slide up along the frontier, which implies reducing orange production. You have to make this tradeoff because you don't have any wasted labor lying around with which you could get more apples without reducing the amount of labor already devoted to orange picking.

All the points below the line are productively inefficient. Consider point *E* in Figure 3-1, which corresponds to producing 300 apples and 300 oranges. You produce at a point like *E* only if you're being productively inefficient. In fact, you can see from Table 3-2 that you can produce these numbers by sending only one worker to pick apples and another worker to pick oranges. You're using just two of your five workers; the labor of the other three workers is either being wasted or not used at all.

In the real world, you end up at points like *E* because of inefficient production technology or poor management. For one reason or another, the resources that are available aren't being used to produce as much output as they possibly could.

Any manager who has five workers to allocate but produces only output combination *E* should be fired! Efficient economies should always be producing at some point on their frontiers because if they are inside, they are wasting their limited resources and not maximizing the happiness that could be gotten from them.

Pushin' the line with better technology

The PPF is a simplification of the real world, derived by allocating one input between just two outputs. The real world is, of course, more complicated, with many different resources allocated among many different outputs. But the principles of limited resources and diminishing returns that show up so clearly on the PPF graph also apply to the much greater variety of both inputs and outputs in the real world.

Another simplification of the PPF is that, other than the particular input you are allocating, you are implicitly holding constant all other productive inputs, including technology. But humanity's level of technological sophistication is constantly increasing, allowing people to produce much more from a given set of resources than before.

Economists represent this increase in productivity by shifting the PPF outward. In Figure 3-2, the shaded area represents new combinations of output that, thanks to better technology, can now be produced using the same amount of resources as before. The PPF is still curved because better technologies don't get rid of diminishing returns. Even with a better technology, if you start increasing the amount of a particular input, you get successively smaller additional increases in output.

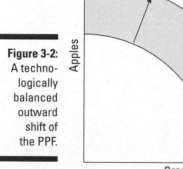

Figure 3-2:
A techno-
logically
balanced
outward
shift of
the PPF.

In Figure 3-2, the new technology shift is _balanced_ in the sense that it increases your ability to produce more of both goods. An example of a balanced technological change would be improvements in fertilizers or pesticides that increase crop yields of both apples and oranges.

But most technological innovations are _biased._ For instance, suppose that you're considering a PPF where the two output goods are wheat and steel. An improvement in steel-making technology obviously allows you to make more steel from your limited resources but has no effect at all on your ability to make wheat. Consequently, as Figure 3-3 shows, the PPF does not shift out evenly. Rather, it shifts out at the end where all your particular input (say, labor) is devoted to steel, but remains fixed at the end where all your particular input is devoted to wheat production.

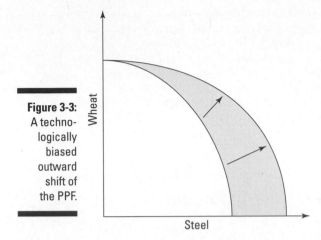

Figure 3-3:
A techno-
logically
biased
outward
shift of
the PPF.

Determining What Should Be Produced

After a society locates the frontier of efficient output combinations, the next step is choosing the point along the frontier that produces the combination of goods and services that makes people most happy. Choosing only from among frontier combinations guarantees *productive efficiency.* Choosing the single frontier combination that maximizes happiness assures *allocative efficiency.*

Because determining where the frontier lies is mostly a matter of engineering and applying current technology to available resources, it engenders little controversy. But deciding which particular combination of outputs a society as a whole should choose is much more complicated. People have preferences both as individuals and as groups about what products make them happiest. An individual choosing a point along his own personal PPF encounters no conflict. He just determines what combination of output makes him happiest and then he produces and consumes it.

The decision-making process becomes vastly more complicated when you consider an entire society's PPF, in which case you're sure to have vigorous disagreement about what combination of output to produce with the society's limited resources. For instance, your neighbor may not mind all the pollution produced by the fact that he likes driving his SUV day and night. If he were living in his own world, the pollution wouldn't matter, but because you live near him, you're affected by the pollution and object. Perhaps you'll seek government intervention that will limit what your neighbor is doing. Similarly, the government argues over what it should produce with its limited resources: Some people favor farm subsidies, while others favor defense spending or programs to aid the poor.

Because of these competing priorities, some sort of decision-making process must be established to determine what will actually get produced and to (try to) make sure that it pleases most of the people most of the time.

In most modern economies, this process is the result of both private and public decisions acting through a combination of free markets and government action. The process is not always smooth, but it has delivered the highest living standards in world history.

Weighing pros and cons of markets and government interventions

When analyzing the ways in which modern economies and societies select a combination of goods and services to produce, you have to realize that current economic laws and institutions are the result of conflicting pressures to either leave markets to their own devices when turning resources into output or use the power of government to intervene in markets in order to secure a different set of outcomes.

Keep the following three factors in mind when considering the fight between leaving the markets alone and intervening:

- Modern economies are hugely complicated, with literally millions of goods and services produced using limited supplies of land, labor, and capital. Markets handle this complexity easily, but government interventions usually don't — meaning that they often risk substantial reductions in productive and allocative efficiency.

- Some goods and services, like cocaine and coal-burning power plants, have negative consequences. These negative consequences bring forth substantial pressure for government intervention in the economy because these markets, if left alone, will produce a lot of these goods and services.

- Some people end up consuming a very large proportion of the goods and services produced, while others end up with very little. Such unequal distribution also brings forth a great deal of pressure for government intervention in the economy in order to equalize living standards.

These factors are both a consequence and a cause of the fact that our modern economies are largely a mix of market production and government intervention. For the most part, what to produce, how much of it to produce, and who gets it is decided by voluntary transactions made by individuals and businesses. But sometimes, the government uses its coercive powers to achieve outcomes that wouldn't happen if individuals and businesses were left to their own devices.

In both cases, a huge apparatus of law and tradition governing economic transactions helps society produce a combination of output that is, hopefully, both productively efficient (so resources are not wasted) and allocatively efficient (so the economy is producing the things that people want most). Next, I outline the benefits and the drawbacks that both markets and governments bring to the economic table.

The magic of markets: Going where no one man can ever go

Market production is the term that economists use to capture what happens when one individual offers to make or sell something to another individual at a price agreeable to both. Markets are very good at producing things that people are willing to pay for. In addition, markets tend to be very efficient if there are many providers of a good or service.

A *competitive market* is one in which many sellers compete against each other to attract customers. In such a situation, each seller has an incentive to sell at the lowest price possible in order to undercut his competitors and steal their customers. Because every firm has this incentive, prices tend to be driven so low that the businesses can just barely make a profit.

A competitive market also tends to guarantee productive efficiency because the best way for sellers to keep prices low is to make sure that they're using all their resources efficiently and that nothing is going to waste. Because competition is ongoing, the pressure to be efficient is constant. Sellers also have a big incentive to improve efficiency in order to undersell their rivals and steal their customers.

In terms of the PPF (which I discuss in the earlier section "Graphing your production possibilities"), market production with a lot of competition tends to ensure not only that economies produce along the frontier, but also that they have frontiers that are constantly being pushed outward as firms improve efficiency.

Markets also have the benefit of figuring out, automatically, the things that people want. To grasp why this is so amazing, consider that we live in a world of nearly 7 billion people. It would be very hard for me or you or any one person to gather enough information to figure out what each of them most wants to buy. It would take several lifetimes to speak with each of them, even just to find out what they want for dinner, let alone all the other things they would most like to purchase on a typical day.

But because production and distribution in modern economies aren't centralized, you don't need to know the big picture. In fact, the real magic of market economies is that they are just a collection of millions and billions of small, face-to-face transactions between buyers and sellers.

For instance, the guy who sells you a TV at the local store has no idea about the total demand for TVs in the world, how many tons of steel or plastic are needed to produce them, or how many other things *weren't* produced because the steel and plastic needed to make the TVs was used for TVs rather than other things. All he knows is that you're willing to pay him for a TV. And if he's making a profit selling TVs, he orders more TVs from the factory. The factory, in turn, increases production, taking resources away from the production of other things. Reallocation of resources also occurs in markets because each resource has a price, and whoever is willing to pay the price gets the resource.

Communism, long lines, and toilet paper

In a *command economy,* all economic activity is done on the orders of the government. Until the fall of the Berlin Wall and the subsequent collapse of communism in the late 1980s and early 1990s, a large part of the world's population lived in countries that had command economies. Sadly, they didn't live very well.

Shortages of everything from sugar to clothing to toilet paper were constant. More seriously, doctors often lacked hypodermic needles and medicines for their patients, and food was often in short supply.

Goods and services weren't allocated using a price system whereby output went to those willing and able to pay for it. Rather, because everyone in a communist country is ideologically equal, the government attempted to give everyone an equal share of the goods and services made. The result, though, wasn't an equal division; instead, there were long lines, with those able to stand in line the longest getting more than their fair share. The lines were so long that people often stood in line for an entire day just to get one roll of toilet paper. If you saw a line forming, you got in it as fast as you could, even if you didn't know what people were standing in line for. Because everything was in short supply, it was almost certainly something you'd want.

What caused this mess? Centralization. In Moscow, government officials called *central planners* attempted to determine the correct amounts to produce for 24 million different items! It was an impossible task. Take, for instance, toilet paper. First, you estimate how many millions of rolls of toilet paper are needed. Then you have to figure out how many trees to cut down to make that much paper and how many railcars you need to carry those trees to paper mills and how many workers it takes to run those mills. At the same time, you have to try to balance production of toilet paper against the other zillion things that also require trees, railcars, and workers.

The entire problem is far too complex and requires far too much information to be solved. The result was that resources were constantly being misdirected and wasted. For instance, food often rotted at farms because no railcars had been scheduled to take it to cities; the officials hadn't accounted for an early harvest, and the railcars were busy elsewhere. In a price system, the farmers would have simply paid to bid the railcars away from other uses. This solution wasn't possible in a centralized economy in which prices weren't used to allocate resources.

In fact, market economies are often called *price systems* because prices serve as the signals that allocate resources. Things in high demand have high prices, and things in low demand have low prices. Because businesses like to make money, they follow the price signals and produce more of what has a high price and less of what has a low price. In this way, markets tend to take our limited resources and use them to produce what people most want — or, at least, what people are most willing to pay for. And they do it all in a completely decentralized manner.

The misdeeds of markets

Markets aren't perfect. In particular, they suffer from two major problems:

- Markets produce whatever people are willing to pay for, even if these things aren't necessarily good for the people or the environment.

- Markets are amoral: They don't in any way guarantee fairness or equity.

The fact that illegal drugs are widely and cheaply available despite vigorous government programs to stop their production and distribution is probably the best example of the robustness of markets. As long as profits are to be made, you can be pretty certain that supply will arise to satisfy any demand. But although it's nice that markets are so hell-bent on giving people what they're willing to pay for, illegal drugs are an excellent example of the fact that markets will deliver things without caring about their social value or their negative consequences.

Along the same lines, producers often do things we don't like while giving us what we want. Child labor and sweatshop labor are primary examples. Often the government must intervene to change these practices when the price system doesn't provide enough incentive for producers to change such objectionable practices.

The other big problem with markets is that they cater to those who have money to spend. The price system gives an incentive to produce only the things that people are willing and able to pay for. If someone is very poor, he can't give producers an incentive to provide him with even basic necessities like medicine and food. Under a pure price system, resources are instead directed toward producing things for those who have money to spend.

A related problem with markets is income and wealth inequality. Because market systems reward those who are best able to provide goods and services that people want to buy, some sellers end up becoming very rich because they're better at providing what people want. This invariably leads to large inequalities in wealth that many people find offensive, even when the money is honestly earned and even though highly productive people make such large contributions toward increasing output and maximizing happiness.

The case for government intervention

Many societies use their governments to intervene and address the problems that markets create or cannot fix. Government interventions in the economy usually take one of three forms:

- **Penalties or bans on producing or consuming goods or services considered dangerous or immoral:** For example, governments may ban drugs or impose "sin taxes" on things like alcohol and tobacco, which, though legal, are thought to be products whose use should be discouraged. However, these bans often work only partially because the market still has large incentives to provide such goods and services.

- **Subsidies to encourage the production of goods and services considered desirable:** For instance, most governments heavily subsidize the education of children and the provision of medical care. They do so because of the fear that insufficient education and inadequate medical care will be provided without the subsidies.

- **Taxes on the well-off to provide goods and services to the less fortunate and to reduce inequalities in income and wealth:** These taxes are put toward things like good parks, clean air, and art, as well as goods and services for the poor. Governments tax individuals and businesses in order to raise the money to provide such things.

In terms of the PPF graph, each of these government interventions causes the economy to produce and allocate an output combination different from the one that society would have ended up with if the markets had made all the production and allocation decisions.

Mo' money for mohair

Mohair is an extremely warm wool that grows on a special kind of goat. During World War II, the U.S. government decided that it needed mohair for the warm jackets worn by bomber pilots in their unheated cockpits. As a result, the government started giving a large subsidy to encourage the production of mohair. Planes have now been heated for 50 years, and bomber jackets are made out of synthetics. But the mohair subsidy remains, and mohair producers receive millions of dollars every year. Why? Because the mohair producers lobby the U.S. government very hard each year to renew the subsidy. For each producer, the subsidy is worth a lot of money. And because only a fraction of one cent of the average tax bill goes to the mohair subsidy, no one protests it. Consequently, the mohair subsidy survives not because it does society any good, but because lobbying pays off in a democracy. Many other government programs are similarly deficient of widespread social benefits.

Depending on the situation, the output combination produced by a government intervention may be better or worse than the market combination in terms of productive efficiency, allocative efficiency, or both. Which combination is, in fact, better depends on the specifics of each case.

The case against government intervention

Government intervention is a powerful force for redirecting economic activity, but it doesn't necessarily make the economy better. In fact, there are at least three good reasons to worry that government interventions in the economy will make things worse:

- ✔ Government programs are often the result of special interest lobbying that seeks to help some small group rather than maximize the happiness of the general population. Special interest lobbying takes resources away from other uses that often benefit numerous people in order to provide benefits to only a few.

- ✔ Even when pursuing the common good, government programs often deliver poor service because they have no competition to create incentives to produce government goods and services efficiently.

- ✔ Government interventions usually lack the flexibility of the price system, which is able to constantly redirect resources to accommodate people's changing willingness to pay for one good rather than another. Government policies take years to pass, and laws are usually written in a very precise manner that doesn't allow for changing circumstances and rapid innovation — things that the price system handles with ease.

Although markets sometimes fail to deliver everything that society wants, government intervention isn't a panacea. Markets are very good at delivering the vast majority of things that people want and can usually do so at the lowest possible cost. Consequently, government intervention should be well thought out lest it make things worse rather than better.

Opting for a mixed economy

In the real world, few societies opt for an extreme type of economy, such as one that is totally market-based or one that features constant and pervasive government intervention. Instead, most societies opt for some mixture of markets, government intervention, and what economists refer to as *traditional production*. In their purest forms, these three types of economy can be defined as follows:

- ✔ **A market economy** is one in which almost all economic activity happens in markets with little or no interference by the government. Because of the lack of government intervention, this system is also often referred to as *laissez faire,* which is French for "to leave alone."

> ✔ **A command economy** is one in which all economic activity is directed by the government.
>
> ✔ **A traditional economy** is one in which production and distribution are handled along the lines of long-standing cultural traditions. For instance, until the caste system was abolished in India during the last century, the production of nearly every good and service could be done only by someone born into the appropriate caste. Similarly, in medieval Europe, you couldn't typically be part of the government or attain high military rank unless you were born a noble.

Because nearly every modern economy is a mixture of these three pure forms, most modern economies fall into the very inclusive category called *mixed economies.* With the exception of a few isolated traditional societies, however, the traditional economy part of the mixture has tended to decline in significance because most production has shifted to markets and because traditional economic restrictions on things like age and gender have become less important (and more illegal).

The result is that most mixed economies today are a mixture of the other two pure types: the command economy and the market economy. The mixtures that you find in most countries typically feature governments that mostly allow markets to determine what's produced, but that also mix in limited interventions in an attempt to make improvements over what the market would do if left to its own devices.

The precise nature of the mixture depends on the country, with the United States and the United Kingdom featuring more emphasis on markets while France and Germany, for instance, feature more emphasis on government intervention. On the other hand, a few totalitarian states like North Korea still persist in running pure command economies as part of their all-encompassing authoritarian regimes.

As I discuss in the sidebar "Communism, long lines, and toilet paper" in this chapter, command economies have all been dismal failures. Even well-intentioned governments can't gather enough information about production and distribution to do a good job allocating resources. In fact, they do a much worse job than price systems do.

Consequently, the opposite extreme, absolutely no government intervention, is an attractive option. Such *laissez faire* systems were first suggested by French economists several hundred years ago in response to the habit of governments of that era to intervene very heavily in economic activity.

However, no pure laissez faire economy has ever existed or probably could ever exist. The simple fact is that properly functioning market economies that use price mechanisms to allocate resources require a huge amount of government support. Among other things, market economies need governments to

> ✔ Enforce property rights so people don't steal
>
> ✔ Provide legal systems to write and enforce contracts so people can make purchases and sales of goods and services
>
> ✔ Enforce standardized systems of weights and measures so people know they aren't being cheated
>
> ✔ Provide a stable money supply that's safe from counterfeiters
>
> ✔ Enforce patents and copyrights to encourage innovation and creativity

Notice that all these things must be in place in order for markets to function. Consequently, a more moderate, more modern version of _laissez faire_ says that government should provide the institutional framework necessary for market economies to function, and then it should get out of the way and let people make and sell whatever is demanded.

However, the vast majority of people want governments to do more than just set up the institutions necessary for markets to function. They want governments to stop the production and sale of things like drugs or to subsidize the production of things that the market economy may not provide a lot of, like housing for the poor. They often also want to tax well-off citizens to pay for government programs for the poor.

Many government programs are so commonplace that you don't even think of them as being government interventions. For instance, free public schools, safety features on cars, warning labels on medicine bottles, sin taxes on alcohol and tobacco, and mandatory contributions to retirement systems are all government interventions in the economy.

The government interventions needed to implement such programs are, in many cases, not efficient. But many people would argue that there's quite a bit more to life than efficiency and that the inefficiencies caused by many government interventions are well worth the benefits that they produce. For such people, the government interventions in question increase overall happiness despite the fact that they are, strictly speaking, inefficient.

Because pure market economies don't deliver everything that many people want, most societies have opted for at least some — and in some cases, quite a lot of — government intervention in the economy. The result is that most economies today are mixed economies, with some aspects of direct command and control of economic activity mixed in with a mostly market economy that uses a price system to allocate resources.

At the end of the day, all government interventions — both good and bad — are the result of a political process. In democracies, the amount of government intervention is, broadly speaking, a reflection of the will of the people. Nations in which people have more trust in markets, like the United States and the United Kingdom, tend to feature mixed economies with less government intervention than nations in which people are more suspicious of corporations and impersonal market forces, like France and Germany.

Encouraging Technology and Innovation

One of the most important jobs of government is helping to promote the invention of new technologies so that we can enjoy higher living standards.

Technology is, in many ways, like any other good that can be provided by a market. If there's a profit incentive to inventing a new technology, business-people will figure out a way to invent it, just as they figure out ways to deliver all the other things that people are willing to pay for.

Businesses and governments spend hundreds of billions of research and development dollars each year attempting to invent new technologies. Governments provide a good deal of direct support through research grants and university subsidies. But a crucial thing to understand about innovation is the indirect role that governments play not by subsidizing new technology but by guarding it.

In particular, the patents granted by governments provide a huge economic incentive for both individuals and businesses to innovate. A patent guarantees inventors of new products or business methods the exclusive right to profit from their innovations, usually for about 20 years in most countries.

Catching up quickly

People in the United States, western Europe, and Japan are richer than those living anywhere else. The interesting thing about this reality, however, is how long it took for these countries to get so rich.

Because these countries have been at the cutting edge of technology for a long time, the only way they've been able to push out their PPF and produce more from the same resources has been to invent new technologies. Historically, this adjustment means that living standards in rich countries grow only about 2 percent per year because they need to invent new technologies in order to raise living standards. At this rate, standards of living take about 30 years to double.

An important thing to realize is that these countries are so much richer than other places not because of some sudden stroke of luck, but because of a long history of slow but steady progress. That slowness, however, also means that other countries that aren't yet as rich can grow very quickly and catch up to the living standards of the richest nations.

Developing nations like China and India can grow much more quickly because they can jump from using older, less productive technologies to the most productive, cutting-edge technologies. Consequently, they're showing growth rates of 6 to 8 percent per year. At these rates, living standards double in less than a decade, and it will take only a couple of generations for China and India to have living standards comparable to those in the United States, western Europe, and Japan.

It's not a coincidence that economic growth in the United States and western Europe took off 200 years ago, right after patents became widely enforced. For the first time in world history, there was a secure financial incentive to use your brain to innovate. Before that time, it was extremely risky to innovate because after all your hard work, others would simply copy your invention and sell it without your permission.

Copyrights for literary, musical, and cinematic works serve a similar purpose. A great deal more art is produced when artists know that they can make a living off their products. Along these lines, the easy duplication and distribution of digital media on the Internet is a troubling development because it has weakened artists' ability to charge for the art that they work so hard to produce.

Governments also have a key role to play in encouraging education. You shouldn't be surprised that every rich country in the world has a policy of universal primary and secondary education, as well as strong universities. Smart new technologies require smart, well-educated researchers, and you don't get them without good educational systems.

Advanced economies also require smart, well-educated workers to implement the new technologies. Consequently, it's very important that education be available to everyone if an economy is to utilize the constant flow of innovative new processes and tools that researchers develop.

Part II

Macroeconomics — The Science of Economic Growth and Stability

The 5th Wave   By Rich Tennant

"Business here is good, but the weak dollar is killing my overseas markets."

In this part . . .

The chapters in this part introduce you to *macroeconomics*, the study of the economy as a whole, which concentrates on economy-wide factors like interest rates, inflation, and the rate of unemployment. I explain what economists believe causes recessions, and I use the famous Keynesian model to illustrate the policies that economists believe can best be used to fight recessions. Finally, I touch upon the factors that economists believe are essential to promoting sustained economic growth and rising living standards.

Chapter 4

Measuring the Macroeconomy: How Economists Keep Track of *Everything*

- -

In This Chapter

▶ Measuring GDP: The total value of goods and services

▶ Decomposing GDP into $C + I + G + NX$

▶ Understanding why free trade is good for you

- -

Macroeconomics studies the economy as a whole. Seen from on high, the production of goods and services is done either by businesses or by the government. Businesses produce the bulk of what people consume, but many goods and services are provided by the government, including public safety, national defense, and public goods like roads and bridges. In addition, the government provides the legal structure in which businesses operate and also intervenes in the economy in order to do things like regulate pollution, mandate safety equipment, and redistribute income from the rich to the poor. (For more on the division of tasks between private businesses and the government, see Chapter 3.)

In order for economists to study the process of production, distribution, and consumption with any real understanding, they need to keep track of exactly how much is being produced, as well as where it all ends up. Consequently, economists have developed a huge accounting apparatus, called *National Income and Product Accounts* (NIPA), to measure economic activity. This system produces numerous useful statistics, including the famous *gross domestic product* (GDP), which measures the total quantity of goods and services produced in a country in a given period of time.

The system can seem arcane, but knowing the accounting is indispensable because it's the basis for all the mathematical models that economists use to understand and predict things like the business cycle, inflation, economic growth, and both monetary and fiscal policy. (Some of these models are presented in Chapters 6 and 7.) So please make sure that you take, uh, proper account of what I'm about to show you.

Using GDP to Track the Economy

Gross domestic product, or GDP, is a statistic that calculates the value of all goods and services produced in a given country in a given period of time. In the United States, the Bureau of Economic Analysis at the Department of Commerce computes this statistic every three months, giving us an idea of how much economic activity took place in the previous quarter or year.

GDP is very important because, other things being equal, richer people are happier people. I'm not saying that money is the only thing that matters in life, but economists evaluate economies by how successfully they maximize happiness, and although money can't buy you love, it can sure as heck buy you a lot of other things that make you happy, such as food, education, and vacations. Consequently, a high and quickly growing GDP is preferable because it reflects lots of economic transactions that provide people with the goods and services they desire. (To examine some reasons why GDP may *not* always reflect increased happiness, see the upcoming section "The good, the bad, and the ugly: All things increase GDP.")

In Chapters 2 and 3, I discuss how people's fundamental economic goal is to maximize happiness given the limited resources that constrain them. Because people like to consume goods and services, measuring GDP allows economists to quantify, in some sense, how well a country is doing at maximizing its citizens' happiness given the country's limited resources. A rising GDP indicates that a country is figuring out ways to provide more of the goods and services that make people happy.

In this section, I show you how and why the economists who tabulate the National Income and Product Accounts (NIPA) break up GDP into its constituent parts. Breaking up the GDP allows you to analyze each part separately and get a good handle on the major factors that influence the production of goods and services. But first, I give you a short explanation of what GDP *doesn't* take account of.

Leaving some things out of GDP

The GDP statistic counts only transactions that involve money, so if you do volunteer work for your parents or if a mother stays home to take care of an infant, that economic activity — though very productive and socially beneficial — doesn't get counted in GDP.

In economies like the United States, GDP is very good at capturing nearly all output that's produced because almost everything that's produced here is subsequently sold. But in a largely rural and agrarian society of small farmers, most production is for consumption within the household, meaning that the output never makes it to the official GDP statistics kept by that country's economists. As countries transition from rural agrarian economic structures with lots of household production to market economies where nearly everything produced is sold for money, the GDP appears to rise because a lot of output is being counted for the first time. However, this apparent change may not be an actual increase in output. These limitations can make comparing the GDPs of various countries misleading.

Gettin' in the flow: Tallying up what counts in GDP

Counting sales where money trades hands can get a little tricky because both a buyer and a seller are involved in every such transaction. The money that the buyer spends has to equal the money that the seller receives. Translated into economist lingo, income has to equal expenditure.

Consequently, you can measure GDP by totaling up all the expenditures in the economy or by counting up all the incomes in the economy. If your calculations are correct, both methods give you the same value for GDP.

When thinking about GDP, you also have to consider the goods and services that are being traded for money. Economists simplify life by saying that all the resources or factors of production of a society — land, labor, and capital (see Chapter 3) — are owned by households. *Households* can be made up of one person or several — think in terms of individuals or families. *Firms* buy or rent the factors of production from the households and use them to produce goods and services, which then are sold back to the households. This process sets up a *circular flow* for resources moving from households to firms, and goods and services moving back the other way, as Figure 4-1 shows.

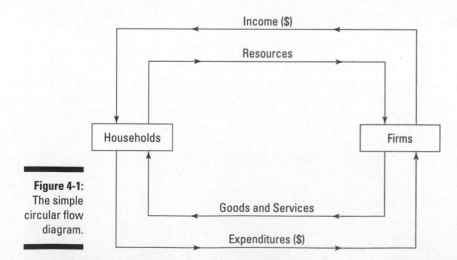

Figure 4-1:
The simple circular flow diagram.

Moving opposite to the flow of resources and goods are payments in dollars. When the firms buy factors of production from households, they have to pay money to the households. That money is income to the households. And when households buy goods and services from the firms, they pay for those goods and services with money, which shows up in the diagram as expenditures.

A key point to understand is that firms are owned by households; they don't exist on their own. As a result, any money that a firm receives when it sells a good or a service flows on as income to some individual or group of individuals. Because of this flow, incomes in Figure 4-1 have to equal expenditures.

Considering flows of income and assets

Although you can use either incomes or expenditures to measure GDP, economists prefer to use incomes because governments make both individuals and businesses keep track of every last penny of income they receive so that it can be taxed. This government requirement provides extensive, accurate data about incomes.

Tracing the flow of income

All the income in the economy flows into one of four categories:

- ✔ Labor receives wages.
- ✔ Land receives rent.
- ✔ Capital receives interest.
- ✔ Entrepreneurship receives profits.

You may recognize the first three of these categories as being the three traditional factors of production that I list in Chapter 3. Obviously, because you need land, labor, and capital to make things, you have to pay for them. That's why some of the income in the economy flows their way. But in a dynamic, competitive economy, you also need people with a willingness to take on business risk and invest in risky new technologies. In order to get them to do so, you have to pay them, which is why some income must also flow to risk-taking entrepreneurs in the form of profits. In fact, I (and many other economists) like to think of entrepreneurship as a fourth factor of production, a factor that must be paid if you want to get stuff produced in a market economy.

Each of the four payments is a flow of money that compensates for a flow of services needed in production:

- ✔ Workers charge wages for the labor services that they provide.
- ✔ Owners of buildings and land charge rents to tenants for the services that real estate and physical structures provide.

> ✔ Firms wanting to obtain the services of capital, such as machines and computers, must pay for them. This payment is considered interest because, for example, the cost of obtaining the services of a $1,000 piece of capital equipment is the interest payments that a firm must make on a $1,000 loan to buy that piece of equipment.
>
> ✔ And, finally, the firm's profits must flow to the entrepreneurs and owners of the firm, who take on the risk that the firm may do badly or even go bankrupt.

Taking assets into consideration

What happens to the flow of income if a firm buys its land and office space rather than rents it? Or if a firm owns its capital outright rather than borrows money to buy it? If a firm owns these things, it no longer has to pay a flow of money in order to obtain a flow of services. Do expenditures still equal incomes?

No need to fear: Incomes still equal expenditures. However, you have to do some fancy accounting to see how this is so. The key to this balancing act is understanding what an asset is.

An *asset* is something durable that isn't directly consumed but that gives off a flow of services that you do consume. For instance, a house is an asset because it provides shelter services. You don't consume the house (just think of all the fiber!); you consume the services it provides. Similarly, a car is an asset because, although you don't consume the car itself, it provides transportation services.

You often have a choice between buying an asset outright and thereby owning all the future services that the asset will provide, or letting someone else own the asset and sell you the services as they're produced. For example, you can buy a house and thereby get all future shelter services that the house will provide, or you can rent the house and get those same services by paying for them each month. For this reason, an asset is considered to be a *stock*, while the services it provides are referred to as a *flow*.

For all assets that a firm owns, accountants put a dollar value on the services that the assets provide based on what those same services would have cost if the firm had rented them. They can then divvy up the firm's total income, calling some of it rent, some of it interest, and some of it profits, as though the owners of the firm are getting three streams of income.

Because the firm's owners provided the money to buy the firm's assets, part of their income is compensation for providing these goods and services, and the rest of their income is counted as compensation for providing entrepreneurship and taking on risk. Consequently, all the money expended on goods and services flows as income to somebody for providing land, labor, capital, or entrepreneurship (the four friendly factors of production). This methodology allows economists to keep saying that incomes equal expenditures even if firms own their own assets.

Following the funds, around and around

The simple circular flow diagram of Figure 4-1 captures the fact that an income exists for every expenditure. However, because the diagram divides the economy only into firms and households, it misses a lot of the action that goes on in the real world. In Figure 4-2, you can see a much more realistic and detailed circular flow diagram that divides the economy into firms, households, and the government, with these entities making transactions through the following three markets:

- ✔ **Markets for factors of production** are where money is exchanged to purchase or rent the land, labor, capital, and entrepreneurship used in production.

- ✔ **Financial markets** are where people who want to lend money (savers) interact with those who want to borrow money (borrowers). In this market, the supply and demand for loans determine the *interest rate,* which is the price you have to pay to get someone to lend you their money for a while. Because most governments run deficits (in other words, they're always in the hole) and have to borrow a lot of money, they're major players in the financial markets.

- ✔ **Markets for goods and services** are where people and the government buy the stuff that firms make.

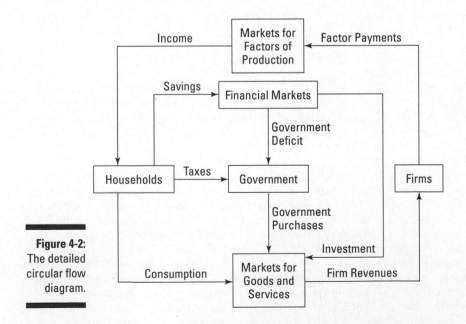

Figure 4-2:
The detailed circular flow diagram.

In Figure 4-2, arrows show the flows of dollars throughout the economy. Firms make factor payments — rent, wages, interest, and profits — to households to obtain the factors of production — land, labor, capital, and entrepreneurship. (See the previous section, "Considering flows of incomes and assets," for more information.) Households take the income they get from selling these factors and use it to pay for goods and services, to pay taxes, or to save. The government buys goods and services using either the tax revenues it takes in or the money it borrows in the financial markets. The financial markets also provide dollars for corporations to make investments. These dollars add to those that firms get from selling goods and services to households and the government.

Note: Not all transactions in the financial markets are relevant to the calculation of GDP. GDP measures currently produced output, and most transactions in the financial markets are trading property rights for stuff produced long ago. (For example, a house that was built 30 years ago has nothing to do with current production, so the sale of the house doesn't factor into this year's GDP. Only the sales of newly constructed houses figure into this year's GDP.)

Counting stuff when it's made, not when it's sold

Newly produced output is counted as part of GDP as soon as it's produced, even before it gets sold. That makes keeping track of the money associated with new production a little tricky.

For example, as soon as construction on a new house is completed, its market value of $300,000 is estimated and counted as part of GDP right then, even though the house may not be sold for months. Suppose construction was completed on December 29, 2004, adding $300,000 to the year 2004's GDP. If the house is subsequently sold on February 21, 2005, it doesn't count in the year 2005's GDP because double counting isn't allowed.

When the house is sold, it's considered old property and not new production. Economists just say that the property right to this now old house has changed hands from the builder to the new owner. Because trading old assets obviously involves no new production, it doesn't count in GDP.

This accounting convention applies to firms producing any sort of output good whatsoever. If Sony produces a TV on December 31, 2004, the value of that TV is counted in the year 2004's GDP, even though it won't be sold to a customer until the next year. A handy way to think about this is to imagine that Sony builds the TV and then, in effect, sells it to itself when it puts the

TV into inventory. This "sale" is what is counted in GDP for the year 2004. When the TV is later sold out of inventory to a customer, it's just an exchange of assets (trading the TV for cash).

The fact that output is counted when it's produced rather than when it's sold is a red flag when interpreting GDP statistics to gauge the health of the economy. High GDP means only that a lot of stuff is being produced and put into inventory. It doesn't necessarily mean that firms are selling lots of stuff.

In fact, it's quite possible that GDP is high but the economy is about to go into a recession because inventories are piling up and managers will soon cut back on production in order to get inventories back down to target levels. Consequently, economists who try to forecast where the economy is heading pay much more attention to inventory levels than they do to last quarter's GDP.

The good, the bad, and the ugly: All things increase GDP

Generally speaking, higher GDP is better than lower GDP because more output produced means higher potential living standards, including better healthcare for the sick and more money to aid the needy.

But higher GDP doesn't guarantee that happiness is increasing because GDP often goes up when bad things happen. For instance, if a hurricane destroys a big section of a city, GDP goes up as reconstruction kicks into gear and lots of new output is produced to replace what was destroyed. But wouldn't it have been better not to have had the hurricane in the first place?

Similarly, higher GDP may be possible in certain situations only if you're willing to tolerate more pollution or greater income inequality. Countries experiencing rapid economic development and quickly rising living standards often also get dirtier environments and more social unrest because some people are getting richer much faster than others. The GDP number doesn't reflect these negative conditions.

GDP also doesn't count the value of leisure. Many of my favorite times have been when I was neither producing nor consuming anything that would count in GDP — sitting on the beach, climbing a mountain, taking a walk, working out with friends. Moreover, an increase in GDP often comes at the price of sacrificing these leisure activities — meaning that when you see an increase in GDP, overall well-being or happiness hasn't necessarily improved.

So although policies that raise GDP are generally beneficial for society, the costs involved in creating the rising output must always be examined.

Introducing the GDP Equation

So far in this chapter, I've only *introduced* you to GDP. Now it's time for you and GDP to make friends so that you can understand all of GDP's little secrets — in particular, its constituent parts and how they behave. The discussion in this section is really interesting in and of itself, but it's doubly useful because it makes the standard Keynesian macroeconomic model (which I introduce in Chapter 6) much easier to understand and manipulate.

The Keynesian model was first developed in 1936 by Cambridge University economist John Maynard Keynes, in his book *The General Theory of Employment, Interest, and Money*. That text was hugely influential — so influential, in fact, that it led to macroeconomics becoming a separate field of study for economists.

Keynes's book was a response to the Great Depression of the 1930s. Because he felt that government policies designed to fight that economic downturn should focus on getting people to increase their expenditures on goods and services, Keynes began his model by using an equation that measures GDP by adding up expenditures.

In the section "Gettin' in the flow: Tallying up what counts in GDP," earlier in this chapter, I explain that you can measure GDP either by adding up all the expenditures made on purchasing goods and services or by adding up all the incomes that are derived from producing goods and services. The two numbers have to be equal. So this switch to the expenditure method of counting up GDP is totally kosher. (It's also the perfect opportunity for you to understand the economy from the point of view of where money gets spent, as opposed to who gets to keep what's earned.)

The expenditure equation for totaling up GDP adds together the four traditional expenditure categories — consumption *(C)*, investment *(I)*, government *(G)*, and net exports *(NX)* — to equal the value in dollars (or whatever currency a given country is using) of all goods and services produced domestically in that period, or the GDP *(Y)*. In terms of algebra, the equation looks like this:

$$Y = C + I + G + NX$$

Although the following sections go into more detail, here's a quick look at the four expenditure variables that total up to GDP:

- ✔ *C* **stands for consumption expenditures** made by households on goods and services, whether domestically produced or produced abroad.

- ✔ *I* **stands for investment expenditures** made by firms on new capital goods including buildings, factories, and equipment. *I* also contains changes in inventories, as any goods produced but not sold during a period have to go into firms' inventories and are counted as inventory investments.

- *G* **stands for government purchases of goods and services** (they've got to buy paperclips over there).

- *NX* **stands for net exports,** which is defined as all a country's exports *(EX)* minus all its imports *(IM),* or *NX = EX – IM. EX* is the number of dollars of our output that foreigners are buying. *IM* is the number of dollars of their output that we're buying.

These four expenditures give us GDP because, as a group, they buy up every last bit of output produced in our country in a given period.

C is for consumption (that's good enough for me!)

Household consumption spending accounts for about 70 percent of GDP — far more than the other three components combined. Many factors affect how much of their income households decide to spend on consumption and how much of it they decide to save for the future.

Microeconomists spend a lot of time studying the various factors that affect such decisions, including expectations about whether the future looks bright or dark and how high or low the rates of return are on savings. (See Part III of this book for everything you ever wanted to know about microeconomics.) Macroeconomists, on the other hand, step back from these factors because, when studying the economy as a whole, what matters is how much total consumption there is rather than why households happen to choose that particular level.

Macroeconomists model consumption very simply, as a function of people's after-tax, or disposable, incomes. You can derive disposable income algebraically using this handy three-step process:

1. **Start with *Y,* the total income in the economy.** In Keynes's equation, *Y* equals total expenditures, but because income equals expenditures, you can use it for income as well. Remember that any money expended by you is income to someone else.

2. **Figure out how much taxes people have to pay.** For simplicity, assume that the only tax is an income tax and that the income tax rate is given by *t.* For instance, *t* = 0.25 would mean a tax rate of 25 percent of people's incomes. Consequently, the total taxes people pay, *T,* will be given by *T* = *t***Y.*

3. **Subtract people's taxes, *T,* from their incomes, *Y,* to figure out their after-tax incomes.** Economists refer to this as *disposable income* and write it algebraically as Y_D. Subtracting taxes from income looks like this:

$$Y_D = Y - T = Y - t{*}Y = (1-t){*}Y$$

After you derive disposable income, you use a very simple model to figure consumption expenditures made by households. The model says that consumption, C, is a function of disposable income and a couple other variables, C_o and c.

$$C = C_o + c*Y_D$$

Lowercase c is called the *marginal propensity to consume,* or MPC. It's always a number between 0 and 1 that indicates the rate at which you choose to consume income rather than save it. For instance, if $c = .9$, then you consume 90 cents of every dollar of disposable income that you have after paying taxes. (You save the other ten cents.)

The actual value of the marginal propensity to consume, c, is determined by the individual and varies from person to person depending on how much of their disposable incomes they like to save. But what is C_o? Think of it as how much people consume even if they have zero disposable income this year. (If you assume that $Y_D = 0$ in the equation $C = C_o + c*Y_D$, then that equation reduces to $C = C_o$.) But where does the money come from to pay for C_o if you have zero disposable income? It comes from your personal savings, which you've piled up over the years.

What the overall equation $C = C_o + c*Y_D$ says is that your total consumption expenditure in an economy will be your emergency level (when you have zero income) C_o plus a part of your disposable income given by $c*Y_D$.

For the rest of this book, I assume that the equation $C = C_o + c*Y_D$ is a good enough model of how consumption expenditures are determined in the economy. It's not perfectly realistic, but it does show that consumption is reduced by higher tax rates and that people make a decision about how much of their disposable incomes to save or consume. The equation allows me to analyze the effects of policies that change tax rates and the effects of other policies that encourage people to spend higher or lower fractions of their incomes.

I is for investment in capital stock (or should it be "I am"?)

Investment is vitally important because the economy's capacity to produce depends on how much capital is available to make output. The capital stock increases when firms purchase new tools, buildings, machines, computers, and so on to help produce consumption goods. Investment is a flow that increases the capital stock of the economy.

But, of course, capital wears out as it's used. Some of it rusts. Some of it breaks down. Some of it is thrown away when it becomes obsolete. All these flows that decrease the capital stock are called *depreciation* by economists.

Naturally, firms must make some investments just to replace the capital that has depreciated. But any investment in excess of depreciation causes the overall size of the capital stock to increase, creating more potential output for people to consume.

The flow of investment spending over any period of time depends on the comparisons that firms make between the potential benefits and the costs of buying pieces of capital. The potential benefits are measured in terms of potential profits, and the costs of buying are measured by the interest rate, regardless of whether or not a firm takes out a loan to buy a given piece of capital.

Why does the interest rate matter so much? Naturally, if a firm needs to take out a loan to buy capital, higher interest rates make it less likely to borrow money because the loan repayment costs will be high. However, even if a firm has enough cash on hand to buy a given piece of equipment, higher interest rates force the firm to decide between using the cash to buy the equipment and loaning it out to someone else. The higher the interest rates, the more attractive loaning it out becomes. Consequently, higher interest rates discourage investment regardless of whether firms have to borrow to fund investment. (See Chapter 2 for the reasons why higher interest rates increase the opportunity cost of investing.)

Economists model the amount of investment expenditure that firms desire to make, I, as a function of the interest rate, r, which is given as a percentage. The equation that I use here is standard in introductory books on macroeconomics (although notation does vary from book to book):

$$I = I_o - I_r^* r$$

This equation is similar in spirit to the consumption equation in the previous section except for the minus sign, which indicates that when the interest rate rises, I falls.

The parameter I_r tells you how much I falls in an entire economy for any given increase in interest rates. For instance, suppose that r rises by one percentage point. If I_r is, say, 10 billion, you know that each one percentage point increase in interest rates will decrease investment by $10 billion.

The parameter I_o tells you how much investment would occur if interest rates were zero. In truth, interest rates never fall all the way to zero, but suppose that they did. Then the second term in the equation would be equal to zero, leaving you with $I = I_o$.

The equation as a whole says that if interest rates were zero, investment expenditures would max out at I_o. But as interest rates rise above zero and keep on rising, investment falls more and more. In fact, rates could potentially rise so high that investment spending would fall to zero.

The relationship between rates and investment is one reason why the government's ability to set interest rates has great bearing on the economy. By setting interest rates, the government can determine how much businesses want to spend buying investment goods. In particular, if the economy is in a recession, the government can lower interest rates in order to raise firms' expenditures on investment and (we hope) help improve the economy.

G whiz! Government, that is

In most countries, a huge portion of GDP is consumed by government. In the United States, government at local, state, and federal levels consumes about 35 percent of GDP. In many other countries, the proportion is even higher. In most of Europe, for instance, it's nearer to 50 percent.

The government gets the money to buy all that output from taxation and borrowing. If a government's tax revenues are exactly equal to its expenditures, it has a *balanced budget*. If tax revenues are greater than expenditures, it's running a *budget surplus*. But if its expenditures exceed its tax revenues, which it can do by borrowing the difference on the financial markets, it's running a *budget deficit*.

Governments borrow by selling bonds. A typical bond says that in exchange for $10,000 right now, the government will give you back $10,000 in ten years and, in the meantime, pay you $1,000 per year for each of the intervening years. If you accept the deal and buy the bond, you're in effect lending the government $10,000 right now and getting a 10 percent per year return until the government gives you back your $10,000 in ten years.

A huge amount of political maneuvering goes into determining how much a government is going to spend in a given year. Many groups lobby for special programs to benefit their hometown or their industry, and no matter what, governments have to provide for essential governmental functions like national defense and law enforcement.

However, economists largely ignore the political machinations that go into determining government expenditures because the economic effects of government expenditure, G, depend on how big the expenditure turns out to be — not on how it got to be that size. Consequently, for the rest of this book, I make the simplifying assumption that government expenditures can be denoted as

$$G = G_o$$

That is, G is equal to some number, G_o, that is determined by the political process. This number may be high or low depending on politics, but in the end you care only about how big or small it turns out to be and can ignore where it came from.

G includes only government expenditures on newly produced goods and services. It doesn't include government expenditures that merely transfer money from one person to another. For instance, when the government taxes me and gives the money to a poor person, that transaction has nothing to do with currently produced goods and services and consequently doesn't count as part of *G.* So, remember that when I talk about *G,* I'm talking about only the government's purchases of currently produced goods and services.

NX: Not a foreign sports car

When your country sells domestically made goods and services to someone or some firm in another country, such sales are called *exports.* When someone in your country buys something produced abroad, such purchases are called *imports. Net exports,* or *NX,* is simply the total value of all exports minus the total value of all imports during a given period of time. When using the expenditure method for totaling up GDP, you add in net exports, *NX.*

But why only *net* exports? Good question, and economists typically do a lousy job explaining why you have to subtract imports from exports in this equation. Here's the skinny.

The whole point of totaling up expenditures to get GDP is to figure out how many total dollars were expended on products made within your own country's borders. Most of that expenditure is made by locals, but foreigners can also expend money on your products. That's exactly what happens when they pay you for the goods that you export to them. Consequently, you have to add in *EX* if you want to get a correct measure of expenditures made on stuff you produce domestically.

The reason you have to subtract your imports of foreign goods is that you must differentiate the total expenditures that domestic residents make on *all* goods and services from their expenditures on *domestically made* goods and services. Total expenditures on all goods and services, both domestic and foreign, are C (see the earlier section, "C is for consumption [that's good enough for me!]"). If you want to get just the part that's spent on domestically made stuff, you have to subtract the value of imports, *IM,* because all money spent on imports is money that's *not* spent on domestically made goods and services. So C – IM gives the amount of money that domestic residents spend on domestically produced output.

The result is that you can write your GDP expenditures equation that totals up all expenditures made on domestically produced output as follows:

$$Y = C - IM + I + G + EX$$

But the equation is normally rearranged to put the exports and imports next to each other like this:

$$Y = C + I + G + EX - IM$$

The reason for rearranging is because *EX – IM* quickly reveals your country's *trade balance*. When *EX – IM* is positive, you're exporting more than you're importing; when it's negative, you're importing more than you're exporting. Economists like it when the math is presented in a way that tells a little story.

International trade is hugely important, and you should have a good understanding of not only why trade balances can be positive or negative, but also why you shouldn't necessarily worry if it's negative rather than positive. I cover this topic in the next section.

Understanding How International Trade Affects the Economy

Modern countries do a huge amount of trading with other countries — so huge, in fact, that for many countries imports and exports are equal to more than 50 percent of their GDPs. So, now's as good a time as any to focus a little more deeply on the *NX* part of the GDP expenditure equation, $Y = C + I + G + NX$.

Understanding how international trade affects the economy is absolutely essential if you hope to have a complete understanding of macroeconomics. It's also important because politicians are constantly suggesting policies like tariffs and exchange rate controls that are aimed squarely at international trade — but whose effects reverberate throughout the domestic economy.

This section explains why trade deficits (negative values of *NX*) aren't necessarily bad and just why it is that engaging in international trade — even when it means sustaining trade deficits — is typically hugely beneficial.

Trade deficits can be good for you!

If your exports exceed your imports, you have a *trade surplus,* whereas if your imports exceed your exports, you have a *trade deficit.* Unfortunately, the words *surplus* and *deficit* carry strong connotations that make it sound like surpluses are necessarily better than deficits. That's just not true, but you wouldn't know it from the rhetoric that politicians throw around. They make it sound as if trade deficits are always bad and always lead to calamity.

To understand why the politicians are wrong (as if you needed any convincing), consider an example of two individuals who want to trade. Each person starts with $100 cash, and each produces a product for sale. The first guy grows and sells apples for $1 each. The second guy grows and sells oranges, also for $1 each. Each of them produces 50 pieces of fruit.

Next, suppose that the guy who grows apples really likes oranges and wants to buy 30 of them for $30, and that the guy who grows oranges wants to buy 20 apples for $20. Each guy is happy to satisfy the other guy's desires, so the apple grower spends $30 buying oranges from the orange grower, and the orange grower spends $20 buying apples from the apple grower.

Their trades shouldn't cause any alarm bells to ring, but when people start looking at their trades using the terms *trade surplus* and *trade deficit,* they often come to the false conclusion that only one of the guys benefits from the trades that, in reality, they both were quite eager to make.

To see where the confusion arises, notice that in the vocabulary of international trade, the apple guy exports only $20 worth of apples but imports $30 worth of oranges. At the same time, the orange guy exports $30 worth of oranges but imports only $20 worth of apples. As a result, you have a situation in which the apple guy is running a $10 trade deficit and the orange guy is running a $10 trade surplus.

Does this mean that the apple guy is worse off than the orange guy? No. Each person started with $150 worth of stuff: their respective $100 cash piles plus $50 each worth of fruit. When they finish trading, they each still have $150 worth of stuff. The apple guy has $90 of cash plus $30 worth of apples and $30 worth of oranges. The orange guy has $110 of cash plus $20 worth of oranges and $20 worth of apples.

Saying that their trading has made either one of them poorer is way off the mark. In fact, both of them are happier with their arrangements of wealth after trading than they were before trading because their trades were voluntary. If the apple guy would have been happier keeping his initial holdings of $100 cash and 50 apples, he wouldn't have traded for oranges. And the same with the orange guy.

As long as international trade is voluntary, all trades enhance happiness. To concentrate on whether a trade deficit or surplus exists is to completely miss the point that international trade is simply a rearrangement of assets between countries that makes everyone happier. Even the country running the trade deficit is happier.

Considering assets — not just cash

To people who hate trade deficits, the fact that the apple guy's cash pile falls from $100 before the trade to only $90 after the trade looks spooky because they're totally focused on the fact that the apple guy is $10 poorer in terms of cash after the trading. And they're even more peeved because that $10 ends up with the orange guy, giving him a commanding $110 to $90 advantage in terms of cash piles.

This perspective misses the fact that the apple guy's overall wealth is still $150 and that he now has a distribution of assets that is more pleasing to him than what he had before. But, if you point this out, deficit haters respond by asking you what happens after the apple guy eats his 30 apples and 30 oranges and after the orange guy eats his 20 apples and 20 oranges. In the end, all that the fruit guys have left are their respective cash piles. Because the apple guy has $20 less cash than the orange guy, he must be worse off by running a trade deficit.

Again, this reasoning misses the point that the apple guy was happier trading and ending up with $90 of cash than he would have been not trading and ending up with $100 in cash. If it weren't for trade, he'd have had a very boring diet of only apples.

Opponents of trade deficits really make things seem scary when they start talking about land trading hands due to international trade. (Oh no, the foreigners are taking over your country!) To see their point, imagine that instead of starting with $100 each of cash, the fruit farmers each start with 100 acres of land worth $1 per acre. The only way for the apple guy to come up with $10 of cash to pay for his trade deficit is by selling 10 acres of land to the orange guy. That is, the overall exchange that they engage in is 20 apples plus 10 acres of land worth a combined $30 in exchange for 30 oranges worth $30. Because 10 of the apple guy's acres of land now belong to the orange guy, deficit haters think the apple guy sold out his country — literally.

Such transfers of property do happen in real life. During the 1980s, the United States ran huge trade deficits with Japan. The result was that Japanese corporations and individuals ended up owning many famous U.S. buildings and companies. This really spooked many jingoistic U.S. politicians, but they missed the point that all trading in life — be it with foreigners or fellow citizens — is designed to make you happy. After all, what good is keeping all your 100 acres of land if you're happier trading 10 of them for foreign-made goods? Or, in the case of the United States during the 1980s, what good is continuing to own Times Square or Columbia Pictures if you'd rather trade them for Honda Accords and Sony VCRs? (The anti-Japanese hysteria at the time was even sillier given that the largest group of foreign owners of U.S. property was, and still is, the British!)

Much to the chagrin of economists, the argument that the point of trade is to make you *happier* doesn't always fly well. A lot of people view trade as an antagonistic contest to dominate other countries by constantly running trade surpluses so that you eventually own all the other guy's assets. To this end, they argue for restrictions on trade designed to rig trade relations so that their own countries always run surpluses. But such policies inevitably fail because any time you put up a tariff barrier or an import tax to discourage imports and improve your trade balance, other countries can do the same. The result of such *trade wars* is that all the barriers, restrictions, and taxes imposed by both sides reduce international trade to a trickle. No one comes out ahead, and no one's happy.

Consequently, for the last 50 years, national governments have increasingly pushed for fewer and fewer restrictions on international trade. This *free trade* movement has resulted in hundreds of millions of new jobs and a vast improvement in living standards and happiness because people all over the world are free to trade and buy whatever they want to make them most happy — even if that means buying from a foreigner.

Wielding a comparative advantage

The argument that even countries running trade deficits are better off because they get to consume a mix of goods and services they couldn't get otherwise rests solely on the benefits of trading things that have already been produced. But an even better argument for international trade is the fact that it actually increases the total amount of output produced in the world, meaning that there is more output per person, and overall living standards rise.

This argument, known as *comparative advantage,* was developed by the English economist David Ricardo in 1817 as a forceful rebuttal against import tariffs known as the *Corn Laws,* which heavily taxed imports of foreign-grown grain at the time. These laws kept the price of grain high, so the nobility that owned the vast majority of farmland favored keeping them. Naturally, the poor were opposed because the laws drove up the price of their basic food supply: bread.

Ricardo pointed out that abolishing restrictions on international trade would, in addition to helping England's poor, actually make England and all the countries it traded with richer by encouraging them to specialize in the production of goods and services that each of them could produce at the lowest possible cost. He demonstrated that this process of specialization would increase total worldwide output and thereby raise living standards.

The logic behind the comparative advantage argument is most easily understood by thinking in terms of people instead of countries. Consider a patent lawyer named Heather and her brother Adam, who works as a bike mechanic. Heather is very good at filing patents for new discoveries, but she's also very good at repairing bicycles. In fact, she's faster at repairing them than her brother. On the other hand, Adam is a smart guy and can file patents, too, although not as quickly as Heather can. Table 4-1 lists how many bike repairs and patent filings each of them could do in one day if they put all their efforts into only one of the activities.

Table 4-1	Productivity for Heather and Adam per Day	
Person	*Patent Productivity*	*Bike Repair Productivity*
Heather	6	12
Adam	2	10

In one day's work, Heather can produce 6 patents or repair 12 bikes, whereas Adam can file 2 patents or repair 10 bikes. Heather is more efficient than her brother at producing both patents and bike repairs because she can convert one day's labor into more of either good than Adam can.

Economists say that Heather has an *absolute advantage* over Adam at producing both goods, meaning that she's the more efficient producer of both; with the same amount of labor input (one workday), she can produce more than her brother. Before David Ricardo came along and invented comparative advantage, the only thing anyone knew to look at was absolute advantage. And when they saw situations like that of Heather and Adam, they concluded (incorrectly) that because Heather is more efficient than Adam at both tasks, she has no need to trade with him.

In other words, people used to incorrectly believe that because Heather is better than Adam at repairing bikes, she should not only work hard as a patent attorney filing lots of patents, but she should also fix her own bike whenever it breaks down. Ricardo pointed out that this argument based on absolute advantage is bogus and that Heather should, in fact, *never* fix bikes despite the fact that she's the most efficient bike repairperson around. The nifty thing Ricardo realized is that the world is better off if each person (and country) specializes.

The key insight of comparative advantage is that the proper measure of cost when considering whether Heather should produce one good or the other isn't how many hours of labor input it takes her to produce one patent or one bike repair (which is the logic behind absolute advantage). Instead, the true cost is how much production of one good you have to give up to produce a unit of the other good.

To produce one patent, Heather must give up the chance to repair two bikes. In contrast, to make one patent, Adam would have to give up the chance to repair five bikes. So, Heather is the lower cost producer of patents and, therefore, should specialize in filing patents. And Adam should specialize in bike repairs because he's the lower cost producer of bike repairs.

On a larger scale, countries should specialize in the production of goods and services that they can deliver at lower costs than other countries. If countries are free to do this, everything that's produced comes from the lowest-cost producer. Because this arrangement leads to the most efficient possible production, total output increases, thereby raising living standards.

Politicians often argue that countries shouldn't be "dependent" on other countries for various goods and services. Any policy that takes this warning seriously by impeding trade and specialization increases costs and makes total output fall.

By letting comparative advantage guide who makes what, free trade increases total world output and thereby raises living standards. Under free trade, each country specializes in its area(s) of comparative advantage and then trades with other countries to obtain the goods and services it desires to consume.

Don't be tricked by absolute advantage. As you see in this section's example, Heather has an absolute advantage at everything but has a comparative advantage only at filing patents. Having an absolute advantage means that you can make something at a lower cost as measured in inputs. (For example, Heather requires fewer hours of labor input to file a patent than Adam does.) However, what matters in life isn't inputs but outputs — the things that people actually want to consume. By focusing on costs as measured in terms of alternative types of output that must be given up to produce something, comparative advantage assures that you're focusing on being efficient in terms of what really matters: output.

Chapter 5

Inflation Frustration: Why More Money Isn't Always a Good Thing

*I*nflation is the word economists use to describe a situation in which the general level of prices in the economy is rising. This doesn't mean that every price of every good is going up — a few prices may even be falling — but the overall trend is upward. Typically, the trend is for prices to go up only a small percentage each year, but people dislike even mild inflations because, face it, who likes paying higher prices? Mild inflation also causes problems like making retirement planning difficult. After all, if you don't know how expensive things will be when you retire, it's hard to calculate with any certainty how much money you need to be saving right now.

Things can go from bad to worse if inflation really gets out of control and prices begin rising 20 or 30 percent per month — something that has happened in more than a few countries in the past century. Such situations of *hyperinflation* usually accompany a major economic collapse featuring high unemployment and a major decrease in the production of goods and services. (For more on prices and how they affect the economy, see Chapter 6.)

The good news, however, is that economists know exactly what causes inflation and precisely how to stop it. The culprit is a money supply that grows too quickly, and the solution is to simply slow or halt the growth of the money supply. Unfortunately, some political pressure is always exerted in favor of inflation so that simply knowing how to prevent inflation doesn't necessarily mean it won't develop.

In this chapter, I tell you some things about money and inflation that you may not already know, including why governments are often tempted to print a lot of money to pay for budget deficits, why doing that is actually a form of taxation, and why there's always a constituency encouraging the government to go ahead and print a ton of money. I also show you why printing lots of money causes inflations, how to measure inflations, and how to measure the effect that inflation has on interest rates. The one thing I won't tell you is how to print your own money — this ain't *Counterfeiting For Dummies.*

Buying an Inflation: The Risks of Too Much Money

It's hard to overstate how important money is to the proper functioning of the economy. Without it, you'd waste most of your time *bartering,* or arranging trades of one good for another — kind of like in kindergarten ("I'll trade you my sandwich for your brownie"). Bartering works well only in the rare circumstance that you run into somebody who has what you want and who wants what you have.

Money provides a medium of exchange so you can still trade for the brownie from the kid next to you, even if you don't have a sandwich. Money can be any good, object, or thing, but its defining characteristic is that it's accepted as payment for all other goods and services. In today's economy, people pay for things using a wide variety of monies, including government-issued coins and cash, checks drawn on private bank deposits, and electronic payments facilitated by credit cards and debit cards. Because it affects nearly every economic transaction that takes place, money is at the heart of *macroeconomics,* the study of the economy as a whole.

Balancing money supply and demand

As with everything in life, balance is essential. If a government prints too much money, prices go up and you get inflation. If a government prints too little, prices go down and you get deflation. But how much money is the right amount? And why does printing too much or too little cause inflation or deflation?

Basically, the value of money is determined by supply and demand (which I discuss in detail in Chapter 8):

✔ The *supply* of money is under government control, and the government can very easily print more money any time it wants to.

✔ The *demand* for money derives from its usefulness as a means of paying for things and from the fact that having money means not having to engage in barter.

For any given supply of money, supply and demand interact to set a value for each unit of money. If money is in short supply, each piece of money is very valuable; fewer pieces of money translate into fewer chances to avoid having to engage in barter. But if the government greatly increases the supply of money, then each individual unit of money loses value because getting enough money together to avoid barter is easy.

Prices and the value of money are *inversely related,* meaning that when the value of money goes up, prices go down (and vice versa). To see how this relationship works, suppose that money is in short supply and is consequently very valuable. Because it's very valuable, it buys a lot of stuff. For instance, one dollar may buy 10 pounds of coffee (that's ten cents per pound). But if money's very common, then each unit isn't very valuable. In this case, one dollar may buy only 1 pound of coffee (that's one dollar per pound). So the greater the supply of money, the higher the prices.

The demand for money tends to grow slowly over time; growing economies produce more stuff, and consumers demand more money with which to buy the available stuff. Depending on how a government reacts to consumer demand for more money, three scenarios are possible:

- ✔ If a government increases the supply of money *at the same rate* as the growing demand for money, prices don't change. In other words, if supply and demand for money grow at equal rates, the relative value of money doesn't change.

- ✔ If the government increases the supply of money *faster* than the demand for money grows, inflation results as money becomes relatively more plentiful and each piece of money becomes relatively less valuable. With each piece of money carrying less value, you need more of it to buy stuff, causing prices to rise.

- ✔ If the government increases the supply of money *slower* than the demand for money grows, deflation results because each piece of money grows relatively more valuable. Buying any given good or service requires less money.

You may be wondering if there's any way to know exactly how much inflation you can expect from printing any given amount of extra money. You're in luck! The *quantity theory of money* states that the overall level of prices in the economy is proportional to the quantity of money circulating in the economy. *Proportional* just means that things go up by equal amounts, so the quantity theory can also be stated this way: If you double the money supply, you double prices.

But *why* would any government want to cause an inflation or a deflation of any size whatsoever? For the answer to that question, read on!

Beating barter: Show me the money!

Historically, people have used a wide variety of things as money:

✔ Seashells were used as money in ancient China, throughout the Pacific, and also by Native Americans.

✔ Boxes of cigarettes were used as money in prisoner-of-war camps during World War II.

✔ Various agricultural products, such as barley or cattle, were used as money by many cultures.

✔ Huge, doughnut-shaped stones were used on the island of Yap in the Pacific.

Eventually, most of the ancient world realized that metal made the best money. Metal doesn't wear out or shatter like seashells; it doesn't get moldy like barley; and it can easily be carried around in your pocket, unlike giant doughnut-shaped stones. Shaping metal money into coins, though, was a later innovation. The first metal monies had other shapes, with early Celts preferring ring money; ancient Mesopotamians being fond of long, helical ribbons of metal; and the Chinese using metal monies cast in the shapes of knives and spades.

Regardless of the shape or substance, nearly every society designated some good or other to serve as money. If they didn't, they were stuck with barter — a fate everyone wanted to avoid.

Giving in to the inflation temptation

Inflation of prices is caused primarily by governments printing more paper money or producing a large amount of cheap-metal coins, which vastly increases the supply of money and makes each piece of money less precious. As sellers demand higher prices to make up for the fact that each piece of money is worth less, you've got inflation.

So why in the world would governments ever print too much money? Good question. Historically, governments circulate more money in three circumstances:

✔ When governments can't raise enough tax revenue to pay their obligations

✔ When governments feel pressure from debtors who want inflation so they can repay their debts using less valuable money

✔ When governments want to try to stimulate the economy during a recession or depression

As you find out more about these three reasons for increasing the money supply, keep in mind what you read in the previous section: If the supply of money increases faster than the demand for money, inflation results. Consequently, no matter what reason a government has for increasing the supply of money, it runs the risk of inflation. And that's true both for good reasons like wanting to help the economy out of a recession, and for bad reasons like helping debtors to repay their loans using less valuable money.

Paying bills by printing bills: Heading for hyperinflation

Governments almost always have debts, and printing extra money can be a tempting way to pay them. Quite often, a government may want to spend more money than it's collecting in tax revenue. One solution is to borrow the shortfall, but another is to simply print up new bills to cover the difference.

Until very recently, printing new bills was difficult because most of the world's paper currencies were backed by a valuable metal, such as gold. Under this system, every piece of paper money circulating in the economy was convertible into a specific quantity of gold so that anyone holding cash could redeem their cash for gold any time they wanted. For instance, in the United States, you could bring $35 cash to the U.S. Treasury and get exactly one ounce of gold.

This *gold standard* made it difficult for the government to devalue the currency by printing too much money because it first had to get more gold with which to back the new money. Because purchasing gold is expensive, governments were effectively restrained from increasing their money supplies.

But in 1971, President Nixon took the United States off the gold standard and put us on the *fiat system,* in which paper currency isn't backed by anything. People just have to accept the currency as though it has value. In fact, *fiat* is Latin for "Let it be!" So when you say *fiat money,* you're basically referring to how a government creates money simply by ordering it into existence. The problem with a fiat money system is that nothing limits the number of little pieces of paper that the government can print up to pay its debts.

Croesus and Kubulai: The kings of money

King Croesus of Lydia is usually given credit for solving the problem of bogus metal money. In the sixth century B.C., Croesus issued the first government-certified coins that guaranteed purity and weight. Lydia was located in what is now western Turkey, and soon all the major trading nations of the Mediterranean were using the new Lydian coins because they were by far the most trustworthy medium of exchange available. The new coinage gave Lydian traders a major advantage, and the kingdom soon became very wealthy, so much so that Croesus was considered the richest man in the world — even richer than King Midas (of *Midas touch* fame), whose gold Croesus minted into coins.

But coins are hard to carry around in large amounts, and it was up to the Chinese emperor Kubulai Khan to create the first paper money in the 13th century. This paper money was actually a kind of precious metal certificate; people holding one of these certificates could go to a government vault and redeem it for gold. Consequently, the pieces of paper were as good as gold, but a stack of paper was a whole lot easier to carry than a heavy bag of coins.

Paper money was such a radical innovation that when Marco Polo came back from China and told Europeans about it, they laughed, unable to conceive of anything other than gold or silver coins serving as money. Their incredulity was hard to overcome, and after paper money fell out of favor in China, it would be centuries before another government issued any again.

The trouble with printing money to pay your debts and obligations is that as soon as the money's out there, people spend it, drive up prices, and cause an inflation. And if you print more and more money, you end up with people offering shopkeepers and producers more and more money for the same amount of goods. It's like a giant auction where everybody bidding on items keeps getting more and more money to bid with.

If a government gets into the habit of rapidly printing new money to pay its bills, inflation can soon reach or even surpass 20 or 30 percent per month, a situation referred to as a *hyperinflation*. Economists hate hyperinflations because they greatly disrupt daily life and ruin the investment climate.

First, hyperinflation causes people to waste huge amounts of time trying to avoid the effects of rising prices. During the Weimar hyperinflation in Germany (which I discuss in the sidebar "Hyperinflation and Hitler"), men working at factories were paid two or even three times a day because money lost its value so quickly. Their wives waited at the factories to immediately take the money to the nearest shops, trying to spend the pay before it lost most of its value. Shopping may be fun, but not when you're desperately racing against outrageously rising prices!

Hyperinflation also destroys the incentive to save because the only sensible thing to do with money during a hyperinflation is to spend it as quickly as you can before it loses even more of its value. People whose life savings were in German marks during the Weimar hyperinflation soon found that what they had worked so hard to amass had become worthless. And people thinking about saving for the future were greatly discouraged because they knew that any money they saved would soon lose all value. The discouragement of saving causes major business problems because if people aren't saving, then no money is available for businesses to borrow for new investments. And without new investments, the economy can't grow.

Feeling printing press pressures: The politics of inflation

Even if the government isn't trying to use inflation to increase tax revenues, a certain political constituency will always pressure it to circulate more money. You may even be a member of this group — they're called *borrowers*.

To understand the politics of inflation, understand that one of the functions of money is as a *standard of deferred payment*. What does that mean? Imagine that you borrow $1,000 to invest on your farm, promising to pay the bank back $1,200 next year. For the past several years, prices in the economy have been stable, and, in particular, the pigs that you raise have sold for $100 each. Essentially, your loan lets you borrow the equivalent of 10 pigs with the promise to pay back 12 pigs next year.

But you've got an idea. You lobby your congressman to lobby the government to print more money. All that new money causes an inflation, after which the price of pigs rises to $200 each. Now you have to sell only six pigs to pay back the $1,200 loan, leaving you with more pigs, you pig!

Hyperinflation and Hitler

History's most infamous hyperinflation hit Germany in the 1920s, during the economically incompetent Weimar Republic. It so badly ruined the German economy that Germans would later vote Adolph Hitler into power because he promised to fix things.

At the end of World War I, Germany faced the prospect of paying off massive debts taken on during the conflict in addition to all the ongoing costs of running a government. Most of its debts were in its own currency, the German mark.

Because the German government had the exclusive right to produce German marks, the debt proved an irresistible temptation to begin printing money to pay its bills. If the government owed a billion marks to a certain firm, it simply printed up a billion crisp, new mark bills and handed them over. If a bunch of schoolteachers hadn't been paid the previous month, the Weimar government simply printed up enough new cash to pay them.

Soon, all the new money caused a wild hyperinflation. In fact, the rate of inflation in Weimar Germany in 1922 was well over 100 percent per month — it reached nearly 6,000 percent by the end of year!

Then things *really* got out of control. Prices went up 1,300,000,000,000 times (this is not a misprint!) in 1923. That year, Germans paid 200,000 marks for a loaf of bread and 2 million marks for a pound of meat. Prices rose so rapidly that waiters at restaurants had to pencil in new prices on menus several times a day. And if you ate slowly, you were sometimes charged twice what was printed on the menu because prices had gone up so much while you were eating! In some places in Germany, people stopped bothering to take the time to count out money. Instead, they tied paper bills into huge bricks and weighed the bricks of cash. For instance, it may have cost two pounds of cash to buy a chicken.

Lenders, of course, oppose the inflationary desires of borrowers. If you were the bank, you would do everything in your power to stop the inflation. If it goes through, not only are your profits ruined, but you're an outright loser. In the first year, your loan of $1,000 is the equivalent of ten pigs. But after the inflation, you get paid back the equivalent of only six pigs. You take a 40 percent loss on the value of your loan. Too much inflation, and a lender ends up being a pig in a poke.

As long as economies use money, lenders and borrowers will always be lined up against each other, both trying to sway the government.

Stimulating the economy with inflation

A much more legitimate reason for governments to print more money has the very respectable name of monetary policy. *Monetary policy* refers to the decisions a government makes about increasing or decreasing the money supply in order to stimulate or slow down the economy.

I go into monetary policy in detail in Chapter 7, but the basic idea is that if the economy is in a recession, the government may print up some new money and spend it. All the goods and services it buys with the new money stimulate the economy immediately. In addition, all those businesses that received money from the government can now go out and spend that new money themselves. And whoever receives the money from them will also go out and spend it to buy things. In fact, this can theoretically go on forever and stimulate a heck of a lot of economic activity — enough to lift an economy out of a recession.

Inflation, angry farmers, and *The Wizard of Oz*

In the second half of the 19th century, U.S. farmers in the newly opened West found themselves deeply in debt to eastern bankers as a result of the technological revolution then sweeping agriculture. Mechanical harvesters, threshers, and other pieces of large and expensive farm equipment greatly increased productivity and output, but the ensuing tremendous increase in supply meant that the prices of agricultural goods plummeted.

Farmers were in a bind because while they were receiving less for their output, they had to keep making large payments on the loans that they had taken out to buy all the expensive new farm equipment. Most farmers settled upon the solution to support political candidates who were in favor of moving the United States from a gold standard to a *bi-metallic,* or gold and silver, standard. Foremost among these candidates was Nebraska senator and two-time Democratic presidential nominee William Jennings Bryant. He argued vigorously for backing U.S. paper money with both silver and gold, because the government could then print more currency than if money were backed only with gold. Although he didn't say so directly, what he wanted was a big inflation.

This political fight pitted western farmers against eastern bankers. The eastern bankers eventually won, and the United States stayed on a gold-only standard. Yet, Americans still have a great cultural legacy of that political fight over inflation — although most people don't realize it.

In 1964, a professor named Henry Littlefield speculated that the book *The Wonderful Wizard of Oz* was a political work meant to support the farmers' opposition to the gold standard. Dorothy is a young farm girl from Kansas who represents rural U.S. citizens; the Tin Man represents city workers; the Cowardly Lion is William Jennings Bryant, whom the author thought was not a strong enough leader; and the Scarecrow is the U.S. farmer. The four travel toward the East on the yellow brick road — a road made of gold — to see the Wizard of Oz, who represents the evil eastern bankers who manipulate the economy by pulling strings and levers behind a curtain. Their destination, Oz, is simply the abbreviation for *ounce,* as in ounces of gold.

After Dorothy and her companions expose the Wizard and the gold standard as frauds, everything is right in the world. The Scarecrow is intelligent, the Lion gets his courage, and the Tin Man never has to worry about rusting (that is, being unemployed) ever again. And in the book, Dorothy returns home thanks to her *silver* slippers. According to Littlefield, the film adaptation used ruby slippers because they looked better on film — a decision that may have led Americans to forget that the story had been intended as much more than a children's book.

If this sounds too good to be true, it is. Why? Inflation. When people start spending all that new money, it drives up prices. Eventually, the only effect of the government's good intentions is that prices will rise and no additional goods will be sold. For example, if the government doubles the money supply, businesses will double the prices they charge because each piece of money is worth half as much as before. Consequently, the total amount of goods and services sold will be the same as before because while there is twice as much money being spent, prices are also twice as high.

The sad upshot is that an increase in the money supply stimulates the economy only when it's a surprise.

If the government can print the money and start spending it before people can raise prices, you get an increase in the amount of goods and services sold. Eventually, of course, people figure it out and raise prices, but until they do, the monetary stimulus works.

Unfortunately, it's hard to keep fooling people. You can surprise people once, but it's much harder the second time and even harder the third time. In fact, if the government keeps trying to surprise people, people begin to anticipate the government, and they raise prices even before the government prints more money. Consequently, most modern governments have decided against using this sort of monetary stimulus and now strive for zero inflation or very low inflation.

Tallying up the effects of inflation

In the United States, prices rise only a small amount each year. However, even moderate inflation causes problems by cutting into the practical benefits of using money instead of barter. You can get a better sense of this fact by looking at the four functions that economists generally ascribe to money and the ways in which inflation screws up each of them:

- ✔ **Money is a *store of value*.** If I sell a cow today for one gold coin, I should be able to turn around and trade that gold coin back for a cow tomorrow or next week or next month. When money retains its value, you can hold it instead of holding cows, or real estate, or any other asset.

  Inflations weaken the use of money as a store of value because each unit of currency is worth less and less as time passes.

- ✔ **Money is a *unit of account*.** When money is widely accepted in an economy, it often becomes the unit of account in which people write contracts. People start using phrases like "$50 worth of lumber" rather than "50 square feet of lumber," or "$1 million worth of shirts in inventory" instead of "20,000 shirts in inventory."

This practice makes sense if money holds its value over time, but in the presence of inflation, using money as a unit of account creates problems because the value of money declines. For instance, if the value of money is falling fast, how much lumber, exactly, is "$50 worth of lumber"?

✔ **Money is a *standard of deferred payment.*** If you want a cow, you probably wouldn't borrow a cow with the promise to repay two cows next year. Instead, you'd be much more likely to borrow and repay in terms of money. That is, you'd borrow one gold coin and use it to buy a cow, after promising to pay back two gold coins next year.

The progressive devaluing of money during a period of inflation makes lenders reluctant to use money as a standard of deferred payment. Suppose a friend asks to borrow $100, promising to pay you $120 in a year. That seems like a good deal — after all, it's a 20 percent interest rate. But if prices are rapidly rising and the value of money is falling, how much will you be able to buy with that $120 next year?

Inflations make people reluctant to lend money. They fear that when the loans are repaid, the repayment cash won't have the same purchasing power as the cash that was lent. This uncertainty can have a devastating effect on the development of new businesses, which rely heavily on loans to fund their operations.

✔ **Money is a *medium of exchange.*** Money is a *medium* (literally meaning "something in the middle") of trade between buyers and sellers because it can be directly exchanged for anything else, making buying and selling much easier. In a barter economy, an orange farmer who wants to buy beer may have to first trade oranges for apples and then apples for beer because the guy selling the beer wants only apples. Money can eliminate this kind of hassle.

But if an inflation is bad enough, money is no longer an effective medium of exchange. During hyperinflations, economies often revert to barter so buyers and sellers don't have to worry about the falling value of money. For example, in a healthy economy, the orange seller can first sell oranges for cash and then trade the cash for beer. But during a hyperinflation, between the time he sells the oranges for cash and buys the beer, the price of beer may have skyrocketed so high that he can't buy very much beer with the cash. During a hyperinflation, economies have to resort to cumbersome bartering.

Another effect of inflation is that it functions as a giant tax increase. This seems strange because you normally think of governments taxing by taking away chunks of people's money, not by printing more money. But a tax is basically anything that transfers private property to the government. Debasing the currency or printing more money can have this effect.

Suppose that the government wants to buy a $20,000 van for the post office. The honest way to go about this is to use $20,000 of tax revenues to buy a van. But a sneakier way is to print $20,000 in new cash to buy the van. By printing and spending the new cash, the government has converted $20,000 of private property — the van — into public property. So, printing new cash works just like a tax. Because printing new money ends up causing an inflation, this type of taxation is often referred to as an *inflation tax*.

Not only is the inflation tax sneaky, it unfairly targets the poor because they spend nearly all their incomes on goods and services, the costs of which go up greatly during an inflation. By contrast, because the rich have the opportunity to save a lot of their incomes rather than spending everything they take in, proportionately they're less affected by an inflation tax. By investing their savings in assets (like real estate) whose prices go up during an inflation, the rich can insulate themselves from a great deal of the harm caused by inflation.

Measuring Inflation: Price Indexes

Inflation can cause lots of problems, so in order for the government to keep inflation under control, it needs a way to measure inflation accurately.

As I explain in the earlier section "Buying an Inflation: The Risks of Too Much Money," the value of money is determined by the interaction of the *supply* of money with the *demand* for money. The supply of money is under the government's control, but the government can't directly ascertain the demand for money, so it has to look at how supply and demand interact in order to determine how much to increase or decrease the money supply:

- If an inflation is in effect, the government knows that the supply of money is increasing faster than the demand for money. If it wants to tame the inflation, it should reduce the supply of money.

- If a deflation is in effect, the government knows that the demand for money is increasing faster than the supply of money. If it wants to end the deflation, it should increase the supply of money.

Because inflation is a *general* increase in prices, the best way to look for it is by seeing whether the cost of buying a large collection of many different things changes over time. If, instead, you look at only one or two prices, you may end up confusing a *relative* price change for a *general* price change. (A relative price change is when one price goes up relative to the others, which remain unchanged.)

Economists arbitrarily define some large collection of goods and services and refer to it as a *market basket*. They then measure inflation by finding out how much money it takes to buy this basket at various times. The best-known market basket is monitored by the Bureau of Labor Statistics. This basket, called the *Consumer Price Index* or the CPI, consists of what the Bureau thinks a typical family of four buys in the United States each month.

In the following sections, I show you how this process works by creating a market basket, seeing how it can be used to measure inflation, and normalizing it to a given base year so that calculating inflation rates between any two years is a breeze. (If I've piqued your interest with this talk of market baskets and the CPI, feel free to check out the Bureau of Labor Statistics CPI Web site at www.bls.gov/cpi/home.htm.)

Creating your very own market basket

The Consumer Price Index involves a large number of products and services — it's a big market basket. Understanding price indexes is easier if you create a simplified index with a very small market basket. In this section, I look at a *very* small market basket containing pizza, beer, and textbooks. Because these three items are typical purchases of college students, I call it the Collegiate Price Index.

For each of the three items in the Collegiate Price Index, I've created prices for 2003, 2004, and 2005 and listed them in Table 5-1.

Table 5-1	The Collegiate Price Index			
Item	*Number Bought*	*2003*	*2004*	*2005*
Pizza	10	$10	$9	$9
Beer	60	$2	$2	$2.25
Textbooks	1	$120	$160	$170

In 2003, one medium cheese pizza costs $10, a cold bottle of beer costs $2, and an overly long, poorly written, incomprehensible introductory economics textbook costs $120. The next year, the price of a medium cheese pizza actually falls to $9 because a new pizza parlor opens up next to the old one, causing a price war. Beer still costs $2, but the college bookstore decides that it can really stick it to students, raising the price of the textbook to $160. (Don't worry about the 2005 column yet. I give you a chance to dig in and calculate inflation using the 2005 numbers later in the chapter.)

So far, so good. But in evaluating the index, you also have to keep track of how many of each item is bought by the typical student each year. For the sake of simplicity, assume that a typical student buys ten cheese pizzas, sixty beers, and one economics textbook each year.

Calculating the inflation rate

To calculate how much inflation your college economy has (or deflation, if the cost of living happens to go down), first total up how much the market basket costs each year. In 2003, it costs $340: $100 on pizza (ten pizzas at $10 each), $120 on beer (60 beers at $2 each), and $120 on economics textbooks (one textbook at $120). The cost of buying the same market basket in 2004 is $370. So the cost of buying the same market basket has gone up by $30.

Now that you've done the adding, you need to do some simple algebra. Economists use the capital letter P to denote how many dollars the defined market basket costs. So in this case, P_{2003} means the cost of buying the market basket in 2003 and P_{2004} is the cost of buying the market basket in 2004. Economics also has a standard practice of denoting the rate of inflation with the Greek letter π (pronounced "pie").

To calculate the rate of inflation, you use a very simple formula:

$$\pi = (P_{Second\ Year} - P_{First\ Year}) / P_{First\ Year} \tag{1}$$

In this case, the formula becomes:

$$\pi = (P_{2004} - P_{2003}) / P_{2003} \tag{2}$$

Substituting in $P_{2003} = \$340$ and $P_{2004} = \$370$, you find that $\pi = 0.088$. Convert this number into a percentage by multiplying by 100, and inflation in the Collegiate Price Index is 8.8 percent between 2003 and 2004. So, on the basis of this number, a student needs 8.8 percent more money in 2004 to buy the simple market basket.

Setting up a price index

The collegiate market basket is a simple example, but when government statisticians compute the Consumer Price Index, they basically do the same thing, just using a lot more goods. They also introduce the concept of a *price index* (or *price level index*) to make calculating and interpreting inflation rates over several years much easier. To set up a price index, they first establish a base year, or index year. Continuing our example, suppose that 2003 is the base year for the Collegiate Price Index. You can then make a handy mathematical transformation so that the price level in 2003 is fixed at the number 100, and the price levels of every other year are set up so that they're relative to the 100 of the base year.

To make P_{2003} = \$340 your base year, divide it by itself. That, of course, gives you 1, which you then multiply by 100 to get 100 (100*1 = 100). This may seem like an idiotic thing to do until you realize that if you do the same thing to the other years, you end up with something very useful. Divide P_{2004} by P_{2003} and then multiply that product by 100 to get 108.8. This number is easy to interpret: It's 8.8 percent larger than 100. Or, put differently, the price level in 2004 is 8.8 percent larger than the price level in 2003. (Of course, you already discovered this inflation rate using equation (1) in the previous section.)

You can keep going, using the numbers for 2005 that appear in Table 5-1. For instance, P_{2005} = \$395. If you divide P_{2005} by P_{2003} and multiply by 100, you get 116.2; the price level in 2005 is 16.2 percent bigger than the price level in 2003.

Figuring the rate of inflation between 2004 and 2005 using these index numbers is also easy. Because the price index level for 2004 is 108.8 and the price index level for 2005 is 116.2, inflation is simply (116.2 – 108.8) / 108.8 = 0.068, or 6.8 percent. (You're using equation (1) here, but you're inputting index numbers instead of actual costs of market baskets.)

Figure 5-1 charts the actual values of the Consumer Price Index from 1983 to 2003. The index was set to a level of 100 using prices that consumers paid on average over the two-year period 1982–1984.

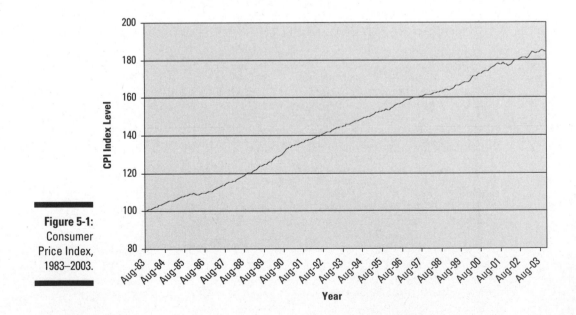

Figure 5-1: Consumer Price Index, 1983–2003.

You can see that the Consumer Price Index grew from its initial level of 100 in 1983 to a level of 185 in 2003. That is, to buy what a typical family of four consumes, you would have needed 85 percent more money in 2003 than you did in 1983. Increases in the money supply drove prices up 85 percent in 20 years.

Determining the real standard of living with the price index

Beyond making inflation easy to measure and interpret, price indexes also make it simple to measure the very important difference between real prices and nominal prices. *Nominal prices* are simply money prices, which can change over time due to inflation. Because nominal prices can change, economists like to focus on *real prices,* which keep track of how much of one kind of stuff you have to give up to get another kind of stuff, no matter what happens to nominal prices.

For example, suppose that in 2003 you make $10 an hour working at a youth camp and the cost of a DVD is $20. The *real cost* of a DVD to you is two hours of work. Suppose that the next year, the prices of all goods double, but your wages also double so that you are earning $20 an hour and a DVD costs $40. The result is that you still have to work two hours to buy a DVD. So although the *nominal* price of a DVD has doubled, its *real* price in terms of labor — how much labor you have to give up to get a DVD — hasn't changed.

By constructing price indexes like the CPI, economists can tell how the *real standard of living* changes for people from year to year. In the example of the previous section (using data from Table 5-1), inflation is 8.8 percent between 2003 and 2004, meaning that the cost of living of a typical college student went up 8.8 percent. So if at the same time student incomes go up only 5 percent, students are actually worse off because costs have gone up faster than incomes. Real living standards — living standards measured in terms of how much stuff you can buy with your income — have fallen.

Identifying price index problems

Using price indexes to track the cost of living isn't a flawless system. Here are three big issues:

> ✔ **The market basket can never perfectly reflect family spending.** The Bureau of Labor Statistics tries to keep track of what a typical family of four purchases when calculating the Consumer Price Index (CPI). But families differ greatly, not only in terms of *what* they buy but also in terms of *how many* of each thing they buy.

✔ **The market basket becomes outdated.** The Bureau of Labor Statistics often waits way too long before including new types of goods in the market basket. For instance, the Bureau took years to include DVD players, even though DVDs were quickly replacing VCRs. If the CPI fails to include popular new products, it's not fully capturing the price changes that matter to consumers.

✔ **The market basket can't account for quality.** Price isn't the only thing that matters to consumers. For example, what if a beer stays the same price but improves in quality from one year to the next? You're getting better beer for the same price, but this isn't reflected in the data. This problem is especially severe for things like computers, cellphones, and video games. For these products, quality improves dramatically year after year while prices either stay the same or go down.

Each of these problems troubles government statisticians, who are constantly coming up with better price indexes and statistical methods to try to overcome them. The Federal Reserve Bank (the government agency charged with determining the money supply) has recently come out with an estimate suggesting that the CPI overstates inflation by 1 to 2 percentage points per year. Most of the overstatement comes from the failure of the CPI to account for new goods and quality improvements.

The main consequence of this overstatement is that the government is overly generous with the cost-of-living increases it grants workers and retirees. Each year, government workers and retirees receive pay increases based upon increases in the CPI. These pay increases are designed to ensure that people's real incomes aren't eroded by inflation, but because the CPI is most likely overstating the rate of inflation each year, the cost-of-living increases are overly generous.

Pricing the Future: Nominal and Real Interest Rates

Because inflation erodes the value of a loan repayment (see "Tallying up the effects of inflation," earlier in the chapter, for details), economists have to distinguish between *nominal interest rates* and *real interest rates*. Nominal interest rates are simply the normal, money interest rates that you're used to dealing with; they measure the returns to a loan in terms of money borrowed and money returned. Real interest rates, however, compensate for inflation by measuring the returns to a loan in terms of units of stuff lent and units of stuff returned. This distinction is very important because it's the *real* interest rate that makes people want to save and invest. After all, what lenders really care about isn't how much money they get back but how much stuff they can buy with it.

Suppose that you borrow $1,000 with the promise to pay $1,100 to the lender in a year. Your nominal interest rate is 10 percent because you're paying back an additional $100, or 10 percent more dollars than you borrowed. But if inflation occurs, the amount of stuff that $100 can buy decreases over time.

For example, say a nice meal for two with a bottle of wine costs $100 right now but will cost $105 next year. Right now, the lender is giving up 10 of these very good meals ($1,000 divided by $100 per meal) in order to give you the loan. Next year, when he gets repaid $1,100, he can buy 10.47 meals at the price of $105. He is giving up 10 meals now in exchange for 10.47 meals next year, meaning that the real rate of interest on the loan is 4.7 percent. Because of inflation, the real rate of interest on the loan is substantially less than the nominal rate.

When lenders and borrowers negotiate a nominal interest rate on a loan, they both try to estimate what the inflation rate will be over the period of the loan. This *expected rate of inflation* is denoted algebraically as π^e. (Don't confuse expected inflation, π^e, with actual inflation, π. The former is what people expect to happen ahead of time, while the latter is what actually ends up happening.) The following sections show you how to estimate and use this rate.

Using the Fisher equation

Economist Irving Fisher came up with a simple formula, known as the *Fisher equation,* that links nominal and real interest rates. Using i to denote the nominal interest rate and r to denote the real interest rate:

$$i - r + \pi^e \qquad (3)$$

This equation simply says that the nominal interest rate is the real interest rate plus the expected rate of inflation. This relationship is very important to borrowers and lenders because while all loan contracts specify a nominal rate of interest, their goal is to achieve a specific real rate of interest, even after any subsequent inflation reduces the value of money. By using the Fisher equation, the borrowers and lenders can determine what nominal interest to charge now in order to achieve a given real rate of return, taking into account the expected rate of inflation.

To see how this works, suppose that a borrower and lender agree that 6 percent is a fair real rate of interest, and they also agree that inflation is likely to be 3.3 percent over the course of one year. Using the Fisher equation, they write the loan contract with a 9.3 percent nominal interest rate. A year later, when the borrower repays the lender 9.3 percent more money than was borrowed, that money is expected to have only 6 percent more purchasing power than the borrowed money, given the expected increase in prices.

Realizing that predictions aren't perfect

Negotiations of the type described in the previous section depend crucially upon estimating the expected inflation rate, π^e, and there are lots of economists whose job descriptions consist primarily of trying to predict future inflation rates. Their predictions are widely reported in the business media, but every person comes up with her own inflation forecast in her own way. Some people listen to the experts, while others make estimates based on their own daily experiences.

Note, though, that because forecasts aren't 100 percent accurate, no one can say for sure what the real rate of return on the loan will be. For example, if the inflation rate turns out to be 9.3 percent in the previous example, then the real rate of return will be 0 percent. On the other hand, if the rate of inflation is 0 percent, then the lender will get back 9.3 percent more money and can buy 9.3 percent more stuff, meaning a real rate of return of 9.3 percent. (See the earlier section "Feeling printing press pressures: The politics of inflation" for a discussion of why borrowers like inflation and lenders don't.)

Figure 5-2 plots actual inflation rates along with average expected inflation rates. The actual rates come from the monthly CPI numbers, and the expected inflation rates come from a poll of consumers taken every month by the University of Michigan. You can see that actual inflation between January 1980 and January 1981 was about 13 percent. By comparison, consumers who were asked in January 1980 what they thought the rate of inflation would be over the next 12 months, on average, told researchers that they expected about a 10 percent inflation rate. So in that particular instance, the inflationary expectations of typical consumers were off by about 3 percent.

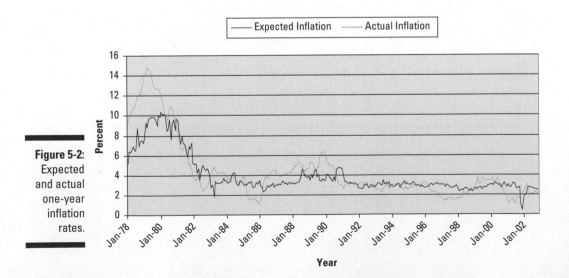

Figure 5-2: Expected and actual one-year inflation rates.

Starting in about 1980, the two sets of numbers have been remarkably close, meaning that people's guesses about inflation in the past two decades have usually been wrong by no more than about 1 percent. Of course, this period also corresponds to a period in U.S. history where the government has been committed to low and stable inflation rates. Such rates aren't that hard to predict, so you shouldn't be surprised that people's guesses have been fairly accurate. During hyperinflations, on the other hand, guesses aren't nearly as good.

Chapter 6

Understanding Why Recessions Happen

. . . .

In This Chapter

▶ Visualizing the business cycle

▶ Hoping for the ideal: Letting price adjustments eliminate recessions

▶ Dealing with reality: Coping with sticky prices and lingering recessions

▶ Linking slow price adjustments to slow wage adjustments

▶ Introducing the Keynesian model

. . . .

*M*acroeconomists' biggest task is to try to prevent — or at least shorten — *recessions,* those periods of time during which the economy's output of goods and services declines. Economists, politicians, and most other people who work for a living despise recessions because of the high toll they exact in human suffering. That's because when output falls, firms need fewer workers. The typical result is massive layoffs, which cause significant increases in unemployment. In large countries like the United States, millions of workers lose their jobs, as well as their ability to support themselves and their families.

In this chapter, I use the *aggregate supply/aggregate demand* model to show you how economists analyze recessions. Typically, recessions begin with what economists like to call *shocks* — unexpected bad events like terrorist attacks, natural disasters, the introduction of bad government policies, or sudden spikes in the cost of important natural resources like oil.

The first big lesson of this chapter is that if the prices of goods and services in the economy were free to adjust to changes in demand and supply caused by shocks, the economy would typically be able to recover quite swiftly. Unfortunately, however, the second big lesson is that not all real-world prices are totally free to adjust to shocks. Rather, some very important prices are quite slow to adjust — they are, as economists like to say, *sticky.* As a result, recessions can linger and cause a lot of harm unless the government intervenes to help the economy recover more quickly. (In Chapter 7, I discuss the best ways for governments to intervene.)

Examining the Business Cycle

Economies go through alternating periods during which the output of goods and services expands and then contracts. In Chapter 4, I explain that Y represents the total output of an economy, so I use Y in this section to conserve some words.

The alternating pattern of economic expansion and contraction, which is illustrated in Figure 6-1, is often called the *business cycle* because businesses are so greatly affected by the changes in output.

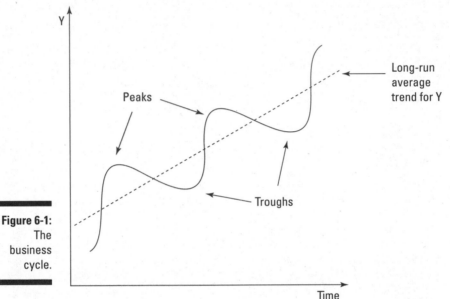

Figure 6-1:
The business cycle.

The solid line in Figure 6-1 represents how output, Y, varies over time. It alternates between troughs and peaks, which helps us identify periods of recession and recovery. Here's how we distinguish between the two:

✔ *Recessions,* or contractions, are the periods of time during which Y falls — that is, after a peak and before the next trough.

✔ *Recoveries,* or expansions, are the periods of time during which Y increases — that is, after a trough and before the next peak.

The dotted line in Figure 6-1 represents the long-run, average growth trend for Y. I've drawn Figure 6-1 so that it has an upward sloping average growth trend for Y, capturing the fact that the economies of most countries now have sustained economic growth. In other words, on average, output tends to rise year after year. Because recessions still happen, however, the actual path of Y given by the solid line fluctuates around the long-run growth path given by the dotted line.

Looking at Figure 6-1, you can see that macroeconomic policy has two very natural goals:

- ✔ **Making the long-run average growth line as steep as possible:** The steeper it is, the faster (on average) output and living standards rise.

- ✔ **Reducing the size of business cycle fluctuations around the long-run average growth line.** Smaller distances between peaks and troughs translate into fewer people suffering through bouts of unemployment when output falls.

In Chapter 7, I explain the policies that economists think are best for achieving these two goals. But in order for Chapter 7 to make sense, I must first explain what causes the business cycle — especially recessions and the high rates of unemployment that accompany them. After all, if you don't understand what's wrong, you can't sensibly fix it.

Striving for Full-Employment Output

Before you can say whether an economy is doing well or doing poorly, you need some objective standard of what "doing well" is. Economists use the concept of *full-employment output* (which is represented by the symbol Y^*) as their measure of how well an economy should be doing.

The idea of full-employment output revolves around the concept of *full employment,* by which economists mean a situation in which everyone who wants a full-time job can get one. *Full-employment output* is how much output is produced in the economy when there's full employment in the labor market.

Please don't confuse full-employment output with the economy's *maximum output,* which is the larger amount of output that would be produced if everyone were forced to work as much as humanly possible.

Also, don't make the mistake of thinking that full employment is the same thing as having a zero unemployment rate. Even when everyone who wants a job can get one, there will always be some unemployment as people voluntarily quit one job to search for a better job. For the duration of their job search, these people are counted as unemployed. Economists call this situation *frictional unemployment,* as though the delay in finding a better job is due to some sort of friction slowing the process down.

As technology improves, full-employment output (Y^*) grows because better technology means that a fully employed labor force can produce more output. But to simplify their analyses, economists usually ignore the long-term growth trend and look only at whether actual output, Y, is currently above or below their best estimates of Y^* at that particular moment.

I'm going to follow this convention, too, for the rest of the chapter. Consequently, you're going to find out how the economy adjusts to situations in which output is either above or below potential output at a given point in time.

As I show you in this chapter, the economy naturally wants to adjust back to Y^* anytime it deviates from Y^*. If that adjustment process was rapid enough, you wouldn't have to worry about business cycles, recessions, and unemployment. If the economy reverted back to Y^* fast enough, recessions would be too brief to cause any serious negative consequences. Unfortunately, the natural adjustment process can be very slow, and as a result, recessions can be quite lengthy and awful.

Returning to Y^*: The Natural Result of Price Adjustments

After an economic shock, such as a natural disaster or a spike in the cost of natural resources, price adjustments tend to return an economy to producing at full-employment output (Y^*). That's right, I said *price adjustments* — not the president, and not the chairman of the Federal Reserve Board. Don't believe me? Read on.

Consider a situation in which the *aggregate* (total) demand for goods and services in the economy falls off: Individuals, firms, and the government demand and buy less output than the economy is currently producing. The result is an excess supply of output which, in turn, leads to lower prices. After all, what does any business do when it can't sell off everything it's producing at the prices it's currently charging? It has a sale. It lowers prices. The lower prices attract more buyers, and soon the business is able to sell off the rest of its output.

This process repeats itself all over the economy during an economic downturn. When aggregate demand falls off due to an economic shock, firms lower prices to make sure they sell off their outputs. This process eventually leads to two outcomes:

✔ Prices all over the economy fall.

✔ The economy again produces at full-employment output, Y^*.

For this process to work well, prices must be able to change quickly; if they can, the economy very quickly returns to Y^*. If, however, price adjustments are slow, the economy may produce less output than Y^* for a significant amount of time. In other words, if prices don't adjust quickly, you can get a recession. And until prices do adjust, the recession lingers.

I've just given you the briefest overview possible of how the economy responds to an economic shock. The following section provides much more detail so you can understand how and why the economy eventually gets back to Y^* (and so you can pass your next exam, if that's your goal).

Responding to Economic Shocks: Short-Run and Long-Run Effects

Economists like to break the time period after an economic shock into two parts, which they call the *short run* and the *long run:*

- The *short run* refers to the period of time in which firms haven't yet made price changes in response to an economic shock.
- The *long run* refers to the period of time after which firms have made all necessary price changes in response to an economic shock.

These definitions are intentionally vague because the speed at which firms adjust prices varies from shock to shock. In this section, I show you that there are major differences between what happens in the short run and the long run.

Defining some critical terms

To see the difference between an economy responding to a shock in the short run versus the long run, begin by looking at Figure 6-2, which is a model of the macroeconomy. The horizontal axis measures the dollar value of the output of goods and services sold in the economy (Y). This number is the same as a country's gross domestic product (GDP), which I discuss in Chapter 4. The vertical axis measures the overall price level in the economy, P.

To understand the meaning of P, consider this: While each individual good and service has its own price, and some of those prices may be going up while others are going down, an overall trend in prices exists for the economy as a whole. P is simply a measure of how the prices of goods and services as a whole behave. If P goes up, then on average prices are rising; if P goes down, then on average prices are falling. And if prices stay the same, then P (of course) stays the same. See Chapter 5 for details about how economists measure P.

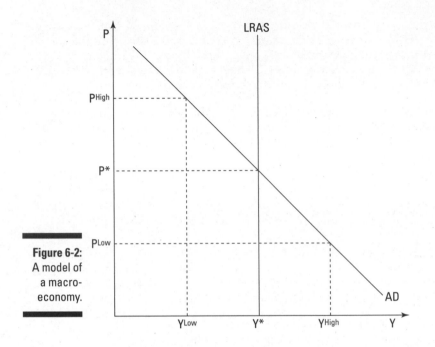

Figure 6-2:
A model of
a macro-
economy.

In Figure 6-2, you see the symbol P^*. This symbol represents the *equilibrium* level of prices. What does that mean? P^* is the price level at which consumers want to buy exactly the amount of full-employment output (Y^*).

How do economists determine P^*? That price level is determined by the intersection of what's called the *long-run aggregate supply curve* (*LRAS*) with the *aggregate demand curve* (*AD*). Before you start hyperventilating, let me explain what these things are:

✔ The *aggregate demand curve* represents the total amount of goods and services that people want to buy.

  Notice that in Figure 6-2, the *AD* curve slopes downward. That's because there's an inverse relationship between the price level and the amount of stuff that people want to buy. *Inverse relationship* simply means that at the higher price level (P^{High}), people want to buy a low level of output (Y^{Low}). But if prices fall to P^{Low}, people demand a much greater amount of output (Y^{High}). The downward slope of the *AD* curve captures the fact that at lower prices, people buy more.

✔ The *long-run aggregate supply curve* represents the amount of goods and services that an economy will produce when prices have adjusted after an economic shock.

In Figure 6-2, you can see that the *LRAS* is a vertical line — it isn't a curve at all! (Do you feel cheated?) The *LRAS* is drawn above the point on the horizontal axis that represents the full-employment output level, Y^*. Why? Because in the long run, changes in prices *always* return the economy to producing at the full-employment output level.

Still don't believe me? You're a tough audience. Keep reading — I'm going to convince you yet!

The tao of P: Looking at price adjustments in the long run

Let's examine what happens if the economy starts out at a price level other than P^*. For instance, look again at price level P^{High} and its corresponding aggregate demand level, Y^{Low}. Obviously, Y^{Low} is less than the economy's full-employment level of output (Y^*). That's important because firms would rather produce at output level Y^*. In fact, they've invested in factories and equipment that will be wasted if they produce at lower levels of output. Consequently, their response is to cut prices in order to increase sales. And they continue to cut prices until the overall price level in the economy falls down to P^*, because that's the price level at which consumers want to buy exactly Y^* worth of output.

Are you worried that all these price cuts will cause firms to lose money? Take heart: Firms don't necessarily lose profits in this situation because their costs are falling at the same time. That's because when the economy is producing at less than Y^*, there are a lot of unemployed workers and a lot of unused productive inputs, like iron and oil. Unemployment puts downward pressure on wages; in other words, having lots of labor readily available means you can hire people at lower wages. And the more piles of unused productive inputs there are, the more their prices fall.

Okay, so the lower prices attract more customers, increase sales, and cause the firms to hire back unemployed workers. This process continues until prices fall all the way to P^*, at which point the economy is operating at full employment again, meaning that all workers who want full-time jobs can get them.

In a similar fashion, prices can't remain below P^* for long. At price level P^{Low}, people want to buy Y^{High} worth of output. But that's more than firms can produce at full employment. The only way to produce that much output is if employees work more than the standard, 40-hour work week. The only way to get them to do so is to pay them more, and the only way to give them higher wages is for firms to raise prices. So with demand exceeding supply, prices are raised until they reach P^*, at which price level the quantity demanded by consumers is exactly equal to the full-employment output level, Y^*.

As you can see, if prices have enough time to adjust, the economy always returns to producing at output level Y^*. Because we're calling the time required for prices to adjust the *long run,* it makes sense to call the vertical line above Y^* the *long-run aggregate supply curve* because it shows how much output the economy will supply after prices have had enough time to adjust to equalize the supply and demand for goods and services. (For much more on supply and demand, see Chapter 8.)

A shock to the system: Adjusting to a shift in aggregate demand

The previous section shows what happens if the prices of goods and services are, on the whole, too high or too low: They eventually adjust to the equilibrium price level (P^*) so the economy can get back to producing at the full-employment output level (Y^*). But what would cause the prices to be too high or too low in the first place? A shock to *aggregate demand* — the total amount of goods and services that people are willing to buy.

First, let's visualize what a shock to aggregate demand looks like: Figure 6-3 shows the aggregate demand curve shifting to the left from AD_0 to AD_1. A leftward shift of aggregate demand is called a *negative demand shock,* and it could be caused, for instance, by a decline in confidence in the economy that makes people want to save more and consume less. (A rightward shift of AD would be called a *positive demand shock.*)

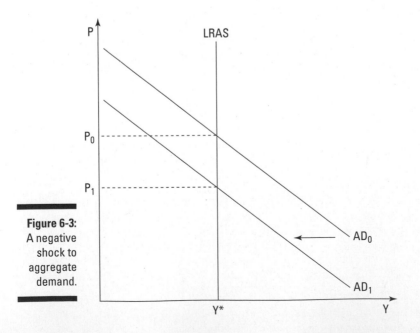

Figure 6-3:
A negative
shock to
aggregate
demand.

The original price level, P_o, was determined by where the original AD_o curve intersected the vertical *LRAS* curve. In the long run, after firms adjust to the demand shock, the new price level, P_1, will be where the new AD_1 curve intersects the vertical *LRAS* curve.

The new price level (P_1) is less than the original price level (P_0). Why? Demand for goods and services decreases after the negative demand shock. The only way to entice consumers to again purchase full-employment levels of output (Y^*) is to lower the cost of buying that much output, so the price level has to fall. It may take firms a while to make the necessary price reductions, but when they do, the economy will again produce at Y^* in the long run.

I hope you're convinced by now that in the long run, after prices have a chance to adjust to whatever shocks occur, the economy will again produce at the full-employment output level, Y^*. That's a huge contrast to what can happen in the short run before prices adjust, which I discuss next.

Dealing with fixed prices in the short run

As I discuss in the previous sections, after an economic shock happens, prices eventually adjust to return the economy to full-employment output (Y^*). However, this process may take a while because in the short run, prices are essentially fixed. Even the managers of the most nimble firms need some time to decide how much to cut prices. And some firms aren't quite as nimble.

Suppose that a firm has printed up catalogs listing the prices of the things it sells. This firm distributes catalogs only once a year, which means it is committed to selling to customers at these prices until the next catalog is sent out. In such a situation, a firm adjusts its production to meet whatever amount of demand happens to come along at these fixed prices. If a lot of people show up to buy at these prices, the firm increases production, typically by hiring more employees. If very few people show up to buy, it reduces production, typically by hiring fewer employees.

Figure 6-4 depicts a situation in which firms have committed to a fixed set of prices and can respond to changes in demand only by adjusting their production levels. The figure shows the horizontal *short-run aggregate supply curve (SRAS)*, which is actually not a curve at all but a straight line. This "curve" corresponds to price level P_o because the firms, in the short run, cannot adjust their prices. Movements right and left along the *SRAS* curve capture the increases and decreases in output that firms have to make as demand for their products varies at the fixed price level.

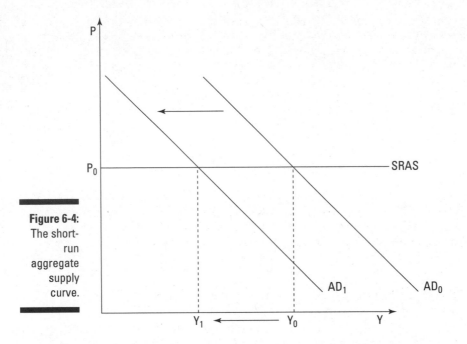

Figure 6-4:
The short-run aggregate supply curve.

Please understand that economists have various complicated ways of explaining how an economy adjusts to a demand shock. I'm cutting the discussion down to the bare bones, which means thinking of the *SRAS* curve as a horizontal line. In more elaborate explanations, the *SRAS* curve is an upward-sloping line. But don't be confused: The basic idea in either case is that the economy moves from having a perfectly horizontal aggregate supply curve right after a shock, to an upward sloping one a little later, to a perfectly vertical one — the LRAS — in the long run. I'm skipping the middle part in order to make the discussion as direct as possible. I use only the initial, horizontal curve and the final, vertical curve, calling the former the *SRAS* and the latter the *LRAS*.

Figure 6-4 also has two aggregate demand curves, AD_o and AD_1, that again show what happens when aggregate demand is reduced as the result of a negative demand shock. The initial level of output that firms produce, Y_o, is determined by the intersection of the original aggregate demand curve, AD_o, with the *SRAS* curve. In other words, at price level P_o, people demand output level Y_o, and firms respond by supplying it.

When the negative demand shock strikes, it shifts aggregate demand leftward to AD_1. Reduced demand means that at the fixed price level, customers are willing to buy less output. Because firms can't change prices, their only recourse is to reduce production down to match the decrease in demand; this reduced level of output (Y_1) appears on the graph where the *SRAS* curve intersects AD_1. Because lower output means that firms need fewer workers, you end up with a recession: Output falls, and unemployment rises.

If you compare Figures 6-3 and 6-4, you can see that the leftward shift in aggregate demand has very different effects in the short run and the long run:

- In the short run when prices are fixed, output falls and unemployment rises.
- In the long run, prices fall and output returns to the full-employment level.

Why the huge difference between the short run and the long run? Firms aren't forever stuck with their original catalog prices. Eventually, they print new catalogs with lower prices. The lower prices entice customers to purchase more, and soon the economy can return to producing at the full-employment output level, Y^*.

Putting together the long and short of it

If you've got the previous sections tucked under your belt, you're now an expert in both long-run and short-run responses to an economic shock. (You should definitely schedule a dinner party so you can impress your friends!) Let's drive this subject home by putting the two very different responses together into one big picture.

Figure 6-5 lets you see how an economy adapts to a negative demand shock both in the short run and in the long run. The economy begins at point A, where the original aggregate demand curve, AD_o, intersects both the *LRAS* and the *SRAS* curves. At point A, the economy is in equilibrium because at price level P_o, the aggregate demand for output equals the full-employment level of output, Y^*. There is neither a surplus nor a shortage that could cause prices to change.

REAL WORLD EXAMPLE

Wal-Mart and Y^*

The two most recent recessions in the United States, in 1991 and 2001, have been very mild — much milder than most previous recessions. The exact reason for this is not totally clear, but many economists believe that one factor is that retailers have gotten much better at quickly adjusting prices when supply doesn't equal demand. The leader in this regard has been Wal-Mart, which has developed the most sophisticated inventory management systems in the retail industry. With these computerized systems, Wal-Mart managers can tell minute-by-minute what's selling and what's not. As a result, the prices of slow-moving items are cut very quickly so that products don't go unsold for weeks or months, as was the case in decades past when inventory was done by hand once a month.

As a result of such innovations, prices can adjust quickly to equate supply and demand. Prices now fall much more rapidly to get the economy back to producing at full-employment output (Y^*). That means shorter, milder recessions.

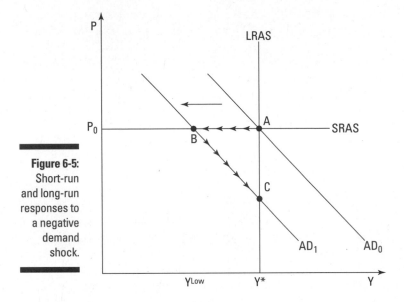

Figure 6-5:
Short-run and long-run responses to a negative demand shock.

The *SRAS* curve is horizontal at price P_o to reflect the fact that after the economy reaches its equilibrium (where AD_o intersects the *LRAS* at output level Y^*), the prices that are determined at that level are fixed in the short run; they can't change immediately even if a demand shock happens to come along.

For instance, suppose that the aggregate demand curve shifts left from AD_o to AD_1 because of a negative demand shock of some sort. Because prices are fixed in the short run at P_o, the economy's first response will be moving from point *A* to point *B*. In other words, because prices are fixed, production falls from Y^* down to Y^{Low} as firms respond to decreased demand by cutting production. (Small arrows indicate the movement of the economy from point *A* to point *B*.)

At point *B,* the economy is operating below full employment, implying that there are a lot of unemployed workers. This high level of unemployment causes wages to fall. As wages fall, firms' costs also fall, allowing them to cut prices in order to attract more customers.

Falling prices cause increased aggregate demand for goods and services, which eventually moves the economy all the way from point *B* to point *C.* (This movement is indicated by arrows on the graph.) When the economy reaches point *C,* it is once again producing at full employment, Y^*.

The short-run and long-run effects of a negative demand shock are basically total opposites of each other:

> ✔ In the short run, prices are fixed while output decreases.

> ✔ In the long run, prices decrease while output returns to Y^*.

If prices don't stay fixed for very long, the economy can quickly move from A to B to C. But if prices are slow to adjust to the negative aggregate demand shock, the economy can take a very long time to get from A to B to C. In such cases, there is a long-lasting recession during which output remains below Y^* and many people are unemployed.

For these reasons, we need to figure out what affects the ability of prices to change quickly. The most important culprit is sticky prices — more precisely, sticky wages.

Heading Toward Recession: Getting Stuck with Sticky Prices

When the economy encounters a negative demand shock like the one depicted in Figure 6-5, price flexibility (or lack of flexibility) determines both the severity and length of any recession that may result. If prices were infinitely flexible — if they could change within seconds or minutes after a shock — the economy would immediately move from point A to point C, and all would be right with the world. But if prices are fixed for any period of time, the economy goes into a recession as it moves from point A to point B before prices eventually fall and bring it back to full-employment output at point C.

In the real world, prices are indeed somewhat slow to change, or, as economists like to say, prices are *sticky*. Interestingly, they tend to be stickier when going downward than upward, meaning that prices appear to have a harder time falling than rising.

The major culprit seems to be one particular price: wages. Wages are the price employers must pay workers for their labor. Unlike other prices in the economy, people are particularly emotionally attached to wages and how they change over time.

In particular, employees don't like to see their wages cut. They have a very strong sense of fairness when it comes to their wages and, as a result, will usually retaliate against any wage cut by working less hard. As a result, managers typically find it counterproductive to lower wages even if a firm is losing money and needs to cut costs.

Cutting wages or cutting workers

Suppose that a negative demand shock hits an economy and greatly reduces sales at a particular company. The firm is losing money, so managers need to figure out a way to cut costs. About 70 percent of this company's total costs are labor costs (wages and salaries). Naturally, labor costs are an obvious target for cuts.

But the managers of the firm realize that if they cut wages, employees will get angry and work less hard. In fact, their productivity may fall off so much that cutting wages may make the firm's profit situation worse: Output may fall so much that sales revenues will decrease by more than the reduction in labor costs. Therefore, cutting wages isn't really a good option.

So, instead, the managers lay off a large chunk of their workforce in order to reduce labor costs. For instance, if sales are down 40 percent, the firm may lay off 40 percent of the workforce. However, any workers who remain employed get to keep their old wages so that they aren't angry and their productivity doesn't fall.

For the reasons I'm showing you here, what you see during a recession is a large increase in unemployment but little decrease in wage rates. The fact that managers are unwilling to cut wages, however, has a nasty side effect: As I discuss in the next section, not cutting wages makes it very hard for firms to cut the prices of the goods and services they sell.

Adding up the costs of wages and profits

Obviously, firms need to turn a profit in order to stay in business. And that means making sure that the price per unit that they charge for their products exceeds the cost per unit of making them.

During a recession, lower aggregate demand means that firms reduce production and sell fewer units. As I discuss in the previous sections, wages are the largest component of most firms' costs — in fact, they're a full 70 percent of the average firm's costs. If a firm can't cut wages for fear of causing worker productivity to drop, it can't reduce its per-unit production costs very much either. In turn, the firm can't cut its prices very much because prices have to stay above production costs if firms are to make a profit and stay in business.

What does all this mean? When demand drops off, prices are typically sticky. They stay high despite the fact that there's less demand for output in the economy. That's the reason behind the economy moving horizontally from point *A* to point *B* in Figure 6-5 after the negative demand shock. With prices sticky because firms can't cut wages, the negative demand shock results in a recession with output falling and unemployment rising because so many workers get fired.

Worse yet, unless prices can somehow begin to fall, the economy won't be able to move from B to C to get back to producing at the full-employment output level (Y^*). Prices do *eventually* fall, but this process can take a long time, meaning that the negative demand shock can cause a long-lasting recession.

Returning to Y^* with and without government intervention

In Chapter 7, I explain how the government can use monetary and fiscal stimuli to get around the sticky prices problem by boosting aggregate demand. Here, I want to give you a preview of how that process works.

Imagine that after the negative demand shock depicted in Figure 6-5 moves aggregate demand leftward from AD_o to AD_1, the government doesn't hang around waiting for prices to eventually fall. Instead, it stimulates aggregated demand so that the aggregate demand curve shifts back rightward and returns to where it started, at AD_o. Taking this action returns the economy to producing at full employment without having to wait for prices to fall.

What if the government doesn't act to stimulate aggregate demand in that fashion? What if the economy is at point B and the government doesn't intervene? In such cases, prices do eventually fall because firms' production costs eventually fall.

As we see in the previous sections, labor costs are very slow to fall because managers don't want to risk alienating workers by cutting their wages. But because there are so many unemployed workers when the economy is at point B, wages eventually decline. Some firms hire unemployed people at lower wages, which reduces their costs, meaning that they can undersell firms that keep wages high. Eventually, such competitive pressures mean that all firms end up cutting wages.

Other costs also decline. That's because during a recession, with output so much diminished, a significant portion of the economy's productive capacity is unused. There are unused factories, unused trucks, unused train cars, and unused ships. There are also large amounts of unused lumber, iron, oil, and other productive inputs.

The owners of these unused inputs lower their prices in order to try to sell them. As their prices fall, firm costs also fall, thereby allowing firms to reduce the selling prices of their output. And as these selling prices fall, the economy moves from point B to point C in Figure 6-5, restoring the economy to producing at the full-employment output level (Y^*). See how nicely it all (eventually) works out?

Achieving Equilibrium with Sticky Prices: The Keynesian Model

Even if this is the first book on economics you've ever laid your hands on, you may have heard the name Keynes before. Who is this guy, and why do economists like him so much?

John Maynard Keynes was the most influential economist of the 20th century. Why? He was the first economist to realize that sticky prices (caused by sticky wages) are the culprit behind recessions. If you read the previous section, you may not have thought the ideas contained there were revolutionary, but trust me: Keynes's insight changed the way people studied economies.

What inspired Keynes to have this insight? He was led to the idea by the horrible state that the economy reached during the Great Depression of the 1930s. Just the name itself — *Great Depression* — gives you some idea how bad things got. Normal economic downturns are called *recessions.* Really bad recessions are called *depressions.* But what happened in the 1930s was so bad that people started calling it the *Great Depression* to indicate just how severe it was.

The Great Depression started with a lingering recession from 1929 to 1933. The United States did not see its output return to its 1929 level until after entering World War II in 1941. To put the Great Depression in perspective, look at Table 6-1, which gives data for each of the seven recessions that the United States has experienced since 1960, plus (on the first line) the same data for the Great Depression.

Table 6-1	The Great Depression and U.S. Recessions since 1960			
Start	*End*	*Duration (Months)*	*Highest Unemployment Rate*	*Change in Real GDP (%)*
8/1929	3/1933	43	24.9	−28.8
4/1960	2/1961	10	6.7	2.3
12/1969	11/1970	11	5.9	0.1
11/1973	3/1975	16	8.5	1.1
1/1980	7/1980	6	7.6	−0.3
6/1981	11/1982	16	9.7	−2.1
6/1990	3/1991	8	7.5	−0.9
3/2001	11/2001	8	6.0	0.5

Source: NBER, Economic Report of the President, Bureau of Labor Statistics

TECHNICAL STUFF

What makes a recession a recession?

In the beginning of the chapter, I define a *recession* as a period of time during which output falls and unemployment rises. But this isn't the only definition. For example, you may read in a textbook or a newspaper article that an economy is in a recession if real GDP falls for two consecutive quarters. But if you look at Table 6-1, you notice that during certain recessions (like the one that began in April 1960), real output actually went up rather than down. So why was that time period labeled a recession?

A lot of factors go into determining what gets labeled a recession. A group of economists at the National Bureau of Economic Research

(NBER) in Cambridge, Massachusetts, gets to "officially" declare when recessions begin and end in the United States. This group has a long set of criteria that begins with output falling and unemployment rising and includes lots of other things, such as how fast factories receive new orders. Sometimes these other factors cause the NBER to feel that the economy has passed a peak and has entered a recession even if output isn't falling.

Check out the NBER's Web site at www.nber.org for lots more information about business cycles and how the NBER goes about declaring recessions.

As you can see, the Great Depression was far, far worse than any normal recession. Nearly 25 percent of the labor force was unemployed, and the initial downturn lasted about four times longer than the 10.7-month average duration of post-1960 recessions.

Total economic output as measured by real GDP (which I discuss in Chapter 5) also fell much more than in a normal recession. Because real GDP adjusts for inflation, it captures changes in the physical quantity of output produced. In recent recessions, output has fallen at most 2 or 3 percentage points. During the Great Depression, it fell 28.8 percent!

As a witness to the Great Depression, Keynes obviously wanted to figure out what could cause such a drastic economic downturn — and what could prevent such devastation from happening again.

Adjusting inventories instead of prices

Not only did Keynes figure out that sticky prices cause recessions; he also developed a hugely influential model that's still presented in many macroeconomics textbooks. This model is a small part of a larger approach to managing the macroeconomy that came to be called *Keynesianism* — an approach that favored large government interventions into the economy rather than the sort of *laissez faire* policies of nonintervention preferred by other people. (For a discussion of the costs and benefits of having the government intervene in the economy, see "Determining What Should Be Produced" in Chapter 3.)

To be fair, I have to point out that Keynesianism has attracted a lot of critics and is not the be-all-end-all of macroeconomics. But the part of it I present here is not controversial. It explains how an economy adjusts to *equilibrium* — a place where aggregate supply matches aggregate demand — in the extreme short run after an economic shock when prices can't change at all.

Look back at Figure 6-4 for a moment. The Keynesian model elaborates on exactly how an economy moves from producing at output level Y_o to producing at output level Y_1 when a shock to aggregate demand happens and prices are fixed at level P_o.

Keynes's model focuses our attention on firms' inventories of goods that have been made but not yet sold. According to Keynes, changes in inventories guide firms to increase or decrease output during situations in which prices are sticky and can't serve as signals of what to do.

To see the novelty of Keynes's inventory idea, understand that if prices could change, then prices (not inventories) would guide firm decisions about how much to produce:

- ✔ If prices were rising, a firm would know that its product was popular and that it should increase output.

- ✔ If prices were falling, the firm would know that the product was not doing well and that it should probably cut output (and maybe get into another line of business!).

In an economy with fixed prices, however, firms need some other way of deciding whether to increase or decrease production. Keynes realized that the guiding force would be changes in inventories.

Keeping an eye on target inventory levels

Inventories are constantly turning over, with goods flowing both in and out. New production increases inventories, while new sales decrease inventories. The two factors interact to determine whether inventories are rising, falling, or staying the same. For instance, if new production equals new sales, inventory levels stay constant. If new production exceeds new sales, inventories rise.

The interaction of new production and new sales is important because each firm has a *target level* of inventories that it likes to keep on hand to meet situations in which sales temporarily run faster than the firm can produce output. The target level is determined by the costs and benefits of having a bigger or smaller inventory on hand.

Having less inventory than the target level is dangerous because the firm may not be able to keep up with sales spikes. Having more inventory than the target level is wasteful because there's no point in having stuff sitting around unsold, year after year. Each firm weighs these costs and benefits to come up with its own target inventory level.

Target inventory levels may vary from year to year depending on whether firms are expecting strong or weak sales. If managers are expecting strong sales, they may plan on increasing inventories, whereas if they are expecting weak sales, they may plan on decreasing inventories.

Keynes realized that aggregate demand shocks (which are, by definition, unexpected) would show up as unexpected changes in firm inventories:

- ✔ Unexpectedly low aggregate demand means that sales slow so much that inventories increase and reach levels higher than firms had planned on.

- ✔ Unexpectedly high aggregate demand means that sales increase so much that inventories decrease and reach levels lower than firms had planned on.

Increasing or decreasing output as inventories fluctuate

Unexpectedly large changes in inventories cause firms to change their output levels as follows:

- ✔ If inventories rise above target levels, firms respond by cutting production. By reducing production rates to less than sales rates, inventories begin to fall down toward target levels.

- ✔ If inventories fall below target levels, firms respond by raising production. By increasing production rates to more than sales rates, inventories begin to rise toward target levels.

The changes in output levels caused by changes in inventories are hugely important because they determine not only whether output (Y) is increasing or decreasing, but also whether unemployment is rising or falling.

For instance, if firms increase production because inventories have fallen below target levels, they need to hire more workers, and unemployment falls. If, on the other hand, firms decrease production because inventories rise above target levels, they need to lay off workers, and unemployment rises.

Adjusting inventories based on planned and actual expenditures

The Keynesian model differentiates between planned expenditures and actual expenditures as follows:

- ✔ *Planned expenditures* are the amount of money that households, businesses, the government, and foreigners would like to spend on domestically produced goods and services.

- ✔ *Actual expenditures* are equal to gross domestic product (GDP), which I discuss in Chapter 4; they are what households, businesses, the government, and foreigners actually end up spending on domestically produced goods and services.

What happens when actual expenditures are different from planned expenditures? Inventories automatically change. For instance, if more money is spent on goods and services than was planned, people are buying up more output than is currently being produced. This situation is possible because firms sell goods from their inventories that were produced in previous periods. On the flip side, if people spend less money on goods and services than was planned, firm inventories rise because firms have to store up all the output that they can't sell.

Keynes represented planned expenditures, *PE,* algebraically with the following equation:

$$PE = C + I^P + G + NX \tag{1}$$

What do all these letters mean? I discuss them in detail in Chapter 4, but here is the short version:

- *C* stands for the amount of output that consumers wish to consume.

- I^P stands for the amount of output that firms plan to buy as investment goods, such as new factories and equipment, as well as any inventory changes that firms plan to make.

   If, later on, firms have to increase or decrease inventories more than they planned, then actual investment, *I,* will not equal planned investment, I^P.

- *G* stands for how much output the government wants to buy for things like building schools or ensuring an adequate supply of paper for paperwork.

- *NX* stands for *net exports* — the value of our exports minus the value of our imports. *NX* tells us the net demand that the foreign sector of the economy has for stuff that we make domestically.

For actual expenditures, *Y,* Keynes used the same equation that we use to calculate gross domestic product (which I discuss in Chapter 4):

$$Y = C + I + G + NX \tag{2}$$

Why can we use the GDP equation to calculate actual expenditures? As I explain in Chapter 4, actual expenditure is equal to national income because every cent of expenditure made in the economy is income to somebody. Furthermore, actual expenditure is also equal to the dollar value of all goods and services produced in the economy because every bit of output that's produced is sold to someone. (Any output that a firm makes but can't sell to customers is counted as being "sold" by the firm to itself as it's placed into inventory. These inventory changes are known as *inventory investment* and are totaled up in GDP as part of the total investment, *I.*)

Having three ways of looking at Y is actually very handy as you become familiar with the Keynesian model. Sometimes it's easier to understand the model if you think of Y as being actual expenditures; at other times it's easier to understand if you think of Y as being national income or output. I switch between these three definitions whenever doing so helps make understanding the model easier.

The only difference between the right-hand sides of equation (1) and equation (2) is the investment variable, which is *planned investment* (I^P) in the first equation and *actual investment* (I) in the second. In other words, the only reason that Y and PE differ is because of differences in investments caused by inventories increasing or decreasing unexpectedly when sales are more or less than planned.

Bringing some algebra into the mix

You knew it was coming: It's time to get algebraic. Our goal? To identify the Keynesian model's economic equilibrium by using our mathematical superpowers. (Now, where did I put those?)

First, we need to define a *consumption function* — a way to calculate total consumption — that we can substitute into equation (1). In Chapter 4, I present the following formula for calculating consumption:

$$C = C_o + c(1-t)Y \qquad (3)$$

For all the details, look back at Chapter 4. For now, what you really need to know about this formula is that higher income (Y) leads to higher consumption (C).

If you substitute equation (3) into equation (1), you get:

$$PE = C_o + c(1-t)Y + I^P + G + NX \qquad (4)$$

If you look carefully, you'll see that this equation shows that the total planned expenditure on goods and services in the economy (PE) depends on the total income in the economy (Y). The higher the total income, the more money people are going to plan to spend.

A good way to simplify this equation is to create a variable called A and to define it as follows:

$$A = C_o + I^P + G + NX$$

If you do that, equation (4) looks a little more palatable:

$$PE = A + c(1-t)Y \qquad (5)$$

The variable *A* stands for *autonomous expenditures,* by which economists mean the part of planned expenditures that doesn't depend on income (*Y*). The part of planned expenditures that does depend on income, $c(1-t)Y$, is known as *induced expenditures*.

To understand induced expenditures, realize that because *t* stands for the income tax rate, $(1-t)Y$ is what people have left over to spend after the government taxes them. And of that amount, the fraction *c* gets spent on consumption, so that $c(1-t)Y$ tells you how much expenditure is "induced" by an income of size *Y.*

Figure 6-6 graphs equation (5) and labels it the *planned expenditure line.*

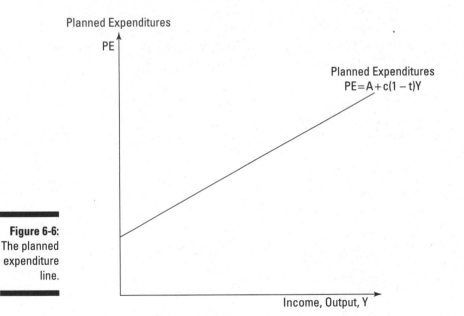

Planned Expenditures

PE

Planned Expenditures
PE = A + c(1 − t)Y

Income, Output, Y

Figure 6-6:
The planned expenditure line.

To find the specific equilibrium of the Keynesian model, realize that all possible equilibriums are captured by the following equation:

$$PE = Y \qquad\qquad (6)$$

This equation can be read as "planned expenditures equal actual expenditures." (Remember that *Y* equals both total income and total expenditure in the economy because all expenditures are income to somebody.)

Any situation where *PE* = *Y* is an equilibrium. Why? Because if the economy could get to the point where *PE* = *Y,* then nobody would have any reason to change their behavior. Consumers would be consuming as much as they planned to consume (*C*). The government would be buying up as much output as it wanted to buy (*G*). Foreigners would be buying as much stuff from us as they intended (*NX*). And, most importantly, firms would be spending exactly as much on investment as they planned — implying that inventories aren't changing unexpectedly.

If planned expenditures equal actual expenditures, you truly have an equilibrium because everybody is getting what they want, and nobody has any incentive to change their behavior.

You can solve for the equilibrium value of output, which I'm going to call $\tilde{Y}$, by substituting equation (5) into equation (6). If you do so, you get the following:

$$\tilde{Y} = \frac{1}{1 - c\,(1 - t)}\,A \tag{7}$$

Showing equilibrium graphically

If the last equation is just too frightening, stick with me. It's much easier to find the Keynesian model's equilibrium graphically. To do so, you plot the $PE = Y$ equation on the same graph as the $PE = A + c(1 - t)Y$ equation, as I do in Figure 6-7. The point where the two lines cross is the equilibrium. At that point, planned expenditures exactly equal actual expenditures in the economy.

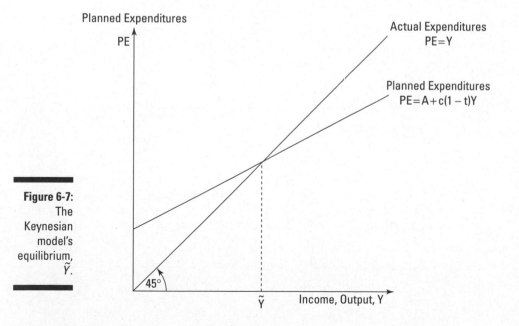

Figure 6-7:
The Keynesian model's equilibrium, $\tilde{Y}$.

This equilibrium is *stable,* by which I mean that if the economy starts out at any income level other than $\tilde{Y}$, it soon moves back to $\tilde{Y}$. The thing that returns it to $\tilde{Y}$ is inventory changes.

To see why this is true, look at Figure 6-8, which exploits a nifty geometric trick about the $PE = Y$ line to show how the economy behaves when it's not producing at the equilibrium output level, $\tilde{Y}$.

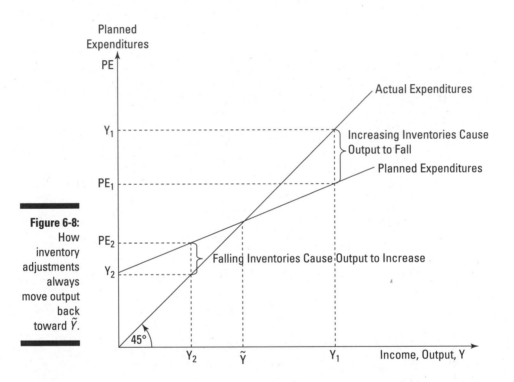

Figure 6-8:
How inventory adjustments always move output back toward $\tilde{Y}$.

The trick is that the $PE = Y$ line shows up on the graph at a 45-degree angle, meaning that it can be used to draw squares — shapes whose sides have the same length. That means you can transpose any value of Y onto the vertical axis. To do so, take any value of Y, go straight up until you hit the 45-degree line, and then go straight sideways until you hit the vertical axis. The point you hit represents as many dollars vertically as Y represents horizontally.

For instance, in Figure 6-8, start on the horizontal axis at output level Y_2, which is less than the equilibrium output level $\tilde{Y}$. If you go up vertically to the 45-degree line and then to the left, you can plot output level Y_2 onto the vertical axis. Why is this useful? Because Y_2 can then be compared directly with the level of planned expenditures, PE_2, that you get by starting at output level Y_2 on the horizontal axis.

As you can see, $PE_2 > Y_2$, meaning that planned expenditures exceed output in the economy. This means that inventories will unexpectedly drop as firms sell part of their stockpiles of inventory to make up for the fact that people are buying up more stuff than firms are currently producing. This drop in inventories will return the economy to equilibrium.

As inventories fall unexpectedly, firms increase production. As a result, Y increases. Furthermore, it continues to increase until it reaches $\tilde{Y}$ because for any value of $Y < \tilde{Y}$, you can see from the graph that planned expenditures will continue to exceed output.

Inventory adjustments also return the economy to equilibrium if it starts out at an output level like Y_1, which is greater than $\tilde{Y}$. As you can see in Figure 6-8, by using the 45-degree line, actual output, Y_1, exceeds planned expenditures, PE_1. In other words, people are buying less (PE_1) than firms are currently producing (Y_1), so inventories will start to rise.

Firms respond to increases in inventories by reducing output. They lay off workers and cut production. As a result, Y falls. It continues to fall until it reaches $\tilde{Y}$ because for any value of $Y > \tilde{Y}$, you can see from the graph that output will continue to exceed actual expenditures.

Boosting GDP in the Keynesian model

Keynes didn't just invent his model to explain how economies with sticky prices reach a stable equilibrium. What he really wanted to do was to use it to show what governments could do during a recession to make things better.

For instance, consider Figure 6-8 once again. Suppose that inventory adjustments have carried the economy to equilibrium income, $\tilde{Y}$, but that $\tilde{Y}$ is less than the economy's full-employment output level, Y^*. In such a case, Keynes asked, what — if anything — should governments do?

Governments could choose to do nothing. Eventually, because $\tilde{Y} < Y^*$, prices will fall and the economy will return to full employment (as it does moving from point B to point C in Figure 6-5). But Keynes argued that governments could speed up the recovery by boosting planned expenditures.

For instance, suppose that the government decides to increase G, government spending on goods and services. If it does so, then PE in equation (4) clearly gets bigger. Because G is a part of autonomous expenditures (A), the increase in G means an increase in A in equation (5). Graphically, a larger A means that the planned expenditure line shifts vertically from PE_1 to PE_2, as shown in Figure 6-9. Given the fact that the actual expenditure line ($PE = Y$) doesn't change, the vertical shift in the planned expenditure line causes equilibrium output to increase from $\tilde{Y}_1$ to $\tilde{Y}_2$.

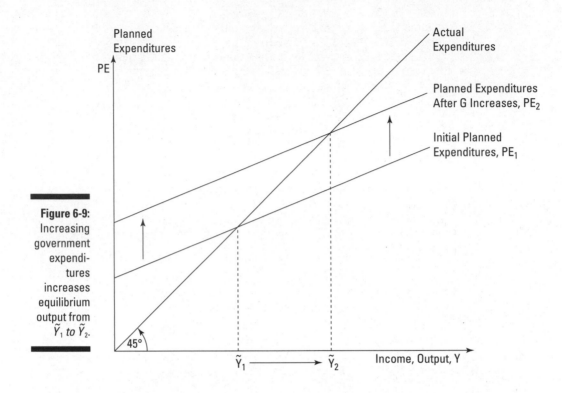

Figure 6-9:
Increasing
government
expendi-
tures
increases
equilibrium
output from
$\tilde{Y}_1$ to $\tilde{Y}_2$.

What Keynes suggested doing was using government policy to increase
planned expenditures by whatever amount was necessary to increase the
economy's short-run, sticky-price equilibrium, $\tilde{Y}$, all the way to the full-
employment output level, Y^*. In Chapter 7, I discuss such policies in greater
detail, including why they don't always work so well in practice.

Chapter 7

Fighting Recessions with Monetary and Fiscal Policy

Monetary and fiscal policy are two of the most important functions of modern governments. *Monetary policy* focuses on increasing or decreasing the money supply in order to stimulate the economy, while *fiscal policy* uses government spending and the tax code to stimulate the economy.

Thanks to the development of good economic theory, it's now possible for governments to use monetary and fiscal policy to mitigate the duration and severity of recessions. This development is hugely important because it gives governments the chance to make a positive difference in the lives of billions of people. Good economic policy can make a nation prosperous, while bad economic policy can ruin it.

Monetary and fiscal policy are not without problems, however, and in this chapter I show you not only how well they can work under the best-case scenario but also their limits and problems when implemented in the real world. By seeing the whole picture, you can decide for yourself when and how monetary and fiscal policy should be used.

The information in this chapter will put you two steps ahead of many politicians and will help you judge when politically-biased economists are trying to pull a fast one. As Joan Robinson, one of the great economists of the 20th century, said, "The purpose of studying economics is not to acquire a set of ready-made answers to economic questions, but to learn how to avoid being deceived by an economist." I totally agree. But don't worry, you can trust *me*.

If you haven't read Chapter 6, I encourage you to do so before tackling this chapter. While my goal with this book is to make each chapter its own entity, so that you can jump in and jump out wherever you need, much of the terminology you encounter in this chapter is introduced and explained in Chapter 6. You may find it easier to tackle monetary and fiscal policy if you have a basic understanding of how recessions work, which is the focus of Chapter 6.

Stimulating Demand to End Recessions

Before looking at monetary and fiscal policy separately and in detail, it's important to realize that the purpose of both is to alter the aggregate demand for goods and services. (The *aggregate demand* is the total demand for goods and services in an economy.) In particular, both can be used to increase aggregate demand during a recession.

Aiming for full-employment output

The ability to use monetary and fiscal policy to stimulate the economy is important because you always want to end a recession and return the economy to producing at the full-employment output level as quickly as possible.

As I explain in Chapter 6, the full-employment output level — symbolized as Y^* — is the amount of output the economy produces at full employment, which occurs when every person who wants a full-time job can get one. If the economy goes into recession and produces less than Y^* worth of output, millions of people lose their jobs because firms need fewer workers to produce the smaller amount of output.

Worse yet, the unemployment rate remains high until output returns to the full-employment level. Monetary and fiscal policy are useful precisely because they can help return the economy to producing at Y^* as soon as possible; they can shorten the period of frustration and misery that the unemployed have to endure.

Take a look at Figure 7-1, which shows how monetary and fiscal policy can be used to stimulate aggregate demand and return an economy to producing at Y^* as quickly as possible after the economy is hit with a negative demand shock. (As I explain in Chapter 6, *negative demand shocks* are things that unexpectedly decrease aggregate demand, such as a drop in consumer confidence.)

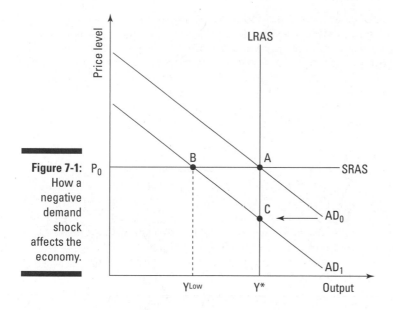

Figure 7-1:
How a
negative
demand
shock
affects the
economy.

In Figure 7-1, the economy begins in equilibrium at point *A,* where the down-ward-sloping aggregate demand curve, AD_o, intersects the vertical long-run aggregate supply curve, *LRAS.* As I explain in Chapter 6, prices in the economy are fixed in the short run. For this reason, the short-run aggregate supply curve, *SRAS,* is horizontal at the initial price level (P_o), which is determined by the intersection of AD_o and *LRAS.* (I explain in Chapter 6, in the section called "Dealing with fixed prices in the short-run," that for simplicity's sake I'm using horizontal *SRAS* curves in this book rather than the upward-sloping curves used in some other books. If you're used to seeing upward-sloping *SRAS* curves, take a quick peek at that section.)

When the negative demand shock comes along, here's what happens:

✔ The aggregate demand curve shifts left to AD_1, reflecting the reduction in spending on goods and services.

✔ With prices fixed at P_o in the short run, the economy's equilibrium shifts leftward from point *A* to point *B,* and output in the economy falls from Y^* down to Y^{Low}.

✔ As output falls, unemployment rises because firms don't need as many workers.

As you can see, the overall result of the demand shock is a recession: a period of declining output and increasing unemployment.

Unfortunately, a recession can take a long time to resolve. As I explain in Chapter 6, if the government takes no action to end a recession, the only way for the economy to return to producing at the full-employment output level is for prices to drop so that the economy's equilibrium can slide down the AD_1 curve from point B to point C. That process is typically very slow because of sticky prices, especially sticky wages, which I describe in Chapter 6. As a result, the economy will have high unemployment and take a long time to get back to producing at Y^* unless the government gets involved.

Shifting the AD curve to the right — or, putting people back to work

The trick that both monetary and fiscal policy accomplish is to increase aggregate demand, which eliminates the need to endure the slow adjustment process that takes the economy from point B to point C (see Figure 7-1). They do this by shifting the aggregate demand curve to the right.

For instance, if the government was able to shift the aggregate demand curve from AD_1 back to AD_o, the economy would jump back to equilibrium point A. That's very nice because it gets the economy back to producing at Y^* without having to go through the slow adjustment process that's needed to get an economy to move from B to C. In human terms, this means that unemployment will end much sooner for millions of workers who can once again find jobs and provide for themselves and their families.

Unfortunately, however, actually implementing aggregate demand shifts to fight recessions isn't easy. Several problems can creep up involving inflation and people's expectations about how increases in aggregate demand affect prices. So before I tackle the details about how monetary and fiscal policy can be used to increase aggregate demand, I first want to explain how inflation (and worries about inflation) can limit their effectiveness.

Generating Inflation: The Risk of Too Much Stimulation

The best way to begin to understand the limitations of economic policies that stimulate aggregate demand is to understand that in the long run, such policies can change only the price level, not the level of output. Why? I'll need several pages to explain the reasons fully, but the explanation comes back to something I discuss at length in Chapter 6: No matter where the aggregate demand curve happens to be — no matter how much stuff consumers are willing (or unwilling) to buy — prices eventually adjust until the economy is once again producing at full-employment output (Y^*). The economy simply doesn't want to stray from Y^* for too long.

I explain the economy's affection for Y^* in Chapter 6, and you can see it in Figure 7-1 as well. The negative demand shock shifts the aggregate demand curve from AD_o to AD_1. If the government does not use some sort of stimulus, the economy slowly adjusts on its own from point A to point B to point C. At point C, the price level will have fallen, and output will have returned to Y^*.

But even if the government applies some sort of stimulus to move the aggregate demand curve to the right of AD_1, the long-run result is always that the economy comes to equilibrium at the point where the aggregate demand curve intersects the long-run aggregate supply (*LRAS*) curve. And, as I show in Chapter 6, the *LRAS* is a vertical line that corresponds to the full-employment output level, Y^*.

An exercise in futility: Trying to increase output beyond Y^*

Because the economy always returns to producing at full-employment output (Y^*), the government can't for any significant period of time keep the economy producing more output than Y^*. To see why this is true, suppose that the government uses monetary and/or fiscal policy to shift the aggregate demand curve from AD_o to AD_1, as shown in Figure 7-2.

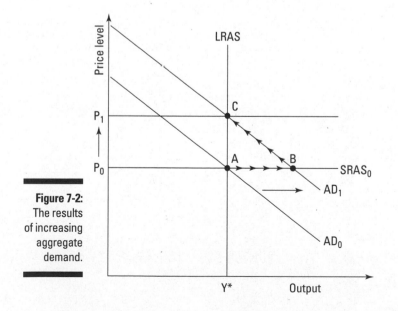

Figure 7-2: The results of increasing aggregate demand.

Before the shift, the economy is in equilibrium at point A, where the original aggregate demand curve, AD_o, intersects the long-run aggregate supply curve ($LRAS$), which is a vertical line above Y^*. At that initial equilibrium, the price level is P_o, and because prices are sticky in the short run (see Chapter 6), the short-run aggregate supply curve, $SRAS_o$, is a horizontal line at P_o.

When the government stimulates the economy and shifts the aggregate demand curve to the right from AD_o to AD_1, the economy initially shifts from point A to point B. That is, because prices are fixed in the short run, the economy adjusts to a temporary equilibrium at B (where AD_1 intersects $SRAS_o$).

The economy's output level at point B is greater than the full-employment output level, Y^*. For this reason, point B is only a temporary equilibrium. That's because the only way that the economy can produce more than Y^* is if it's using more labor than is used at Y^*. There are only two ways this can happen:

- Firms convince existing workers to work overtime.
- Firms increase the total number of workers by tempting people like retirees, who wouldn't normally be in the labor force, to take jobs.

Both ways of increasing the labor supply increase labor costs:

- To get existing workers to consistently work overtime, firms must pay them high overtime wages.
- To tempt people like retirees to join the workforce, firms must increase wages (because, obviously, these people weren't tempted to work at the old wages).

Either way, production costs rise. And as they do, firms pass them on to consumers by raising the prices they charge for goods and services.

That is why the economy moves from point B to point C in Figure 7-2. As prices rise because wages are increasing, the economy moves up the AD_1 curve (as indicated by the arrows). Wages, and hence prices, continue to rise until the economy is once again producing Y^* worth of output at point C. At that point, there's no need for further wage increases; the economy is once again producing at Y^*, and firms don't have to increase wages to try to produce more than that level.

A temporary high: Tracing the movement of real wages

If you look at Figure 7-2 and consider the movement from A to B to C caused by the government's stimulus program, you can see that the only long-run consequence is an increase in the price level from P_o to P_1. After a period of increased production, the economy is back to producing at the full-employment output level, Y^*.

You can take two critical lessons away from this example:

✔ The government can't permanently keep output above Y^*.

✔ The government can't permanently keep more people employed than the number employed at Y^*.

Real wages are the reason these two lessons are true. What are real wages? Wages measured not in terms of money, but in terms of how much stuff workers can buy with the money they're paid.

Real wages are crucial to understanding how government stimulus affects the economy because people don't work hard for money in and of itself — they work hard for the things that money can buy. This distinction is important because as the economy reacts to the government's shifting of the aggregate demand curve from AD_o to AD_l, real wages increase only temporarily. While they're higher, workers supply more labor. But when they fall back down to their original levels, workers go back to supplying their original amount of labor.

Raising nominal wages while prices are stuck

Confused? Stick with me. To see how this works, let me concentrate on the situation of a banana-loving worker named Ralph. When the economy is at point A in Figure 7-2, Ralph is paid $10 per hour, and his favorite food, bananas, costs $1 per pound. This implies that his *real wages* — his wages measured in terms of what they can buy — are 10 pounds of bananas per hour. At that real wage, Ralph is willing to work full-time.

When the government stimulates the economy and shifts the aggregate demand curve from AD_o to AD_l, workers like Ralph initially benefit because real wages initially rise. That's because in order to produce more output than Y^*, firms have to raise *nominal wages* (wages measured in money) in order to get workers to produce more. Because prices are initially sticky at price level P_o, the increase in nominal wages means an increase in real wages.

In Ralph's case, suppose that the price of bananas remains at $1 per pound because of sticky prices, but Ralph's nominal wage rises to $12 per hour because the company he works for needs more labor. Ralph's real wage increases from 10 pounds of bananas per hour to 12 pounds of bananas per hour.

This increase in real wages motivates workers to supply all the extra labor that's required to produce higher levels of output. (In Figure 7-2, this is what's going on at point B.) Because nominal wages have gone up but prices haven't, the resulting increase in real wages causes workers to supply more labor, which in turn allows firms to produce an output level greater than Y^*.

Moving back to Y* and to original real wages

Unfortunately, as firms begin to pass on the costs of increased wages as higher prices, real wages begin to fall. Suppose that because of higher labor costs, the price of bananas rises to $1.10 per pound. At that price, Ralph's real wage falls from 12 pounds of bananas per hour down to 10.91 pounds of bananas per hour. (To get 10.91, divide Ralph's $12 per hour money wage by the $1.10 per pound price of bananas.)

In Figure 7-2, the decrease in real wages happens as the economy moves along the aggregate demand curve from point B to point C. As prices rise, real wages fall. Prices will continue to rise until they've risen so far that real wages return to where they originally were at point A before the government stimulated aggregate demand.

In Ralph's case, the price of bananas continues to rise until they cost $1.20 per pound. At that price, his higher nominal wage of $12 per hour once again buys him 10 pounds of bananas per hour; his real wage is back where it started.

This boomerang effect in the real wage makes total sense. Because the economy returns to producing at Y^*, you only need to motivate workers to supply enough labor to produce Y^*, not anything extra. Workers like Ralph were willing to supply that amount of labor at point A for a real wage of 10 pounds of bananas per hour. After the economy has moved to point C, they'll once again be willing to supply that amount of labor for the same real wage.

Obviously, not every worker is fixated on bananas like Ralph. But I hope you get the idea: If both wages and prices rise by 20 percent, real wages remain unchanged and, consequently, the amount of labor that workers supply ends up unchanged.

Because this is true, government stimulus policies, like the one shown in Figure 7-2, that shift aggregate demand from AD_o to AD_1 can't permanently increase the amount of labor being employed by firms. Neither can these policies permanently increase workers' real wages. These effects are at best temporary; they last only as long as it takes for the economy to adjust from A to B to C.

You may think that a temporary increase in employment and output is pretty good, however, and that the government should still go ahead and increase aggregate demand from AD_o to AD_1. Unfortunately, as I'm about to show you, if people know about the stimulus ahead of time, the economy may adjust directly from A to C and eliminate the ability of the aggregate demand shift to stimulate the economy even temporarily.

Failing to stimulate: What happens when a stimulus is expected

In the previous section, I explain why an increase in aggregate demand that tries to increase output beyond Y^* can do so only temporarily, until prices adjust. In this section, I show you that prices may adjust so quickly that the stimulus may fail to increase output at all, even temporarily.

Respecting the importance of price stickiness

As I show in Figure 7-2, any increase in output after aggregate demand shifts rightward from AD_o to AD_1 depends on prices being sticky in the short run. In other words, the economy moves from point A to point B along the horizontal short-run aggregate supply curve, $SRAS_o$, only if the price level is fixed at P_o in the short run.

In Chapter 6, I explain that a lot of evidence shows that prices have a hard time falling during a recession. In particular, firms don't like to cut wages and insult their workers. They know that if they cut wages, workers will become angry and refuse to work hard, and the resulting decline in productivity will make the firm's profit situation even worse.

As a result, there's a lot of *downward wage stickiness* in the economy — by which economists mean that nominal wages only rarely decline. As I explain in Chapter 6, downward wage stickiness leads to *downward price stickiness,* because firms can't cut their prices below production costs if they want to turn a profit and stay in business. (Keep in mind that labor costs are, for most businesses, the largest part of production costs. If firms can't cut wages, they can't cut the price of their output.)

Realizing that prices aren't very sticky upward

Notice that in the previous section I talk only about *downward* stickiness; I don't say anything about prices or wages having trouble rising. In fact, there seems to be very little in the economy that can cause *upward* wage stickiness or *upward* price stickiness.

Quite the contrary, wages and prices seem quite free to rise if demand increases relative to supply. Business contracts and labor contracts may limit price and wage increases for a while, but as soon as these contracts expire, prices and wages are free to rise.

Anticipating (and undermining) a stimulus

The lack of upward price stickiness implies two very important things for any government attempting to stimulate the economy into producing more than the full-employment output level (Y^*):

✔ If prices and wages can rise quickly, the economy will produce more than Y^* only very briefly. That is, it will move from A to B to C in Figure 7-2 very quickly — so quickly that the stimulus will cause output and employment to rise above Y^* only very briefly.

✔ If people can see a stimulus coming, that stimulus (which attempts to increase output beyond Y^*) is likely to generate only inflation and no increase in output whatsoever. In other words, if people can anticipate an increase in aggregate demand, the economy may jump directly from point A to point C, so that the price level rises without there being even a temporary increase in output.

To see why this is true, suppose that the government preannounces a big stimulus package that will shift aggregate demand from AD_o to AD_1 in a few months' time (see Figure 7-2). Because workers and businesses can learn macroeconomics just as well as the politicians running the government, they realize that the only long-run effect of the upcoming stimulus will be for prices to rise from P_o to P_1.

In addition, workers understand that real wages will remain unchanged in the long run because both their nominal wages and their cost of living (given by the price level) will increase by equal amounts. As a result, they know that in the long run, the stimulus won't help them at all. Indeed, their only hope for gains is based entirely upon the short run, when nominal wages should go up and the price level should stay the same. In other words, they hope to benefit from the movement from A to B in Figure 7-2.

But firms aren't stupid. They don't want to have their profits reduced because wages are rising while prices are fixed. So they simply anticipate everything. Because prices eventually have to rise from P_o to P_1 and wages eventually have to rise by an equal amount, firms get ahead of the wage increases by raising prices as soon as they can.

Nothing prevents firms from raising prices because there's nothing in the economy causing upward price stickiness. So, if firms can see the stimulus coming ahead of time, they simply raise prices as soon as they can in order to make sure that prices and wages are going up at the same pace. As a result, the price level jumps from P_o to P_1.

Of course, at the same time, firms raise wages by an equal percentage in order to keep real wages the same. They want to keep workers motivated to supply the labor necessary to produce Y^* worth of output.

As you can see, if a government tries to stimulate the economy past producing at Y^*, and if the stimulus is understood and anticipated by everyone in the economy, it may not work at all. Prices and wages may simply jump from point A to point C, meaning that the stimulus fails to stimulate because output stays constant at Y^* while prices and wages go up simultaneously.

Having rational expectations

The phenomenon I describe in the previous section is an example of *rational expectations,* a term that economists use to describe how people rationally change their current behavior in anticipation of future events. In this case, firms rationally decide to raise prices immediately when they find out that the government will be increasing aggregate demand from AD_o to AD_1 in the future.

Indeed, firms' only rational course of action is to immediately raise prices because if they left prices alone at P_o, they'd be volunteering for the decrease in profits that results when the economy moves from point *A* to point *B* (when nominal wages rise while prices stay constant). By immediately raising prices and shifting the economy directly from *A* to *C*, they can avoid that situation altogether.

Rational expectations is one of the most important ideas in macroeconomics because it tells you that there are strong limits on the government's ability to control the economy. People don't just sit around like potted plants when the government announces a policy change. They change their behavior. And sometimes, as in the case I describe in the previous section, their behavioral change completely ruins the government's ability to achieve its objective of stimulating the economy.

A little inflation may help employment

Economists have thought a lot about the best way to run monetary policy. Interestingly, many have concluded that it should always be just a little bit overstimulating so that there's always a modest 1 or 2 percent inflation rate. The idea is that modest inflation rates help to smooth out the labor market by giving firms a sneaky way to increase profits if they run into a temporary slowdown in sales.

As I point out in Chapter 6, wages are typically sticky downward because if you cut workers' wages, they get mad and give less effort. The result of this phenomenon is that when the demand for a firm's output slows and labor costs need to be cut to restore profitability, managers usually fire a portion of the workforce and keep the remaining workers at their old wages rather than keeping all the workers on the job at lower wages.

The pressure to make such layoffs is reduced if there's inflation, because the inflation drives up the selling price of the firm's output. If managers keep nominal wages fixed while that's happening, profits improve and lessen the need to fire anyone.

However, workers' real wages will fall. That's because while nominal (money) wages are fixed, the cost of living keeps rising due to the inflation. But because firm profits are helped along by inflation, there's less of a need to lay off workers. So, while the workers lose in some sense by seeing their real wages fall, many benefit because they still have jobs, whereas otherwise they would have been laid off.

As I explain monetary and fiscal policy in more detail in the rest of the chapter, you can see other examples of rational expectations limiting the effectiveness of government policy. Be sure to notice how, in every case, changes in people's behavior reduce the impact of government policy initiatives.

Figuring Out Fiscal Policy

Fiscal policy concerns itself with how governments tax and spend. It overlaps macroeconomics because modern governments have many opportunities to increase aggregate demand by making changes in fiscal policy. These changes fall into two main categories:

- ✔ Increasing aggregate demand indirectly by lowering taxes so that consumers have larger after-tax incomes to spend on buying more goods and services.
- ✔ Increasing aggregate demand directly by buying more goods and services.

The first category involves decreasing government revenues, and the second involves increasing government spending. Because the government's budget deficit is defined as tax revenues minus spending, both types of fiscal policy are likely to increase government budget deficits. This fact is very important because large and ongoing government budget deficits may lead to many economic problems, including inflation. As a result, the fear of large budget deficits constrains the magnitude of fiscal policy initiatives.

As you read about fiscal policy in the following sections, keep this fear of large budget deficits in mind because it limits the size of the aggregate demand shifts that a government can undertake. For instance, if you look back at Figure 7-1, the government may want to use fiscal policy to shift aggregate demand rightward from AD_o to AD_1, but if doing so would involve an overly large budget deficit, it may have to settle for a smaller shift that moves the economy only part of the way back to producing again at full-employment output (Y^*).

Increasing government spending to help end recessions

If an economy gets into trouble, one of the first things that politicians call for is increased government spending. The idea is that if people are unemployed and unsold goods are sitting around gathering dust, the government can come in with a lot of money and buy up a lot of the unsold products. The result of this action is that the government generates so much demand that businesses start hiring the unemployed in order to increase output to meet all the new demand.

The hope is that this stimulus jumpstarts further demand. When people who were formerly unemployed start getting paychecks again, they start spending more money, which means that demand rises. When this happens, the economic recovery should be self-sustaining so that the government doesn't need to continue to spend so much money.

Paying for increased government spending

Politicians naturally like suggesting increases in government spending because such increases make them look good, especially if they can get some of the new spending earmarked specifically for their own constituents. However, nothing in life is free.

There are only three ways to pay for increased government spending:

- ✔ The government can print more money.
- ✔ The government can raise taxes.
- ✔ The government can borrow more money.

As I discuss in Chapter 5, printing lots of new money to pay for increased government spending leads to large bouts of inflation, which bring with them economic chaos and recessions. Consequently, governments nowadays almost never resort to printing more money to pay for increased government purchases of goods and services.

Raising taxes is also problematic because if you're trying to get out of a recession, you want consumers to spend as much as possible on goods and services. If you raise taxes, consumers reduce their spending. You may offset some of the decreased private spending by immediately turning around and spending all the tax revenue, but clearly this is not the way to stimulate aggregate demand in the long run. The government may as well just let its citizens spend their money in the first place.

Borrowing and spending: The most common solution

What governments need to do to combat recessions is figure out a way to increase their own spending without decreasing private spending. The solution is borrowing.

By borrowing money during a recession and spending it, the government can increase its purchases of goods and services without decreasing the private sector's purchases. Who does the government borrow from? You, and other people like you.

At any given moment in time, people want to save a certain part of their incomes. They can use these savings to buy many different kinds of assets, including stocks and bonds issued by corporations, real estate, mutual funds, and annuities. But they can also use their savings to buy government bonds, which are, in essence, loans to the government.

By offering more bonds for sale, the government can redirect some of the savings that people are making away from purchases of other assets and into purchases of government-issued bonds. By selling bonds, the government can get ahold of lots of money that it can spend on goods and services, thereby turning what otherwise would have been private spending on assets into public spending on goods and services.

Dealing with deficits

Increasing government spending and financing it through borrowing is clearly a good way to increase the overall demand for goods and services. But it has the potentially nasty side effect of creating a *budget deficit,* which is the dollar amount by which government spending exceeds tax revenues during the current year. Any current budget deficit adds to the *national debt,* the cumulative total of all the money that the government owes lenders.

The problem with budget deficits and the national debt is that they have to be paid back someday. Consider a ten-year bond that pays a 6 percent rate of return. When you buy the bond from the government, you give it $1,000. In return, the government promises to do two things:

✔ To give you back your $1,000 in ten years

✔ To give you $60 per year (a 6 percent return) until you get your $1,000 back

So, the government gets $1,000 right now to spend on goods and services to boost the economy, but it has to figure out where to get $60 per year to give you your interest payments and also where to get $1,000 in ten years when the bond matures.

Relying on the security of future tax revenues

Obviously, the only reason that people are willing to lend the government any money by buying bonds is because they believe that the government will eventually pay them back. The reason they have confidence in that happening is that governments have the exclusive right to tax things. Essentially, all government borrowing is secured by future tax revenues.

But the link between taxes and bond repayments is not direct. In other words, just because a government has a lot of bonds coming due, it doesn't necessarily have to raise taxes all of a sudden to get the money to pay off the bonds. That's because governments often refinance the bonds that are coming due; they simply issue new bonds to get enough cash to pay off the old bonds. This process is referred to as *rolling over the debt* and is routinely practiced by governments everywhere.

But don't think that this is all just a huge scam to indefinitely defer paying off the debt. The only reason that investors are willing to participate in a rollover is they've got confidence that the government can always use its tax powers to pay off its debts. Investor confidence allows governments to keep on borrowing, whether to fund new borrowing or to roll over old debt.

Paying the debt by printing money: A devastating choice

Sometimes, investor confidence in the government turns out to have been misplaced. As I discuss in Chapter 5, governments have another (rather diabolical) way to pay off their bonds besides using tax revenues: They can print lots of money.

A $1,000 bond obligates the government to pay you back $1,000 worth of money. The bond doesn't say where that $1,000 comes from. So the government is free to print $1,000 worth of new bills and hand them to you. This solution may seem okay at first, but when you and all the other bond holders with newly printed cash go out into the economy and start spending that new money, you drive up prices and cause an inflation.

As I point out in Chapter 5, big inflations destroy economic activity. During a big inflation, prices lose much of their meaning, and people are much more mistrustful and reluctant to engage in long-term contracts or make long-term investments because they don't know how much money will be worth in the future.

Knowing the potential horrors of inflation, people tend to worry any time they see a government running large budget deficits or piling up a very large debt. They worry that the government may find itself in a position in which it can't raise taxes high enough to pay off its obligations (or it isn't willing to anger voters by raising taxes that high). Investors worry that if this situation occurs, the government may resort to printing money to pay off its debts. And doing so would ruin the economy.

Printing money to pay government debts would also badly hurt most bond-holders because most of them would get their cash after prices have gone up, meaning that their cash won't buy much stuff. Consequently, when people really begin to worry that a government may start printing money to pay off its debts, it gets harder and harder for the government to find anyone willing to buy its bonds. In such a situation, the only way for the government to get anyone to buy its bonds is to offer higher and higher interest rates as a compensation for people's worries that the money they'll eventually get back won't be worth much. These higher interest rates then make the government's situation even more desperate because any debt rollovers have to be done at the higher interest rates.

Furthermore, because an inflation affects all bonds, not just the ones issued by the government, interest rates all across the economy rise if people fear an inflation is coming. This situation can have bad economic consequences *immediately* because higher interest rates dissuade consumers from borrowing money to buy things like cars and houses, and they also discourage firms from borrowing money to buy new factories and equipment. Consequently, just the expectation that a government may print money at some point in the future to pay off its bonds can cause immediate harm to the economy. (This is another example of rational expectations in action; see the section "Having rational expectations," earlier in the chapter.)

Most governments try to keep their debt level and their deficits under control so that no one seriously worries that the government will ever be tempted to print money to pay off its bonds.

Dissecting Monetary Policy

Monetary policy is the manipulation of the money supply and interest rates in order to stabilize or stimulate the economy. In modern economies, monetary policy has come to be regarded as the most powerful mechanism that governments have at their disposal to fight recessions and reduce unemployment — even more powerful than fiscal policy.

Monetary policy is put into practice by first changing the supply of money in order to manipulate interest rates. Because interest rates affect everything from the demand for home mortgages by consumers to the demand for investment goods by businesses, they have a huge and pervasive effect on stimulating or depressing economic activity.

To give you a complete picture of how monetary policy functions, I first review what money is. I then show you that it's actually possible to have too much money and how that fact is related to interest rates and inflation. That, in turn, gives you the insight necessary to understand how the government can affect interest rates by changing the amount of money that's floating around in the economy.

Identifying the benefits of fiat money

Money is an *asset,* meaning that it holds its value over time. Other assets include real estate, precious metals like gold, and financial assets like stocks and bonds. But money is unique because it's the only asset that's universally acceptable as a means of payment for goods and services.

As I explain in Chapter 5, money makes an economy much more efficient because it eliminates the need to engage in barter. But the need to verify the authenticity of money (so that people are willing to accept it) has meant that the responsibility for producing money and suppressing counterfeits has fallen to governments.

That, in turn, brings up its own potential problems, because governments always face the temptation to print more money in order to pay off old debts or buy lots of newly produced goods and services.

Historically, one way to limit governments' ability to print up more money to pay off bills was to put them on a *metallic standard.* Under such a system, governments couldn't print more bills without backing them with a precious metal, like gold. For instance, the United States used to have a gold standard under which $35 of currency could be redeemed for one ounce of gold. You could literally bring $35 of bills to the U.S. Treasury and exchange it for an ounce of gold.

What this meant for monetary policy was that the government couldn't arbitrarily increase the supply of paper money because for every $35 of new bills it wanted to print, it had to buy an ounce of gold with which to back them. The high cost of buying gold limited the money supply.

As I note in Chapter 5, such a system is great for preventing big inflations because the only way you ever get a big inflation is if the government prints a huge amount of new money. (When that new money begins circulating, it drives up prices.)

Preventing inflations is a good thing, but using a metallic standard turns out to have some big drawbacks. That's because using a metallic standard causes the supply of money to be pretty much fixed over time, meaning that even if the economy could use a little bit more or a little bit less money to make it work better, the government can't do anything because the supply of money is fixed by the amount of gold the government has in its vaults.

In particular, the metallic standard means that you can't use monetary policy to stimulate your economy if it gets into a recession. One of the reasons that the Great Depression was so bad everywhere around the world was that nearly every country was on a gold standard when the calamity began. This meant that governments were unable to increase their money supplies in order to help their economies. It also explains why the countries that quit their gold standards earliest had the shortest and mildest recessions; after they quit, they were free to print new money to stimulate their economies. On the other hand, countries like the United States and England that stubbornly stuck to their gold standards had the most prolonged and painful economic downturns.

Largely because of that experience and the desire to use monetary policy if needed, every country in the world has abandoned the gold standard in favor of *fiat money.* Under a fiat money system, the government simply prints up as many bills as it likes, declares them to be money, and puts them out in the economy. (*Fiat* means "let it be" in Latin.) The great benefit of this system is that the government can arbitrarily increase or decrease the money supply in whatever way will best help to stimulate the economy.

For the rest of this chapter, I use M to denote the total supply of money floating around the economy. For instance, "M = \$1.3 trillion" means that the sum of the face values of all the bills and coins in the economy is \$1.3 trillion.

Realizing that you can have too much money!

Monetary policy works by manipulating the supply of money in order to change the price of borrowing money, which is the interest rate. The key to making monetary policy work is the fact that the demand for money depends on the interest rate.

Imagine that I hand you \$1 million, and you can do whatever you want with it. Suppose that you're frugal and decide to save every last penny, at least for a year, because you think that'll give you enough time to figure out how to best blow the money.

My question to you is: Should you keep all your new wealth in cash?

The correct answer is "NO!"

Holding your wealth in cash is, to be blunt, really stupid because cash earns no interest. Even if you put the money into a checking account, you'd get at least a tiny bit of interest. Even 1 percent of interest on a million dollars is \$10,000. Why would you give that up? Even better, if you use the cash to buy government bonds, you may get 5 or 6 percent. That's \$50,000 or \$60,000 more than you'd get if you kept your wealth in the form of cash.

Clearly, the higher the interest rate you can get on other assets, the more incentive you have to convert your cash into other assets. In fact, the only thing preventing people from converting all their wealth to other assets and never holding any cash is the fact that money lets them buy things. Beyond that function, money is not any better than any other asset; in fact, it's worse in terms of its rate of return because the rate of return on cash is always zero.

In Figure 7-3, I've created a graph that demonstrates how much money people demand to hold at any particular interest rate. I denote money demand as M^D. The nominal interest rate, i, is on the vertical axis. (For an explanation of nominal interest rates, see Chapter 5.) The horizontal axis is measured in dollars.

As you can see from the downward slope of the money demand curve, the higher the interest rate, the less money people want to hold. This graph simply represents the idea that cash, with its zero interest rate, is a worse and worse place to park your wealth if you can get higher and higher returns in alternative assets. In other words, the higher the interest rate on other assets, the more you're going to want to economize on your cash holdings.

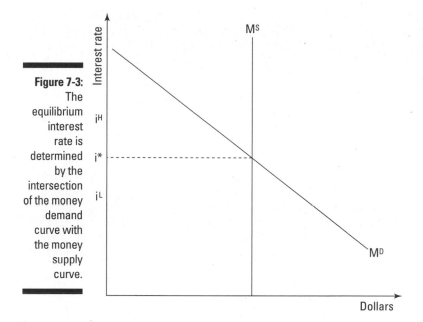

Figure 7-3: The equilibrium interest rate is determined by the intersection of the money demand curve with the money supply curve.

Figure 7-3 also contains the vertical money supply curve, where M^S stands for money supply. This curve is vertical because the government can decide how much money it wants to print and circulate without regard to the interest rate.

The M^D and M^S curves cross at interest rate i^*. This interest rate is the *equilibrium* interest rate because it's the only one at which the total number of dollars of money that people want to hold are equal to the total number of dollars that the government has circulated.

More importantly, i^* is a *stable equilibrium,* meaning that if interest rates ever deviate from it, they will be pushed back to i^* by market forces. But before this fact is going to make sense, I need to take a few paragraphs to explain how interest rates are determined in the bond market. Pay close attention because bond markets are *the* place where interest rates for the whole economy are determined. Bond markets have a huge effect on everything else that goes on in the economy.

Getting the basics about bonds

A *bond* is a financial asset for which you pay a certain amount of money right now in exchange for a series of payments in the future. There are two kinds of payments, face value payments and coupon payments:

✔ The *face value payment* is printed on the face of the bond certificate and comes on the date the bond expires.

> ✔ The *coupon payments* are typically made twice per year until the bond expires. They're called *coupon payments* because before computerized recordkeeping, you would literally clip a coupon off the bottom of the bond certificate and mail it in to receive your payment.

Typically, bonds expire after 1, 5, 10, or 20 years.

Bonds do not guarantee any sort of rate of return. They promise only to make the coupon and face value payments on time. The rate of return depends on how much you pay for the right to receive those payments.

If you think I'm speaking in tongues right now, bear with me. Imagine a really simple kind of bond called a *zero-coupon bond* (so named because there are no coupon payments). The only payment this bond will ever make is the face value payment that comes when the bond expires. And to make things really simple, suppose that it will pay its owner exactly $100 exactly one year from now.

If you're the bond owner, the thing you have to understand is that the rate of return the bond will pay depends on how much you pay for it right now. Suppose that you were naive enough to pay $100 for the bond right now. Your rate of return would be zero percent because you paid $100 for something that will give you $100 in a year.

On the other hand, suppose that you pay only $90 for the bond right now. Your rate of return will be about 11 percent because ($100 − $90)/$90 = 0.111, or 11.1 percent. If you could buy the bond for only $50, your rate of return would be 100 percent because you would double your money in a year's time.

Here's a fact that you should memorize. The rate of return on a bond *varies inversely* with how much you pay for it. Because the amount of money you get in the future is always fixed, the more you pay for it right now, the less is your rate of return. Higher bond prices imply lower rates of return.

Seeing the link between bond prices and interest rates

The fact that bond prices vary inversely with interest rates is the key to understanding why i^* is a stable equilibrium in Figure 7-3. In this section, I explain the link.

First, consider interest rates that are higher than i^*, such as i^H. When interest rates are higher than i^*, the amount of money supplied exceeds the amount of money demanded. What this means is that people have been given more of the asset called money than they want to hold. So what they do is try to reallocate their portfolio of assets by using the excess money to buy other assets.

One of the things that people buy is bonds. But with all this new money being thrown at the limited supply of bonds, the price of bonds rises. Now be careful. What happens to interest rates when bond prices rise? They *fall*. That's why if you start out at an interest rate that's higher than i^*, interest rates will fall back down toward i^*. Excess money drives up the price of bonds, which lowers interest rates.

On the other hand, for interest rates like i^L that are lower than i^*, the amount of money demanded exceeds the amount of money supplied. Because people want more money than they have, they're going to try to get it by selling non-cash assets like bonds in order to convert those assets into the cash they want.

Imagine that everybody does this by trying to sell their bonds. With all the selling, bond prices fall, meaning that interest rates will *rise*. In fact, bond prices will continue to fall and interest rates will continue to rise until they are back at i^*, because that's the only rate of interest at which people are satisfied holding the amount of money, M^S, that the government has decided to circulate.

It's important to understand that the movements back to the equilibrium interest rate, i^*, are very quick. Any excess money demand or excess money supply never lasts very long because rapid adjustments in the price of bonds move the interest rate to its equilibrium.

An important consequence of the fact that interest rates adjust so quickly is that the government can print whatever amount of money it wants to, knowing that interest rates will adjust to get people to want to hold exactly that amount. This gives the government a very useful policy tool to manage the economy because it can think one step ahead and create whatever interest rate it wants by printing the appropriate amount of money. In the next section, I show you how it does this.

Changing the money supply to change interest rates

Monetary policy works because governments know that interest rates adjust in order to get people to hold whatever amount of money the government decides to print. The interest rate is, in some sense, the price of money, and it reacts in a way similar to other prices. That is, if the money supply suddenly increases, the price of money falls, and vice versa.

You can see this fact graphed in Figure 7-4, in which the government increases the money supply from M^S_o to M^S_1. This action shifts the vertical money supply line to the right and lowers the equilibrium nominal interest rate from i^*_o to i^*_1.

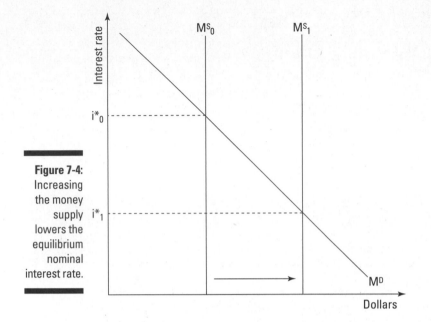

In the United States, changes in the money supply are controlled by the Federal Reserve Bank, which is often just referred to as *the Federal Reserve* or *the Fed*. The Fed has the exclusive right to print currency in the United States, which means that it could make M^S as big as it wanted to by printing more money and handing it out. However, the Fed actually relies on a more subtle method for changing the money supply, a method that economists call *open-market operations*.

The term *open-market operations* refers to the Fed's buying and selling of U.S. government bonds. That is, open-market operations are transactions that take place in the public, or open, bond market. Depending on whether the Fed buys or sells bonds, the money supply out in circulation in the economy either increases or decreases:

✔ If the Fed wants to increase the money supply, it buys bonds because in order to buy bonds the Fed must pay cash, which then circulates throughout the economy.

✔ If the Fed wants to decrease the money supply, it sells bonds because the people to whom the Fed is selling the bonds have to give the Fed money, which the Fed then locks away in a vault so that it no longer circulates.

By buying or selling bonds in this way, the amount of money out in circulation (M^S) can be very precisely controlled, meaning that the Fed can, in turn, keep tight control over interest rates.

Lowering interest rates to stimulate the economy

Now that you understand the actual mechanics by which the Federal Reserve (or similar institutions in other countries) manipulates interest rates, you are ready to see how monetary policy affects the economy.

The basic idea behind monetary policy is that lower interest rates cause both more consumption and more investment, thereby shifting the aggregate demand curve to the right. Here's how:

✔ Lower interest rates stimulate consumption spending by consumers by making it more attractive to take out loans to buy things like automobiles and houses.

✔ Lower interest rates stimulate investment spending by businesses because at lower interest rates, a larger number of potential investment projects become profitable. That is, if interest rates are 10 percent, businesses are only willing to borrow money to invest in projects with rates of return of more than 10 percent. But if interest rates fall to 5 percent, all projects with rates of return higher than 5 percent become viable, so firms take out more loans and start more projects. (For more on how interest rates affect investment, see Chapter 4.)

When trying to remember how monetary policy works, keep in mind that it's actually a very simple three-step process. When the Fed wants to help increase output, it initiates the following chain of events:

1. **It buys U.S. government bonds in order to increase the money supply.**

2. **The increased money supply causes interest rates to fall because the prices of bonds get bid up.**

3. **Consumers and businesses respond to the lower interest rates by taking out more loans and using the money to buy more goods.**

The hard part is remembering the counterintuitive fact that higher bond prices mean lower interest rates. But if you have a hard time remembering that, don't be embarrassed. Many economists get stuck on it, too.

Understanding how rational expectations can limit monetary policy

The government's ability to use increases in the money supply to stimulate the economy is limited by rational expectations and the fears that people have about inflation. Specifically, investors understand that increases in the money supply can cause inflation (as I discuss in Chapter 5). This understanding means that whenever the Federal Reserve increases the money supply in order to lower nominal interest rates, it has to do so with some moderation in order to avoid causing inflationary fears that can offset the stimulatory effect of increasing the money supply.

Graphing the results of money supply increases

Take a look at Figure 7-5, which shows an economy in recession at point *A* where aggregate demand curve AD_o intersects short-run aggregate supply curve $SRAS_o$, which is fixed at price level P_o. The Federal Reserve then increases the money supply to lower interest rates and stimulate the economy, which causes the aggregate demand curve to shift rightward to AD_1.

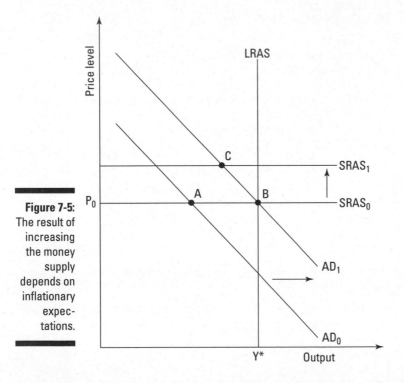

Figure 7-5:
The result of increasing the money supply depends on inflationary expectations.

At this point, two things can happen, depending on people's inflationary expectations:

> ✔ If people believe that the price level will remain fixed at P_o, the rightward shift in aggregate demand will move the economy's equilibrium rightward along the $SRAS_o$ curve from point *A* to point *B*.

✔ If people believe that the price level will jump in response to the increase in the money supply, the short-run aggregate supply curve will shift up vertically by the amount that the price level is expected to increase. That means that the economy's equilibrium will move from *A* to *C*, where AD_1 intersects the new short-run aggregate supply curve, $SRAS_1$.

Because output increases less if the economy moves from *A* to *C* than if it moves from *A* to *B*, the Fed obviously has to be careful about inflationary expectations when trying to stimulate the economy by increasing the money supply. If people expect inflation to occur, their actions can offset some of the stimulus that an increased money supply is expected to bring with it.

Realizing how inflationary expectations affect interest rates

The underlying problem is that the Federal Reserve has only partial control over interest rates. In particular, it controls money supply but not money demand. This is a problem because if people think that an increase in the money supply will cause inflation, they increase their money demand because they're expecting to need more cash to buy things at higher prices.

So while the increase in the money supply tends to lower interest rates, as shown in Figure 7-4, the increase in money demand caused by inflationary fears tends to increase interest rates. Because higher interest rates tend to decrease investment, any increase in interest rates caused by inflationary fears works against the stimulus that the Fed is attempting to apply to the economy by increasing the money supply.

This decrease in the effectiveness of monetary stimulus is why the big shift in aggregate demand in Figure 7-5 doesn't shift the economy all the way back to producing at Y^*. With people expecting inflation, part of the stimulus ends up causing inflation rather than stimulating the economy to produce more output.

Keeping inflationary expectations low to help monetary policy work well

Since the 1970s, most countries have been very cautious when using monetary policy. That's because during the 1970s, countries learned the lesson of the previous section — that if people believe an increase in the money supply is going to cause inflation, an increase in the money supply may mostly end up causing inflation rather than providing stimulus.

An extreme case of this situation can be seen in Figure 7-6, where output remains unchanged at the recessionary level Y^{Low} despite an increase in the money supply that causes aggregate demand to shift rightward from AD_o to AD_1. The problem is that higher inflationary expectations cause the short-run aggregate supply curve to shift up vertically from $SRAS_o$ to $SRAS_1$, fully offsetting the increase in aggregate demand. The short-run equilibrium shifts from *A* to *B*, but the only effect is a higher price level with no increase in output.

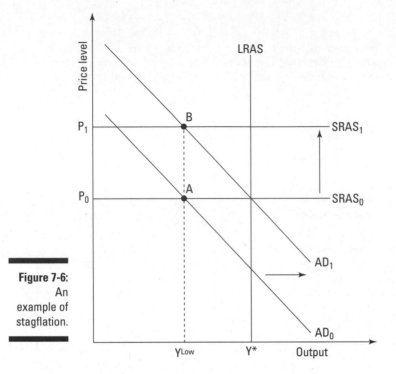

Figure 7-6:
An example of stagflation.

The situation in Figure 7-6 came to be referred to as *stagflation,* by which economists meant that the economy simultaneously had a stagnant output level coupled with inflation.

The experience of stagflation during the 1970s taught the Federal Reserve (and its equivalents in other countries) that monetary policy works best if people believe that the Fed is *not* going to cause inflation. Consequently, these days, the Fed makes only moderate increases in the money supply when it wants to stimulate the economy. These increases end up being more effective than larger increases because they don't trigger inflationary fears.

Part III

Microeconomics — The Science of Consumer and Firm Behavior

The 5th Wave   By Rich Tennant

"This is classic voodoo economics, Bernice, right down to the chicken blood it's written in."

In this part . . .

Microeconomics focuses on the decision-making behavior of individual people and individual firms. In this part, I show you that economic models assume that individuals make decisions in an attempt to maximize happiness, and firms make decisions in an attempt to maximize profits. The pleasant but surprising thing is that in the context of competitive markets, firms pursuing profits and individuals pursuing happiness end up using society's limited pool of resources in the most efficient manner possible — meaning that properly functioning competitive markets produce the best combination of goods and services from society's limited pool of resources. However, markets aren't always set up correctly, so I also cover situations like monopolies and "lemons markets" to show you what happens when things go wrong and how they can be fixed.

Chapter 8

Supply and Demand Made Easy

. . . .

In This Chapter

▶ Explaining why a higher price decreases the quantity demanded of a good or service

▶ Showing why a higher price increases the quantity supplied of a good or service

▶ Demonstrating that demand curves slope down while supply curves slope up

▶ Focusing on market equilibrium

▶ Understanding how shifts in demand or supply affect market equilibrium

▶ Identifying policies that prevent market equilibrium

. . . .

*T*he supply and demand model of markets is the economics profession's most famous contribution to human understanding. This model has become famous because it's so useful in so many areas, shedding light on exactly how markets set prices and allocate resources, as well as giving accurate predictions about how government policies will affect the behavior of markets.

For instance, this model can tell you why the price of gas goes up during the summer and why the price of wheat goes down after a good harvest. It can also predict — correctly — that agricultural price supports will cause an overproduction of food and that rent control will lead to a shortage of housing.

If you have time to learn only one thing in economics, it should be supply and demand. Nothing else in this book will bring you nearly as great a practical reward as the contents of this chapter. After reading it, you should have new insights on virtually everything you read about commerce, business, and politics.

At the same time, don't overdo it. The supply and demand model is a model of how markets function, but not everything in life is a market. Economics has gotten a bad name because sometimes it seems that economists try to explain everything using supply and demand. That's why the famous English historian Thomas Carlyle once sneered, "Teach a parrot the terms 'supply and demand' and you've got an economist."

I begin this chapter by introducing you to markets. I then explain supply and demand separately and show you how to draw and manipulate supply curves and demand curves; the demand curves capture the behavior of buyers, while the supply curves capture the behavior of suppliers. The next step is to watch the curves interact to see how markets function both when left to their own devices and when subject to government regulation or intervention.

Making Sense of Markets

In the modern economy, most economic activity takes place in *markets,* places where buyers and sellers come together to trade money for a good or service. A market doesn't have to be an actual place, and many markets nowadays are fully computerized and exist only in cyberspace. But no matter what sort of institutional arrangement markets have, they all tend to behave in the same way, which means we can study markets in general instead of having to study each one separately.

It turns out that a very simple model called *supply and demand* does an excellent job of describing how markets work, and it does so regardless of what good or service is being bought and sold.

This model very reasonably separates buyers from sellers and then summarizes each group's behavior with a single line on a graph. The buyers' behavior is captured by the demand curve, while the sellers' behavior is captured by the supply curve. By putting these two curves on the same graph, economists can show how buyers and sellers interact to determine how much of any particular item will be sold, as well as the price at which it will be sold.

But before I get to that handy graph, I need to explain to you exactly where the two curves come from and how you can manipulate them to capture different sorts of human behavior. I tackle the demand curve first, and then the supply curve.

Deconstructing Demand

People want to buy things, and economists refer to that desire as *demand.* When they say *demand,* economists aren't referring to pie-in-the-sky dreams or to mere wishful thinking along the lines of, "I want a billion jillion scoops of ice cream!" Rather, when they say *demand,* economists mean how much of something people are both *willing and able* to pay for. So while I may want a billion jillion scoops of ice cream (butter pecan, please!), that's not my demand in the sense that economists use it. Rather, my demand is three scoops because that's how much I'm willing and able to buy at the price that my local ice cream shop charges.

Getting our terms straight

Let me be even more precise in my terminology: What I've actually just described is my *quantity demanded,* which refers to how much I demand at a specific price given my income and preferences. By contrast, when an economist uses the word *demand,* he means the whole range of quantities that a person with a given income and preferences will demand at various possible prices.

To get a better handle on the difference between these two concepts, you have to understand that economists divide everything that can possibly affect the quantity demanded into two groups: the price and everything else.

Prices have an *inverse relationship* with the quantity demanded. In other words, the higher the price, the less people demand (if all the other things that could possibly affect the quantity demanded are held constant).

Chief among the other things that affect quantity demanded are tastes and preferences. For instance, no matter how low the price gets, I won't buy even a single container of Cherry Garcia ice cream because I think it's gross. At the same time, however, lots of people love Cherry Garcia so much that even if the price got very high they'd still be willing to buy quite a bit of it.

No matter how much a container of Cherry Garcia costs, the people who love it will always have a higher quantity demanded than I will. Because this is true for every possible price, we say that they have a *higher demand* than I do.

Another important factor is income. As you get richer, you increase your purchases of certain goods that you've always liked and can now afford to buy more of. These are called *normal goods.* On the other hand, you decrease your purchases of things that you were buying only because you were too poor to get what you really wanted. These are called *inferior goods.* For example, new cars are normal goods, while really old, poorly running used cars are inferior goods. Similarly, freshly made organic salads are normal goods, while three-day-old, discounted bread is an inferior good.

Given the complexity of variables such as preferences and income, why do economists insist on dividing everything that could possibly influence your quantity demanded into only two groups, the price and everything else? They do this for two reasons:

- ✔ They want to concentrate on prices.
- ✔ When you translate the concept of demand into a graph and create a demand curve, prices have a very different effect than do the other variables. This point is what I show you next.

Graphing the demand curve

I've drawn a demand curve in Figure 8-1. Let's say that this demand curve represents the demand for cabbages. On the vertical axis is the price of cabbages, measured in dollars. The horizontal axis is the number, or quantity, of cabbages that are demanded at any given price.

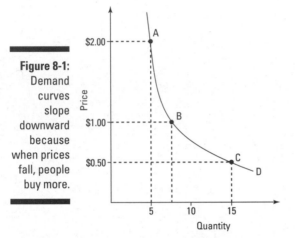

Figure 8-1: Demand curves slope downward because when prices fall, people buy more.

As you can see, the demand curve slopes downward, reflecting the fact that there's an inverse relationship between the price of cabbages and the number of cabbages people want to buy. For instance, consider point *A* on the demand curve. At a price of $2 per cabbage, people demand five cabbages. However, as you can see by looking at point *B,* if the price drops to $1 per cabbage, people demand eight cabbages. And if the price drops to only $0.50 per cabbage, they demand fifteen cabbages.

Price changes: Moving along the demand curve

When you consider the relationship between the price and the quantity demanded at each price, it's crucial to understand that increases or decreases in price simply move you *along* the demand curve.

In the previous section, I mention that economists divide all the variables that could affect demand into two groups, price and everything else. Geometrically, this division is reflected in the fact that price changes move you along the demand curve, while the other variables combine to determine exactly where the curve is located and how it's shaped.

For instance, if people hated cabbages, you wouldn't find them buying five of them when the price is $2, as they do at point *A* in Figure 8-1. Rather, if people hated them, they'd be buying zero no matter what the price, and the demand curve would look very different.

Other changes: Shifting the demand curve

Because the nonprice factors determine where the demand curve is and how it's shaped, if any of these factors changes, the demand curve *shifts* its location.

For instance, suppose that a government health study comes out saying that cabbages make people really attractive to members of the opposite sex. Naturally, this is going to increase the demand for cabbages. Geometrically, the effect is to shift the demand curve to the right. I've illustrated this effect in Figure 8-2, where the demand curve before the study is announced is labeled *D,* and the demand curve after the study is announced is labeled *D'.*

Figure 8-2: An increase in demand causes the demand curve to shift right from *D* to *D'.*

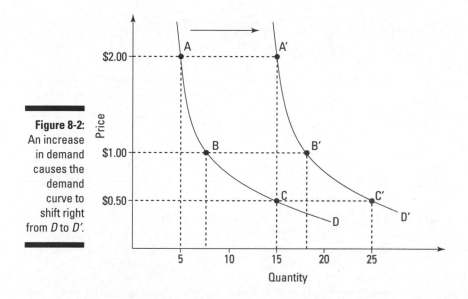

Whenever a demand curve moves, economists say that there has been a *shift in demand.* In this case, demand has increased, whereas if the curve had shifted to the left, you would say that demand decreased.

Implicit in this way of describing the movements is the fact that the quantities demanded either increase or decrease *while holding prices constant.* I need to emphasize this point: You *have* to distinguish between changes in quantities demanded that occur because the price changes (these are movements along a given curve) and changes in quantities demanded that occur because something besides the price changes (these are shifts of the entire curve).

To see the difference, compare point *A* and point *A'.* Both points share the same price of $2 per cabbage, but thanks to the recently released government study, people now demand 15 cabbages at that price (at point *A'*) rather than 5 cabbages at that price (at point *A*). Because the price is the same for the two points, you *know* that the change in the quantity demanded was caused by something other than price. Similarly, you can look at what happens to the quantity demanded while holding the price constant at $1: It increases from 8 before the study to 18 after, moving from point *B* to point *B'*.

It's very important to remember that anything besides the price that affects the quantity demanded *shifts* the demand curve. In our example, a positive research study causes people to demand more cabbages. But many other factors could influence people's demand, including changes in their income or wealth and changes in their tastes or preferences. Whenever any of these nonprice factors changes, the demand curve shifts either left or right.

Opportunity costs: Determining the slope of the demand curve

The slopes of demand curves depend on how people view the tradeoffs that changing prices force them to make. For instance, imagine that the price of a good you currently buy falls from $10 down to $9. How do you respond? Well, that depends on how you feel about the good in question relative to other goods you could spend your money on:

- ✔ You may buy a lot more of the good in question because extra units bring you a lot of happiness, and you're consequently grateful to be able to purchase them for $9 instead of $10.

- ✔ You may barely increase your buying because, while it's nice that you can now buy the good for $9 instead of $10, extra units just don't make you all that much happier. In such a situation, the best thing about the price cut is that it frees up money to buy more of other things.

In terms of demand curves, these different reactions lead to different slopes. The person who buys a lot more when the price falls has a flat demand curve, while the person whose purchases barely budge when the price falls has a steep demand curve.

To make this discussion more concrete, consider Figure 8-3, where I've drawn two separate demand curves on two separate graphs. The one on the left is my demand for pecans. The one on the right is my sister's demand for pecans.

Notice that my demand curve has a very steep slope while my sister's demand curve is very flat. The difference is completely the result of differences in how we react to price changes. You can see this by comparing my quantity demanded at point *A* with my quantity demanded at point *B*. Even though the price doubles from $1 per bag of pecans to $2 per bag of pecans, my quantity demanded falls only from six bags to five bags. By contrast, when the price doubles from $1 per bag to $2 per bag, my sister's quantity demanded falls hugely, from fifteen bags to only five bags.

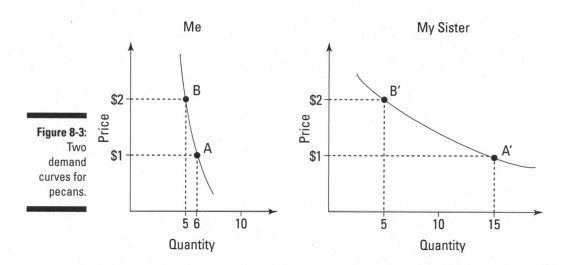

Figure 8-3:
Two
demand
curves for
pecans.

Loosely speaking, this means that my sister is much less attached to pecans than I am. When I see the price double, it barely reduces my quantity demanded, meaning that I'm willing to give up a lot of other things that I could have spent the money on in order to keep buying almost as many pecans as before.

My sister, on the other hand, reacts very differently. Although she initially buys more pecans than I do when the price is only a dollar, doubling the price causes her to cut her pecan buying by ten bags. What this says is that when the price doubles, she decides that she would be better off cutting back sharply on pecan purchases in order to spend her money on other things. In plain English, she's not nearly as attached to pecans as I am. (Pecan pie, pecan peanut butter cookies, butter pecan ice cream . . . mmmmmm!)

Defining demand elasticity

Economists have borrowed the word *elasticity* to describe how changes in one variable affect another variable. If they say *demand elasticity,* they're referring to how much the quantity demanded changes when the price changes. In Figure 8-3, my demand curve has a lot less demand elasticity than does my sister's because the same change in price causes my quantity demanded to fall much less than my sister's quantity demanded.

Extreme cases of demand elasticity are illustrated in Figure 8-4 using two demand curves, the first being perfectly vertical and the second being perfectly horizontal.

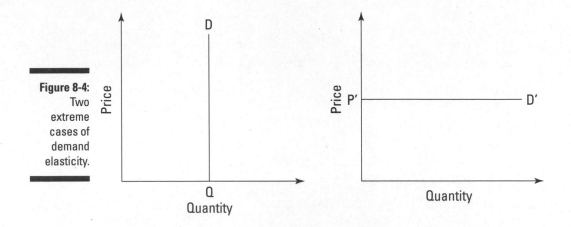

Figure 8-4:
Two extreme cases of demand elasticity.

The vertical demand curve, *D,* is said to be *perfectly inelastic,* because exactly *Q* units are demanded no matter what the price is. You may be wondering just what sort of a good would have such a demand curve, and the answer is lifesaving drugs. If you need exactly *Q* units to keep living, you'll pay any price asked. Ransoms in kidnappings are also probably like this, because people will pay any price to get their family members back. Also, drug addicts probably feel this way about their drugs; they're so desperate to get high that they don't care about the price.

On the other hand, the horizontal demand curve, *D',* is said to be *perfectly elastic.* To understand this name, try to imagine a very gradually sloping demand curve that's almost — but not quite — horizontal. On such a very shallowly sloped demand curve, even a small change in price causes a big change in the quantity demanded. Indeed, the flatter a demand curve becomes, the greater is the change in the quantity demanded for any given price change. For instance, look at Figure 8-3 one more time. Compare how a $1 change in the price of pecans causes a much bigger change in my sister's quantity demanded on her flatter demand curve than it does on my steeper demand curve.

You can think of a perfectly horizontal demand curve as being the most extreme case of this phenomenon, so that even the tiniest change in price brings forth an infinite change in quantity demanded. That is, if prices are above *P'* in the right-hand graph in Figure 8-4, you buy nothing, while if prices are at *P'* or just a penny less, you buy a whole lot. (*Infinite* is a whole lot.)

A concrete example of such a situation would be if you worked for a large restaurant chain and had to buy tons of ketchup. Your choices are brand X and brand Y, but because they taste exactly the same, the only thing that matters is the price. Consequently, if the price of brand X is even the slightest bit lower than brand Y, you'll buy tons of brand X and none of brand Y. If the price of X is even slightly higher than that of brand Y, you'll buy tons of Y and none of X.

Please realize that demand curves that are perfectly elastic or perfectly inelastic are not normal. Nearly all demand curves slope downward, meaning that moderate changes in prices bring forth moderate changes in quantities demanded. In Chapter 9, I explain why this is so by looking at how consumers make tradeoffs between different goods in order to maximize the happiness that they can get from spending their limited budgets. But before I get to that, I'm going to introduce you to the demand curve's partner in crime, the supply curve.

Sorting Out Supply

We now move on to how economists view the *supply* of goods and services. The key underlying concept is that supplying things is costly, and you have to pay people to supply the things you want. Even more interesting, though, is the fact that the more you want them to supply, the higher their costs of supplying each additional unit. In other words, the first units tend to be relatively inexpensive to produce, while later units become more and more costly to produce. (In Chapter 10, I explain why this holds true.)

Because production costs rise as you produce more output, if you want producers to make more and more, you have to pay them more and more. This fact implies that supply curves slope upward.

Graphing the supply curve

Let's use cabbages again as an example. (They served us nicely in the previous discussion of demand.) Imagine that a farmer named Babbage likes to grow cabbage. In Figure 8-5, I graph Mr. Babbage's supply of cabbages and label it *S*. (I was tempted to label it B^S, for *Babbage's Supply,* but I didn't want you telling your friends that my book was full of B^S.)

The horizontal axis gives the number of cabbages supplied, while the vertical axis gives the price per cabbage that you have to pay to get Mr. Baggage to supply you any given number of cabbages. Thus, point *A* says that you have to pay Mr. Babbage 50 cents per cabbage if you want him to supply you with five cabbages.

Because Mr. Babbage's production costs rise as he tries to grow more and more cabbages, you have to pay him $1 per cabbage if you want him to grow you ten cabbages, as shown by point *B*. And you have to pay $1.50 per cabbage if you want fifteen cabbages, as shown by point *C*.

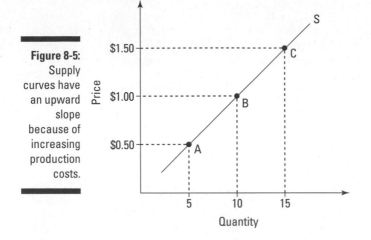

Figure 8-5:
Supply
curves have
an upward
slope
because of
increasing
production
costs.

Keep in mind that the points on the supply curve don't represent the prices that Mr. Babbage *wants* to receive for any given amount of cabbages — obviously, he wants to receive a gazillion dollars for each one. Rather, what each dollar amount on a supply curve represents is the minimum that you could pay him and still get him to produce the desired amount. At point *A,* you can get him to produce five cabbages if you pay him 50 cents per cabbage; if you offer him 49 cents per cabbage, he won't do it. Why not? Because he has costs, and he can cover them at 50 cents per cabbage but not at 49 cents per cabbage.

Separating sales price and production cost

As with demand curves, economists split all the things that can affect the quantity supplied into two groups: the price and everything else. The things that go into *everything else* all relate to the costs of supplying the good in question.

When you see a particular supply curve, you should imagine that it derives from a particular production technology used by the supplier. Because each possible technology creates its own unique relationship between output levels and costs, some technologies give rise to steeply sloped supply curves, while others generate fairly flat supply curves. (See Chapter 10 for all the details on firms' supply curves.)

Regardless of exactly how the curve is sloped or where it's positioned, the fact that costs increase as output increases means that you need to offer a higher and higher price to the supplier if you want to obtain more units. And that's basically why prices move you along supply curves. The next two sections explain these ideas in more detail.

Price changes: Moving along the supply curve

Varying the price of an item moves you along a given supply curve because the supply curve represents the minimum payment you need to give the supplier in order for him to supply the amount of output you want.

To see how this works, let's think about cabbages again. Consider what happens if you offer to pay Mr. Babbage $1 per cabbage, and then you let him choose how many cabbages he wants to produce. Given his supply curve in Figure 8-5, he's going to want to produce exactly ten cabbages and no more. That's because for cabbage number one through cabbage number nine, the cost of production is less than what you're paying him. For example, consider point *A*. At point *A*, his production costs are 50 cents per cabbage. That means that if you're going to pay him $1 per cabbage, he'll be making a nice profit. Similarly, because his cost per cabbage for producing six cabbages is also less than $1 per cabbage, he'll also want to make number six. The same is true of cabbages seven, eight, and nine.

At ten cabbages, Mr. Babbage is indifferent, because his cost per cabbage is $1 and you're offering him $1. In such cases, economists assume that he'll produce the tenth just to keep the buyer happy. But notice that Mr. Babbage would not produce at point *C* if you were offering him $1 per cabbage. That's because his cost of production there is $1.50 per cabbage, and he would lose money.

So here's how to think about the supply curve and how it responds to price changes: Suppliers look at whatever price is being offered and make as many units as are profitable, but no more. Because costs rise with each additional unit produced, the only way to get suppliers to produce more is to offer them higher prices. Therefore, raising or lowering prices moves you *along* the supply curve as the suppliers' quantities supplied respond to changing prices.

Cost changes: Shifting the supply curve

Because a supplier's cost structure determines where his supply curve is located and how it's sloped, changes in the cost structure cause changes in the supply curve. In Figure 8-6, Mr. Babbage's costs of production increase because the government imposes a new organic farming law under which he's required to grow cabbages without using pesticides. In response, he has to hire lots of extra workers to kill pests with tweezers instead of simply spraying cheap chemicals.

Because his costs of production have increased, the minimum you have to pay him to get you to produce any given level of output also goes up. Consequently, his supply curve can be thought of as shifting upward vertically from S_o to S_1.

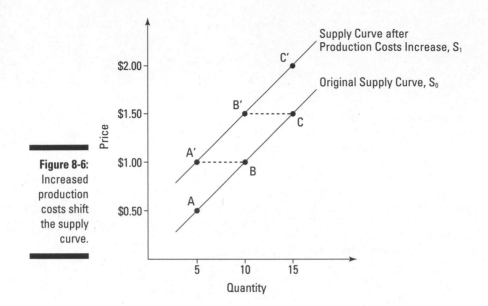

Figure 8-6:
Increased
production
costs shift
the supply
curve.

I've drawn the shift to show that Mr. Babbage's cost of production is 50 cents higher for each cabbage no matter how many cabbages are produced. Compare points A and A'. Before the new environmental regulation, Mr. Babbage was willing to produce five cabbages if you paid him 50 cents per cabbage. After the policy change, you have to pay him $1.00 per cabbage if you want him to grow you five cabbages.

Similarly, points B and B' show that before the regulation, he would grow you ten cabbages if you offered him $1 per cabbage. Now, you have to offer him $1.50 per cabbage if you want him to grow ten.

The important thing to remember is that anything that changes producers' costs structures will shift their supply curves. Things that make production more costly will shift supply curves up, while things that lower costs will shift supply curves down.

Keep in mind that it's also perfectly kosher to think of supply curves as moving left and right when cost structures shift. For instance, consider the quantity supplied at a price of $1.00 both before and after the cost increase. Before the cost increase, Mr. Babbage is willing to supply you ten cabbages for $1.00, putting you at point B on the original supply curve. But after the cost increase, he's willing to supply you only five cabbages for $1.00, putting you at point A' on the shifted supply curve. Similarly, at a price of $1.50, Mr. Babbage was previously willing to supply you with fifteen cabbages (point C), whereas after the cost increase he's willing to supply only ten cabbages at that price (point B').

It's perfectly fair to say that the supply curve shifted *left* when costs increased. And you can quickly extrapolate that a decrease in costs would shift the supply curve to the *right*.

Having two ways to interpret supply curve shifts is actually rather handy. In some situations it's easier to think of the shifts as either right or left, while in others it's easier to think of them as up or down.

Understanding extreme supply cases

Two extreme supply curves help to illustrate how production costs and prices combine to determine the quantity that will be supplied at any particular price. I've illustrated these two cases in Figure 8-7.

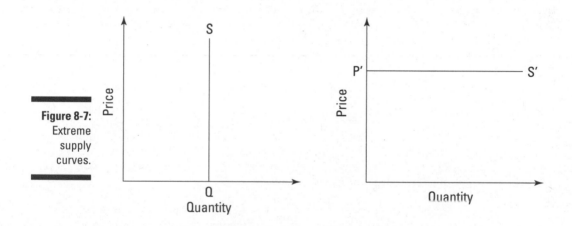

Figure 8-7: Extreme supply curves.

The graph on the left shows a vertical supply curve and illustrates what economists call *perfectly inelastic supply*. The graph on the right with a horizontal supply curve illustrates what economists call *perfectly elastic supply*. I talk about each curve in the next two sections.

Paying any price: Perfectly inelastic supply

The left graph of Figure 8-7 illustrates a situation in which the price has no effect on the quantity supplied. As you can see in the graph, no matter how low or how high the price, the quantity *Q* is supplied. Because the quantity supplied is completely unresponsive to the price, it is said to be *perfectly inelastic,* and supply situations that look like this are usually referred to as situations of *perfectly inelastic supply.*

I expect you're curious about what things have perfectly inelastic supply curves. The answer is unique things that cannot be reproduced. Examples include:

✔ **The Hope Diamond:** Because it's one of a kind, and there would still be only one Hope Diamond no matter how much anyone wanted to pay, its supply curve is vertical.

✔ **Land:** As comedian Will Rogers said back in the early 20th century, "Buy land. They ain't making more of it."

✔ **The electromagnetic spectrum:** There's only one set of radio frequencies, and we all just have to share because there's no way to make more.

An interesting thing about such situations is that there are no production costs. Because of this, offering the owner a price is not an incentive in the way it is when you pay a producer enough to make something for you. Rather, the price serves solely to transfer the right of ownership and usage from one person to another.

Historically, the fact that the quantity of land supplied has nothing to do with production costs has been the justification for property taxes. The way governments see it, they can tax land as harshly as they want because there's no need to worry that the amount of land — and, consequently, the tax base — will ever decrease.

Producing however much you want: Perfectly elastic supply

The right-hand graph in Figure 8-7 illustrates the polar opposite case, where the supply curve is perfectly horizontal. The idea here is that the supplier is producing something that has nonincreasing costs. No matter how many units you want her to produce, it always costs her only P' dollars to make a unit. Consequently, whether you want one unit produced or one jillion units produced, you pay her only P' dollars per unit.

In the real world, there probably aren't any supply curves that are truly perfectly elastic because production costs typically rise with output levels (as I explain in Chapter 10). But a few supply curves do come close. For instance, the supply curve for pencils looks nearly perfectly elastic because pencil companies seem to be able to increase production levels by millions of units with only very small increases in costs.

Interacting Supply and Demand to Find Market Equilibrium

In previous sections I discuss demand and supply curves separately. Now it's time to bring them together so they can interact to show you how markets determine the amounts, as well as the prices, of goods and services sold.

Finding market equilibrium

In Figure 8-8, I've drawn a demand curve and a supply curve on the same axes and labeled them *D* and *S,* respectively. There are three things you *must* remember about the demand and supply model when staring at this graph:

Figure 8-8: The market equilibrium price and quantity happen where the demand curve crosses the supply curve.

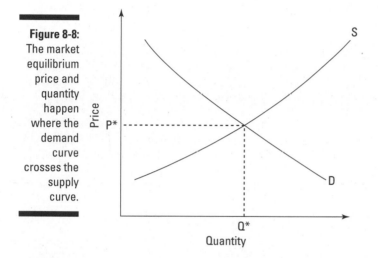

✔ The *equilibrium* of the supply and demand model is where the demand and supply curves cross. (Just remember: X marks the spot!)

✔ The price and the quantity where the curves cross will be, respectively, how much the good or service in question costs and how much of it gets sold. This price and this quantity are known as the *market price* and the *market quantity.*

✔ The market price and market quantity represent a stable equilibrium such that market forces will *always* push the price and quantity back to these values. Consequently, the market price and market quantity are also called the *equilibrium price* and the *equilibrium quantity.*

I label the market price and market quantity as P^* and Q^*, respectively. What makes this price and this quantity special is that at price P^*, the quantity that buyers demand is equal to the quantity that producers wish to supply.

Put slightly differently, you can see starting at price P^* and moving to the right horizontally along the dotted line that buyers demand Q^* at that price and sellers supply Q^* at that price. Because demand equals supply, both producers and consumers are content. The consumers get exactly the quantity that they want to buy at price P^*, and the producers sell exactly the quantity that they want to sell at price P^*.

Economists call situations like these, where everybody is happy, *equilibriums*. That's because with everyone getting everything that they want, nobody is going to cause any changes.

What's even more interesting is the fact that at any other price besides P^*, there is always some sort of pressure brought to bear either by buyers or sellers to bring the model back to the market equilibrium price and quantity. The pleasant result is that no matter where the market starts, it always ends back at equilibrium.

Before I talk more about the supply and demand model's equilibrium, you should know one other very important thing. Notice that at the market equilibrium quantity, Q^*, the price that buyers are charged, P^*, is on the supply curve. This means that suppliers are just barely getting enough money to motivate them to supply quantity Q^*. In other words, suppliers aren't able to exploit buyers. This result tells us that capitalism is not inherently exploitative. Quite the contrary: If there's real competition, producers just barely make enough money to make it worth their while to stay in business. (I talk much more about this subject in Chapter 11.)

Demonstrating the stability of the market equilibrium

The market equilibrium is called a *stable equilibrium* because no matter where the demand and supply model starts off, it always gravitates back to the market equilibrium. This is very nice because it means that markets are self-correcting, and if you know where the demand and supply curves are, you know where prices and quantities will end up. Especially gratifying is the fact that the actions of the market participants — buyers and sellers — move the market toward equilibrium without the need for any outside intervention, such as government regulations.

I want to prove to you that the market equilibrium is indeed stable. In the next section I focus on the fact that if prices start higher than P^*, they fall down to P^*. After that, I show you that if prices start lower than P^*, they rise up to P^*. The fact that prices always move toward P^* indicates that the market equilibrium is stable.

Excess supply: Reducing prices until they reach equilibrium

In Figure 8-9, you can see what happens when you have a price like P^H that starts out higher than the market equilibrium price, P^*. At price P^H, the quantity demanded by buyers, Q^D, is less than the quantity supplied by sellers, Q^S. (I use dotted lines to show where P^H intersects the demand and supply curves.) Economists refer to such a situation as *excess supply,* and it can't be an equilibrium because sellers aren't able to sell everything they want to sell at price P^H.

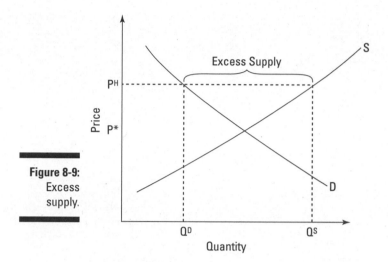

Figure 8-9:
Excess
supply.

In fact, of the total amount that sellers want to sell, Q^S, only the amount Q^D is sold, meaning that the remaining amount, $Q^S - Q^D$, remains unsold unless something is done. Well, something *is* done. Sellers see the huge pile of unsold goods and do what any store does when it can't sell something at current prices: They have a sale.

Sellers lower the price and keep lowering it until supply no longer exceeds demand. You can see in Figure 8-9 that this means sellers keep lowering the price until it falls all the way down to P^*, because that's the only price at which the quantity demanded by buyers equals the quantity that sellers want to supply.

Excess demand: Raising prices until they reach equilibrium

Figure 8-10 shows a situation opposite to the one we just saw. The initial price, P^L, is lower than the market equilibrium price, P^*. You can see that in this case, the problem is not excess supply but rather *excess demand* because at price P^L, the amount that buyers want to buy, Q^D, exceeds the amount that suppliers want to sell, Q^S.

In other words, there is a shortage of $Q^D - Q^S$ units. As a result, buyers start bidding the price up, competing against each other for the insufficient amount of the good.

As long as the price is less than P^*, some degree of shortage exists, and the price continues to be bid up. This means that whenever you start out with a price less than P^*, the price is pushed back up to P^*, returning the market to its equilibrium — the only place where there is neither a shortage nor an excess supply.

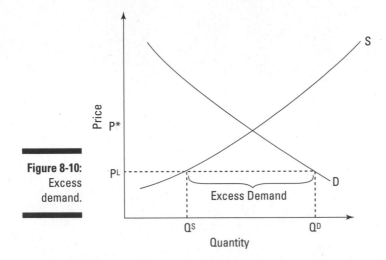

Figure 8-10:
Excess
demand.

Adjusting to New Market Equilibriums when Supply or Demand Changes

As we see in the previous sections, for any given supply and demand curves, market forces adjust the market until the price and quantity correspond to where the demand and supply curves cross. When they reach that point — the market equilibrium — the price and quantity don't change. They stay right there as long as the demand and supply curves don't move.

In this section, I show you how prices and quantities *do* adjust if the demand and supply curves change. I illustrate by first showing you a demand curve shift, followed by a supply curve shift.

Reacting to an increase in demand

Take a close look at Figure 8-11, which shows what happens if the demand curve shifts to the right from D_o to D_1 while the supply curve S stays the same. Before the shift, the market equilibrium price is P^*_o, and the market equilibrium quantity is Q^*_o. When the demand curve shifts to the right to D_1, the price momentarily stays the same at P^*_o. But this price can't last because with the new demand curve, there is now an excess demand. That is, at price P^*_o, the quantity demanded, Q^D_1, exceeds the quantity supplied, Q^*_o.

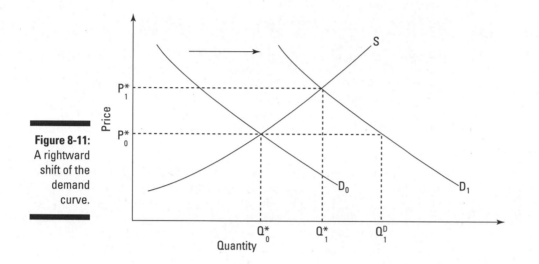

Figure 8-11:
A rightward
shift of the
demand
curve.

As I discuss in the previous section, any such shortage causes buyers to bid up the price. The result is that the price rises and continues to rise until it reaches P^*_1, the price where demand curve D_1 crosses supply curve S.

Note that when moving from the first equilibrium to the second, the equilibrium quantity increases from Q^*_o to Q^*_1. This result makes good sense because if demand increases and buyers are willing to pay more for something, you would expect more of it to be supplied. Also, the price goes up from one equilibrium to the other because to get suppliers to supply more in a world of rising costs, you have to pay them more.

A much more subtle thing to realize, however, is that the slope of the supply curve *interacts* with the demand curve to determine how big the changes in price and quantity will be. Think back to the perfectly vertical supply curve of the left-hand graph of Figure 8-7. For such a supply curve, any increase in demand *only* increases the price because the quantity can't increase. On the other hand, if you are dealing with the perfectly horizontal supply curve of the right-hand graph of Figure 8-7, a rightward shift in demand *only* increases the quantity, because the price is fixed at P'.

When you consider these two extreme cases, it hammers home the point that in a situation like Figure 8-11, neither demand nor supply is in complete control. Their interaction jointly determines equilibrium prices and quantities and how they change if the demand curve or the supply curve shifts.

Reacting to a decrease in supply

To show you how the market equilibrium changes when the supply curve shifts, consider Figure 8-12 in which the supply curve shifts from S_o to S_1 because of an increase in production costs. (As I discuss in the earlier section "Cost changes: Shifting the supply curve," this increase in costs can be considered to shift the supply curve either up or to the left. In Figure 8-12, I've drawn a vertical arrow to indicate a vertical shift, but I could have just as correctly put in a left arrow to indicate a leftward shift.)

The shift in supply will cause the market equilibrium to adjust. The original equilibrium is at price P^*_o and quantity Q^*_o, which is the point where the demand curve, D, and the original supply curve, S_o, cross. When production costs increase, the supply curve shifts to S_1.

Figure 8-12:
A vertical shift of the supply curve.

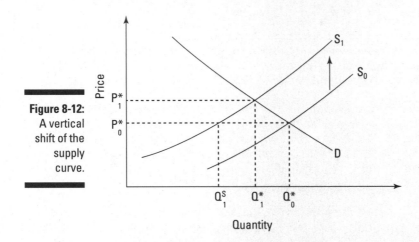

For a moment, the price remains at P^*_o. But this price cannot continue because the quantity demanded at this price, Q^*_o, exceeds the quantity supplied, Q^S_1. This situation of excess demand causes the price to be bid up until reaching the new equilibrium price of P^*_1, at which price the quantity demanded equals the quantity supplied at Q^*_1.

If you compare this situation of increasing costs with the situation of increasing demand in the previous section, you notice that in both cases the equilibrium price rises. However, be sure to note that equilibrium quantities went in opposite directions. An increase in demand causes an increase in equilibrium quantity, but an increase in costs causes a reduction in equilibrium quantity.

The reason that the equilibrium quantity falls is because the increase in production costs doesn't just affect the producer. In order to stay in business, the producer has to pass along the cost increase. But when he passes the increase along, it has a tendency to discourage buyers. The result is that the equilibrium quantity falls because some buyers are not willing to pay the higher costs. Those who still want to buy are willing to pay the higher costs — a fact that is reflected in the increased market price.

Constructing Impediments to Market Equilibrium

Left to its own devices, a market always adjusts until the price and quantity are determined by where the demand and supply curves cross. The market equilibrium price has the very nice property that everyone who wants to buy at that price can do so, while everyone who wants to sell at that price can also do so. (The quantity demanded equals the quantity supplied.)

However, the market price is not always the politically expedient price, and governments often interfere in the market to prevent the market equilibrium from being reached. Such interventions happen either because politically influential buyers think the market price is too high, or because politically influential sellers think the market price is too low.

Unfortunately, if the government intervenes to help the people who are complaining, it creates a whole new set of problems and, in some cases, even hurts those whom the intervention is designed to help. To explain how this happens, I first explain price floors and then price ceilings. Price floors keep prices from falling to the market equilibrium, while price ceilings prevent them from rising to the market equilibrium. (Obviously, you use only one or the other!)

Raising price ceilings

Sometimes the government intervenes in a market to ensure that the price stays below the market equilibrium price, P^*. Because prices below the market equilibrium would normally rise, such policies are called *price ceilings* because they prevent the price from rising as high as it would if left alone. Prices hit the ceiling and then go no higher.

To see how this works, and the problems it creates, look at Figure 8-13, in which the price ceiling P^C lies below the market equilibrium price of P^*. To make clear that we have a ceiling that the price can't rise above, I've drawn a solid horizontal line starting from P^C and extending right.

The problem here is that at the ceiling price, the quantity demanded, Q^D, far exceeds the quantity supplied, Q^S. This may not seem like such a big problem, but the shortage has to be dealt with somehow. You have to figure out a way to allocate the insufficient supply among all the people who want it.

What happens is that people end up waiting in lines, or *queues,* to get the limited supply. Let me tell you a little story about my grad school days at Berkeley, a town in which there were price ceilings for how much rent a landlord could charge — a policy euphemistically referred to as *rent control.*

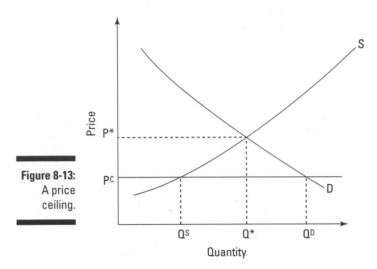

Figure 8-13: A price ceiling.

Because rents were kept far below their market equilibrium value, there were always many more people who wanted to rent than there were apartments available. The result was that any time an apartment became available, you stood in line with — literally — 200 people to fill out a rental application. With so many potential renters hoping for one apartment, the landlord could take his pick — hence rental applications were often five to ten pages long and asked you *everything.* If you weren't picked, you had to go get in the next line for the next apartment that happened to come on the market.

It didn't matter if you had enough money to pay higher rent. It didn't matter if you were much more desperate than other potential renters. Because the government had artificially created an excess demand, you had to wait in line and hope and pray that you'd get an apartment.

The main result of the policy was that thousands of people wasted tens of thousands of hours each year waiting in line — and some of them still didn't get apartments! Even worse was the fact that the policy actually reduced the total number of apartments available in the city of Berkeley. You can see this by the fact that $Q^S < Q^*$ in Figure 8-13. That's a perverse result for a policy that was intended to help provide low-cost housing for the poor. And it serves as a warning to anyone considering interfering with markets: While you may not like the market price and market quantity, it may be better than what you'll get if the government interferes.

Propping up price floors

The opposite sort of market intervention is a *price floor*, by which the government keeps the price above its market equilibrium value. An example of this situation is shown in Figure 8-14, where the floor price, P^F, is greater than the market equilibrium price, P^*. To make it clear that prices can't fall below P^F, I've drawn a solid horizontal line at that price.

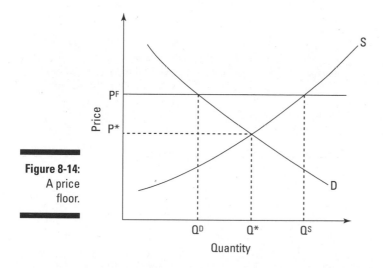

Figure 8-14:
A price
floor.

The problem here is that at price P^F, the quantity supplied, Q^S, is much bigger than the quantity demanded, Q^D. The normal response to such a situation of excess supply would be for the price to fall. The way the government prevents this and keeps the price propped up is by stepping in and buying up the excess supply.

In other words, of the total amount Q^S that's supplied at price P^F, regular consumers demand and purchase Q^D. The remainder, $Q^S - Q^D$, must be purchased by the government. That doesn't sound so bad until you read about price floors in agriculture, which are usually referred to euphemistically by proponents as *price supports* (as in, "You poor thing! All you need is a little *support!*").

Price supports generate huge piles of crops that nobody wants to buy. For instance, thanks to supporting the price of milk, each year the U.S. government must buy up hundreds of thousands of gallons of milk that nobody wants to buy at the high price the government is maintaining to help dairy farmers.

First World supports, Third World suffering

A perverse result of agricultural price supports in rich countries like the United States and the nations of the European Union is the great damage they inflict on developing nations. For instance, the U.S. price of sugar is three times the world price because the United States restricts imports of cheaper foreign sugar in order to help U.S. food production giants like Archer Daniels Midland. The result is that thousands of poor Third World farmers who could otherwise make a living selling sugar to Americans and Europeans are left without a livelihood.

Even worse is what the United States does with some of the many tons of excess agricultural products that pile up due to its agricultural price supports. Not wanting to sell the excess in the United States and thereby depress U.S. prices, the government often sends the stuff free to developing countries as food aid. That sounds nice and friendly, but when all that free wheat hits Nigeria, it puts Nigerian farmers out of business.

Interfering with markets is typically a bad thing. There are almost always unexpected side effects that end up hurting people that the policy wasn't expected to harm. Furthermore, such policies are also typically inefficient, costing more to the losers than they benefit the winners.

What does the government do with the milk? It turns it into cheese that it can't sell (because it's also supporting the price of cheese) and stores the cheese in huge refrigerated warehouses — indefinitely! And yes, this is all done at the taxpayer's expense.

The U.S. government used to support the price of oranges, and it would have to buy and literally burn tons of oranges each year because burning them was the easiest way to get rid of the excess supply. But because people protested that sort of wastefulness, the government has now switched policies for some crops. The government now pays farmers *not* to farm. That way, the farmers still get paid, but there's no worry about an excess supply that has to be destroyed.

For both price ceilings and price floors, the message you should take away is that great mischief is typically caused if you interfere with the markets. (Yet, deep inside, I'm actually hoping that the government decides to support the salaries of academic economists. I'd love to end up getting paid *not* to teach.)

Chapter 9

Getting to Know *Homo Economicus*, the Utility-Maximizing Consumer

This chapter gets behind the demand curve (which I introduce in Chapter 8) by showing you how people come to choose the things they choose. This decision-making process is very important because human wants are what drive the economy. Firms don't randomly produce goods and services; they produce the things that people want to buy and are spending money on.

The thing that makes studying this process hard is the fact that people have so many different things they can spend their money on. If an economist was asked to research how you would spend $100 in a store that sold only blueberry muffins, his job wouldn't be so hard. What's impressive is that economists have come up with a way to explain how you would spend $100 in a store that has hundreds or even thousands of items for sale.

Even more impressive is the fact that an economist can explain not only which items you would buy but also how many of each you would buy. In other words, economists can explain not just *what* you demand, but also the *quantities* you demand, which is where demand curves come from.

I start the chapter by discussing *utility,* which is how economists measure human happiness. Economists assume that people act in ways that maximize their happiness, but our actions are constrained, especially by limited budgets. I explain how people navigate these constraints to get the most happiness possible given the limits involved. Finally, I show how these decisions underlie and explain the slope and position of demand curves.

Knowing the Name of the Game: Constrained Optimization

Later in this chapter I discuss *how* people choose what to buy when they buy. First, let's focus on *why* they must choose.

The reason that people must make choices is because their means for satisfying their wants are limited. There's never enough money or time to do everything that you desire. Consequently, you need to choose wisely to get the most happiness out of the limited resources that you do have.

Economists and engineers refer to problems of this sort as *constrained optimization problems* because people are trying to optimize their happiness given the fact that they're constrained by their limited resources. The rest of this chapter shows you how economists model the way that people go about solving their everyday constrained optimization problem: deciding how to best spend their limited incomes on available goods and services — choosing not only which things to buy, but how much of each.

Finding a Common Denominator to Measure Happiness: Utility

In order for people to choose between the exceedingly different goods and services available in the economy, they must have a way of comparing them all. Comparing costs is pretty easy; you just compare prices. But how do you compare the benefits of various goods and services? How do you assess whether it's better to spend $20 on Swiss chocolate bars or on a new plaid shirt? In what ways are chocolate and shirts even comparable?

Obviously, people do manage to make the comparison and rank the two choices. The way economists imagine that people do this is by assigning a common measure of happiness to each possible thing they could buy and use. Economists call this common measure of happiness *utility,* and they imagine that if they could somehow get inside your brain and measure utility, they could do so using a unit that they very uncreatively refer to as a *util.*

Some people very naturally object to assigning specific numbers of utils to different things — for instance, 25 utils to the pleasure associated with eating a brownie, or 75 utils to the pleasure associated with watching a sunset. Making such specific assignments is called *cardinal utility* (like cardinal numbers: 1, 2, 3 . . .). People object to cardinal utility because it's not clear that people make such assessments — after all, how many utils do you think you receive from a sunny day or an infant's smile?

A much less objectionable thing to do is to think in terms of *ordinal utility,* a system in which you simply rank things. For instance, instead of saying that the sunset has a utility of 75, which makes it preferred to the brownie with a utility of 25, you can simply say that sunsets are preferred to brownies. This system has a much more intuitive feeling for most people and eliminates the need to try to measure things using the imaginary unit called the util.

Even better, it's been proven mathematically that you can describe the same human choice behavior using ordinal utility that you can using cardinal utility, which means that economists don't *have* to use cardinal utility.

But I'm going to anyway!

Why? Because it's much easier to explain the crucial concept of diminishing marginal utility using the cardinal utility system. You can also explain diminishing marginal utility using the ordinal system, but the math is so hard that it's normally taught only to Ph.D. students. So please forgive me if the cardinal utility system seems a bit unrealistic, but it's really the best way to convey this incredibly important idea.

Getting Less from More: Diminishing Marginal Utility

People get bored even with things they like and get tired of repetition and sameness. Economists have to take account of this when studying how people choose to spend their money.

For instance, if I haven't had any pizza in a long time, I'll get a huge amount of utility from eating a slice. The melted cheese, the basil and garlic in the sauce, and the warmth in my mouth all make me very, very happy.

But the thrill of pizza is dampened by eating that first slice so that if I eat a second slice, it's still very good, but not as good as the first. And if I have a third slice, it's not as good as the second. And if I keep eating and eating and eating, the additional slices of pizza will soon get sickening and produce pain instead of pleasure if I eat them.

This phenomenon isn't limited to pizza; it applies to nearly everything. Unless you're addicted to something, you get tired of it as you have more of it, and each additional unit brings you less happiness than the previous unit.

To make this phenomenon more clear, look at Figure 9-1, which shows my cumulative, total utility as I eat more and more slices of pizza. For instance, my total utility after eating one slice of pizza is 20 utils. After eating two slices, it's 36 utils. And after three slices, it's 50 utils.

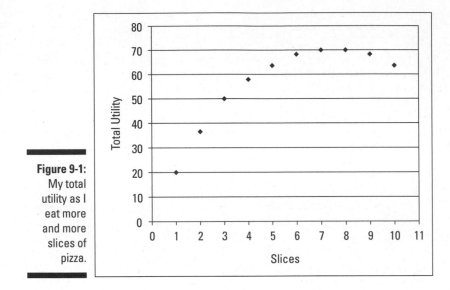

Figure 9-1:
My total
utility as I
eat more
and more
slices of
pizza.

If you look at these numbers, you should notice that the extra utility each additional slice brings me is decreasing:

- ✔ **First slice:** My total utility increases by 20 utils, from 0 to 20 utils.

- ✔ **Second slice:** The increase is only 16 utils; my total utility increases from 20 utils to 36 utils.

- ✔ **Third slice:** My utility increases only 14 utils, from 36 to 50.

Economists refer to this phenomenon as *diminishing marginal utility* because the extra utility, or *marginal utility,* that each successive slice brings with it decreases relative to the marginal utility brought by the previous slice. Diminishing marginal utility is simply a reflection of the fact that people get fed up or bored with things. Or, in the case of food and drink, their appetite decreases with each unit they consume.

Look at what happens in Figure 9-1 after slice number eight. My total utility actually goes down, because slice number nine is making me a little sick. And if I have slice number ten, I'm even sicker, so total utility falls again.

What this decrease in total utility implies is that marginal utility must be negative for slices nine and ten. Look at Table 9-1, which gives both the total and marginal utilities I get for each slice. As you can see, the data matches Figure 9-1 and shows that while my total utility increases for slices one through seven, it stalls at slice number eight and falls for slices nine and ten.

Table 9-1	Total and Marginal Utility as I Eat Ten Slices of Pizza	
Slice	*Total Utility*	*Marginal Utility*
1	20	20
2	36	16
3	50	14
4	58	8
5	64	6
6	68	4
7	70	2
8	70	0
9	68	−2
10	64	−4

The right column shows that I feel diminishing marginal utility as I eat more and more slices of pizza, because the marginal utility that comes with each additional slice is always less than that of the previous slice. Specifically, while my marginal utility is 20 utils for the first slice, it falls to 0 utils for slice eight and then actually becomes negative for slices nine and ten because eating them makes me ill.

In Figure 9-2, I plot out the marginal utility that I get for each slice of pizza. You can see quite clearly from the downward slope of the points that my marginal utility diminishes as I eat more and more slices of pizza.

You have to be careful not to confuse diminishing marginal utility with *negative* marginal utility. As you see in Table 9-1 and Figure 9-2, there is diminishing marginal utility for all slices of pizza starting with the second, because each successive slice has a smaller marginal utility than the previous one. But the marginal utilities are still positive for all slices up to slice seven, and they become negative only for slices nine and ten.

That fact implies that you enjoy eating every slice up to and including the seventh slice because doing so brings you an increase in utility (happiness). So don't think that just because marginal utility is diminishing for a particular slice, you wouldn't want to eat it. Marginal utility can be diminishing but still positive. The only slices you'll outright want to avoid are the ninth and tenth.

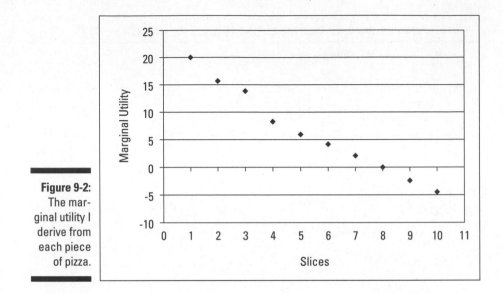

Figure 9-2:
The marginal utility I derive from each piece of pizza.

Choosing Among Many Options When Facing a Limited Budget

The phenomenon of diminishing marginal utility makes studying human choices very interesting because whether I prefer chocolate ice cream or vanilla ice cream can't be determined in the abstract. Rather, it depends on what I've already eaten.

If I haven't had any ice cream for months and you ask me whether I want chocolate or vanilla, I'll say chocolate. But if you ask me whether I want chocolate or vanilla after I've just eaten a gallon of chocolate, I'm going to say vanilla because I've already more than satisfied my chocolate cravings.

So the answer to the question "Chocolate or vanilla?" isn't as straightforward as it seems. Your preferences exhibit diminishing marginal utility, and even something that you normally like a lot won't bring you much marginal utility (additional happiness) if you've just indulged in it a lot.

This fact ends up leading to a very simple rule about how people make decisions when faced with limited budgets. But before I state the rule, let me give you an example that will help explain it. In this example, I have $10 to spend and, because I'm going to the local student bar, the only two things I can spend the money on are pints of beer and slices of pizza.

Trying to buy as much (marginal) utility as you can

I'm now thinking about how to best spend my $10, and the intelligent thing to do is to think in terms of buying up as much utility as I can with my limited budget. Both beer and pizza make me happy, but my goal isn't just to be happy; it's to be as happy as possible given my limited budget. So I want to make sure that every dollar buys me the maximum possible amount of utility.

Keep in mind that I don't care where utility comes from. One util from beer makes me just as happy as one util from pizza; all I care about is buying up as many utils as possible.

To do that, the key concept turns out to be the price of utility. Beer and pizza clearly have prices measured in dollars, but what is the price of a util?

Well, it depends. Take a look at Table 9-2. The first three columns repeat the data from Table 9-1 that gave my total and marginal utilities for ten slices of pizza. But the final two columns include new data and are labeled, respectively, "MU per dollar at $1 per slice" and "MU per dollar at $2 per slice." (*MU* stands for *marginal utility*.)

Table 9-2		Determining the Price of Utility for Pizza		
Slice	*Total Utility*	*Marginal Utility*	*MU per Dollar at $1 per Slice*	*MU per Dollar at $2 per Slice*
1	20	20	20	10
2	36	16	16	8
3	50	14	14	7
4	58	8	8	4
5	64	6	6	3
6	68	4	4	2
7	70	2	2	1
8	70	0	0	0
9	68	−2	−2	−1
10	64	−4	−4	−2

What I've done in these last two columns is to calculate how much it costs to get some additional happiness (marginal utility) if the way you're getting it is by buying slices of pizza.

Consider the fourth column, which assumes that each slice of pizza costs $1. If you buy one slice, it brings you a marginal utility of 20 utils at a cost of $1. So the MU per dollar of the first slice is 20.

But now consider spending a second dollar to buy a second slice of pizza. Because that second slice brings with it a marginal utility of only 16 utils, the MU per dollar spent here is only 16. And because diminishing marginal utility continues to decrease the marginal utility of each additional slice of pizza, each additional dollar you spend buys you less additional utility than the previous dollar.

The final column of Table 9-2 shows you that the MU per dollar that you get from pizza depends on how much each slice of pizza costs. If pizza costs $2 per slice, each dollar spent brings you less marginal utility than when pizza cost only $1 per slice.

For instance, because each slice now costs $2, when you buy the first slice and it brings you 20 utils, you're getting only 10 utils per dollar spent. Similarly, while the second slice still brings you 16 additional utils of happiness, because it now costs you $2 to get those utils, your MU per dollar is only 8 utils.

In Table 9-3, I give you the same sort of information as in Table 9-2, but this time it's for my total utility, marginal utility, and MU per dollar when I'm drinking beer that costs $2 per pint.

Table 9-3		Determining the Price of Utility for Beer	
Pint	Total Utility	Marginal Utility	MU per Dollar at $2 per Pint
1	20	20	10
2	38	18	9
3	54	16	8
4	68	14	7
5	80	12	6
6	90	10	5
7	98	8	4
8	104	6	3
9	108	4	2
10	110	2	1

As you can see from the third column, I exhibit diminishing marginal utility with regard to beer, as my MU for each beer falls from 20 utils for the first pint down to only 2 utils for the tenth pint. As a result, my MU per dollar spent in the fourth column falls from ten per dollar for the first pint down to only one per dollar for the last pint.

Allocating money between two goods to maximize total utility

Tables 9-2 and 9-3 show you how much utility I can get by spending money on either pizza or beer. The trick now is to see how I can get the most possible utility for my limited budget of $10.

As a first attempt, consider the two extreme options: blowing all the money on pizza, or blowing all the money on beer. (Pizza costs $1 per slice, and beer costs $2 per pint.)

If I spend all $10 on pizza, I can buy 10 slices of pizza, which would give me a total utility of 64 utils. On the other hand, if I spend all $10 on beer, I can buy 5 pints at $2 each and thereby get 80 total utils. If these were my only two options, I would clearly prefer to spend all my money on beer because it brings me more utils than does buying only pizza.

However, there's a much better thing to do. I can get even more total utility if I wisely mix up my consumption a bit and spend some of my money on beer and some of it on pizza.

The way I get the most utility possible out of my $10 is simple: I take each of the ten dollars in turn and spend it on whichever good will bring more utility. I don't think of my task as buying slices of pizza or pints of beer. Rather, my job is buying utility. For every dollar spent, I want to buy as much utility as possible, and I don't care whether that utility comes from beer or pizza.

The only thing complicating this process of spending each dollar on whichever good will bring the most utility is the fact that I have diminishing marginal utility for both beer and pizza, meaning that the amount of utility I'll be able to buy with each extra dollar spent will depend on how much beer or pizza I've already bought. But given the information in Tables 9-2 and 9-3, I can figure out the best thing I should do with each dollar:

    ✔ **Dollar 1:** What should I do with the first dollar? From the fourth column of Table 9-2, you can see that if I spend that dollar on pizza, I can buy 20 utils of utility. On the other hand, the fourth column of Table 9-3 tells you that if I spend that first dollar on beer (along with a second dollar because pints cost $2), I'll get only 10 utils of utility. So, the obvious thing to do with the first dollar is to buy pizza rather than beer.

✔ **Dollar 2:** If I use my second dollar to buy a second slice of pizza, I'll get 16 utils of utility. If I buy beer with that second dollar (along with a third dollar because the price of a pint is $2), I'll get only 10 utils for that second dollar because it will be spent on buying the first pint. So once again, it's better to spend this dollar on pizza rather than beer.

✔ **Dollar 3:** I also want to spend the third dollar on pizza rather than beer because I'll get 14 utils of marginal utility rather than 10 utils. (Remember, this dollar would buy the *first* pint of beer, which brings 10 utils of utility.)

✔ **Dollars 4 and 5:** At dollar number four, everything changes. That's because if I spend a fourth dollar on pizza, it will bring 8 utils. However, if I spend that fourth dollar (along with the fifth dollar) on a pint, I get an MU per dollar of 10 utils (for each of those dollars). So, I should spend dollars four and five on buying the first pint of beer.

✔ **Dollars 6 and 7:** I should also spend dollars six and seven on beer, because I'll get an MU per dollar of 9 utils for my second pint, whereas I'll get only 8 utils if I spend the sixth dollar on a fourth slice of pizza.

✔ **Dollars 8, 9, and 10:** For dollar number eight, the MUs per dollar are tied. If I use this dollar to buy a fourth slice of pizza, I get 8 utils. I'll get the same by spending the dollar on a third pint of beer. So what I should do is spend my last three dollars buying a fourth slice of pizza and a third pint of beer.

In Table 9-4, I list where I should spend each of my ten dollars. Notice that the total utility I can purchase with my ten dollars is 112 utils. That's much better than the 64 utils I would get spending all the money on pizza or the 80 utils I would get spending it all on beer. By spending each dollar in sequence on whichever good brings the most utility, I've done much better than I could by spending the money on only one good or the other.

Table 9-4	How I Optimally Spend Each Dollar in My Budget	
Dollar	*Good Chosen*	*MU per Dollar*
1	Pizza	20
2	Pizza	16
3	Pizza	14
4	Beer	10
5	Beer	10
6	Beer	9

Dollar	Good Chosen	MU per Dollar
7	Beer	9
8	Pizza	8
9	Beer	8
10	Beer	8
Total utils		**112**

Also notice that I end up buying four slices of pizza and three pints of beer. Given this budget and these prices, my quantity demanded of pizza is four slices and my quantity demanded of beer is three pints. The process of maximizing utility is also the basis of demand curves and the relationship between quantity demanded and price. (I discuss demand curves in Chapter 8 and return to them later in this chapter, in the section "Deriving Demand Curves from Diminishing Marginal Utility.") In the next section, I present the magic formula for choosing where to spend your money in any situation.

Equalizing the marginal utility per dollar of all goods and services

In the previous section, I go through a rather tedious process to determine how to best spend $10 on beer and pizza. Making these decisions doesn't always take so long. In this section, I explain a simple formula that guides people to maximize the total utility they can get out of spending any budget — no matter how many goods there are to choose from or how much they each cost.

To keep things simple, let me begin by showing you the version of the formula that applies to deciding how to best spend your budget when there are only two goods or services to choose from. When you get the hang of the two-good version, the multigood version is effortless.

Let me call the two goods X and Y, and let me say that their respective prices are P_X dollars for each unit of X and P_Y dollars for each unit of Y. Also, their respective marginal utilities are MU_X and MU_Y. The formula looks like this:

$$\frac{MU_x}{P_x} = \frac{MU_y}{P_y}$$

(1)

Inflation and allocation in the real world

An interesting thing to notice when you stare at equation (1) or equation (3) in this chapter is that if all the prices in the denominators were to suddenly go up by the same multiple, all the equalities would remain intact, meaning that people would still choose to buy the same amounts of every good. In other words, if there was suddenly an inflation that exactly doubled all prices, people would still choose to buy exactly the same quantities of everything as they did before.

The intuition behind this result is that if my income doubles at the same time that the prices of everything I buy double, nothing has really changed. I can still purchase exactly the same quantities of goods and services as I used to purchase before the inflation. And since those quantities were the ones that were maximizing my utility before, they'll still be maximizing my utility now. As a result, you may mistakenly conclude that inflation doesn't matter.

But in Chapter 5, I tell you about the great horrors of inflation. These horrors are caused by the fact that you never, in real life, see a *perfect* inflation like the one I just described in which the prices of all goods and services go up by exactly the same amount and at exactly the same time.

Instead, what happens is that the prices of different goods and services go up at different rates, so the fractions in equations (1) and (3) are thrown completely out of whack because their denominators change at different rates. When that happens, people start drastically changing their quantities demanded in an attempt to reestablish equality between all their marginal utilities per dollar. As they do this, chaos results; some firms find demand suddenly falling for their products, while others find it suddenly rising.

So don't let equations (1) or (3) make you think that inflation doesn't matter in the real world. It does.

What it means is that if a person has allocated her limited budget optimally between the two goods, then at the optimal quantities of X and Y the marginal utilities per dollar of X and Y will be equal.

This relationship holds true in the example in the previous section. Look back at Table 9-4. When I optimally spend my $10 on beer and pizza, the optimal amounts of each are four slices of pizza and three pints of beer. From the third column of Table 9-4, you can see that marginal utilities per dollar for the fourth slice of pizza and the third beer are indeed equal at 8 utils per dollar, just as the formula in equation (1) dictates.

Seeing why the marginal utilities per dollar must be equal

In this section, I demonstrate *why* marginal utilities per dollar have to be equal if you want to maximize your utility when spending a limited budget. If marginal utilities per dollar aren't equal, you'll want to keep rearranging your purchases until they are. The examples in this section show you why.

First, imagine that I choose some other quantities of each good, so that for the final unit of X and the final unit of Y that I purchase,

$$\frac{MU_x}{P_x} > \frac{MU_y}{P_y} \tag{2}$$

For instance, let pizza be X and beer be Y. From Tables 9-2 and 9-3, you can see that if I purchase four pints of beer and two slices of pizza, the MU per dollar for the fourth pint of beer is 7, while the MU per dollar for the second slice of pizza is 16. Clearly, the MU per dollar of pizza is much bigger than the MU per dollar of beer if I spend my limited budget in this way.

But this way of spending my budget isn't optimal. The reason is that the money I'm spending on what is currently the final unit of X (pizza) buys more marginal utility than the money I'm currently spending on the final unit of Y (beer). If I can get more utility by spending a dollar on X than I can on Y, I should take money away from spending on Y in order to spend it on X. And as long as the inequality in equation (2) holds true, I should continue to take money away from Y in order to increase spending on X.

Consider a more extreme example. Suppose that I spend all $10 buying five pints of beer. You can see from Table 9-3 that the marginal utility per dollar of the last dollar spent on beer is only 6. By contrast, if I took that dollar away from beer and used it to buy a first slice of pizza, the pizza would bring me 20 utils (see Table 9-2). Clearly, I should reduce my beer buying in order to increase my pizza buying.

I should continue to buy fewer beers and more pizza until I arrive at the combination of four slices of pizza and three beers. That is, I should rearrange my spending until the marginal utilities per dollar of both beer and pizza are equal, as in equation (1).

The same rule applies if I start out spending all my money on pizza. If I buy ten slices of pizza, you can see from Table 9-2 that the marginal utility of the tenth slice is actually –4 utils. Meanwhile, the marginal utility per dollar of the first dollar spent on beer is 10. I should clearly take money away from pizza and use it to increase my purchases of beer.

Applying the formula to multiple goods and services

You want to remember the rule represented in equation (1). It simply says that in order to maximize total utility, you should rearrange your purchases so that for the final units of each good, the marginal utilities per dollar are equal. If that isn't true, one of the goods offers you a higher amount of happiness for each dollar spent, meaning that you want to rearrange your purchases to spend more on that good. Only when equation (1) holds will you not want to rearrange any more, because neither good offers you more happiness per dollar than the other.

Also realize that equation (1) can be generalized to apply to many goods. For example, in the case of three goods, you would arrange your buying so that for the last unit of each of the three goods X, Y, and Z:

$$\frac{MU_x}{P_x} = \frac{MU_y}{P_y} = \frac{MU_z}{P_z} \qquad (3)$$

If any of the three goods has a higher marginal utility per dollar than the others, you'll rearrange your purchases to buy less of the others and more of that good. And you keep rearranging until equation (3) holds true.

Deriving Demand Curves from Diminishing Marginal Utility

Diminishing marginal utility is one reason demand curves slope downward. You can get a hint of this from Figure 9-2, where you see that the marginal utility that comes with each successive piece of pizza decreases. If your goal is to use your money to buy up as much utility as possible in order to make yourself as happy as possible, you'd be willing to pay less and less for each successive piece of pizza, as each successive piece of pizza brings with it less utility than the previous piece.

However, Figure 9-2 is not a demand curve, for two reasons:

✔ It doesn't take into account the effect prices have on the quantity demanded.

✔ It looks at only one good in isolation, whereas the quantity demanded of a good is determined by finding the solution to the more general problem of allocating a limited budget across all available goods in order to maximize total utility.

In other words, you can't look at each good in isolation. How much of it you want to buy depends not only on its price but also on the prices of everything else and how their marginal utilities vary as you buy more or less of them.

Seeing how price changes affect quantities demanded

In the example I've been using in this chapter, I've had to decide how to best spend $10 when my choices are slices of pizza or pints of beer. I want to make one change to that example: Let's say that pizza now costs $2 per slice rather than $1 per slice. What I want to show you is how this price change affects the quantity demanded of both pizza and beer.

The changes in quantities demanded result from the fact that the new, higher price of pizza reduces the marginal utility per dollar of pizza. Doubling the price of pizza means that the marginal utility per dollar spent on each slice of pizza is exactly half of what it was before. You can see this by comparing the fourth and fifth columns of Table 9-2. Because the increase in price lowers the marginal utility that each dollar spent on pizza buys, it's naturally going to affect where I spend my limited budget of $10.

As you may expect, a higher price of pizza will lead me to eat less pizza and drink more beer. You can prove this to yourself by spending, in order, each of my dollars so that I buy whichever good has the higher marginal utility. (The section "Allocating money between two goods to maximize total utility," earlier in the chapter, walks you through the process.) The results of doing so are summarized in Table 9-5.

Table 9-5	How I Optimally Spend My Budget When the Price of Pizza is $2	
Dollar	**Good Chosen**	**MU per Dollar**
1	Pizza	10
2	Beer	10
3	Beer	10
4	Beer	9
5	Beer	9
6	Pizza	8
7	Beer	8
8	Beer	8
9	Beer	7
10	Beer	7
Total utils		**86**

By comparing Table 9-5 with Table 9-4, you can see that raising the price of pizza from $1 to $2 has affected not only my quantity demanded of pizza but also my quantity demanded of beer. For pizza, my quantity demanded has fallen from four slices down to only two. For beer, my quantity demanded has increased from three pints to four pints.

The increase in the price of pizza has also made me poorer in the only sense that really matters: I'm less happy. Due to the price increase, the total number of utils that I can purchase with my $10 budget has fallen from 112 down to only 86. Despite rearranging my quantities consumed of beer and pizza to make the most of the new situation, the price increase still hurts me overall.

Graphing the price and quantity changes to form a demand curve

I can use the information about how my quantity demanded changes when price goes up to plot out two points on my demand curve for pizza: four slices demanded at a price of $1, and two slices demanded at a price of $2. In Figure 9-3, I've plotted these two points and sketched in the rest of the demand curve. As you look at the figure, keep in mind two things:

✔ The downward slope of the pizza demand curve derives in part from the diminishing marginal utility of pizza, but . . .

✔ As the price of pizza changes, the quantity demanded of pizza does not change in isolation; it changes as the result of rearranging the quantity demanded of both beer and pizza in order to maximize total utility.

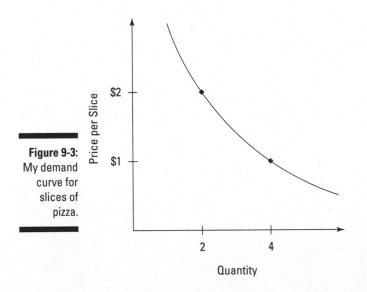

Figure 9-3:
My demand curve for slices of pizza.

Demand curves for individual goods aren't made in isolation. Certainly, a relationship exists between a good's price and its quantity demanded. However, when the good's price changes, that change affects the entire budgeting decision — not just for that good, but for *every* good. The resulting change in the good's quantity demanded is just part of the overall rearrangement of spending that strives to keep maximizing total utility given the new price.

Consider how the increase in the price of pizza affects the demand curve for beer. My quantity demanded of beer went from three pints to four pints when the price of pizza increased from $1 to $2. But the price of beer was unchanged. What this means is that the demand curve for beer must have *shifted* (which I explain in Chapter 8).

I illustrate this shift in Figure 9-4. Point *A* on demand curve *D* shifts over to become point *A'* on demand curve *D'*. Events like this, where changes in the price of one good affect the quantity demanded of another good, are called *cross-price effects*. By contrast, when a change in a good's own price affects its own quantity demanded, you have *own-price effects*. Please note that while cross-price effects cause demand curves to shift, own-price effects cause movements along given demand curves.

The direction of a cross-price effect depends on the situation. In this chapter, I allow consumers to purchase only two goods, beer and pizza. The result is that when the price of pizza goes up, they switch some of their purchasing power over to buying beer — or, as economists say, they *substitute* from one good to the other (see the sidebar "Complementary goods and substitute goods"). That's why when the price of pizza goes up, the demand curve for beer in Figure 9-4 shifts to the right.

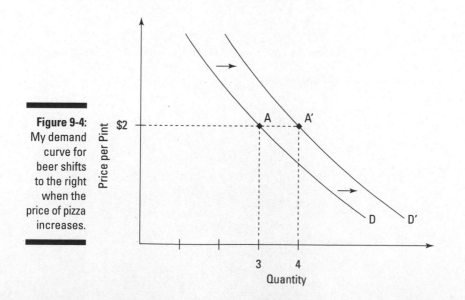

Figure 9-4:
My demand curve for beer shifts to the right when the price of pizza increases.

Complementary goods and substitute goods

Some things just go together. Hot dogs and hot dog buns. Hamburgers and ketchup. Shoes and shoelaces. In each of these pairs, the goods in question are more useful or more pleasing when consumed along with the other member of the pair.

Because such goods complement each other, economists refer to them as *complementary goods*. An interesting thing about complementary goods is that changes in the price of one complement affect the other complement. For instance, if hot dogs go on sale, not only do people buy more hot dogs; they also buy more hot dog buns. And more mustard is sold, too.

By contrast, consider *substitute goods* — goods that serve similar functions so that if the price of one goes up, people switch to the other one. For instance, if the price of train travel goes up,

more people drive cars. And if the cost of regular mail goes up, more people use e-mail.

Both complementary goods and substitute goods are the result of cross-price effects. An increase in the price of a complement causes the quantity demanded of its pair to fall, while an increase in the price of a substitute causes the quantity demanded of its pair to rise.

As you look around the economy, make sure you think of it as one great big organic whole, where things don't happen in isolation. When the price of one good changes, it doesn't affect just that good, but also many other goods that are either substitutes or complements. And if the prices of the substitutes or complements change, too, as a result of the initial price change, then all their substitutes and complements are also affected. It's like a gigantic ripple effect.

But in the real world, where many other consumption goods are available, the demand curve could very well shift the other direction. For instance, some people like drinking beer only when they eat pizza. For them, an increase in the price of pizza may decrease *both* the amount of pizza eaten and the amount of beer drunk.

Such people think of beer and pizza as bundle. An increase in the price of one member of the bundle increases the price of the entire bundle. These people would buy less of each member of the bundle in order to free up money to spend on the many other consumption goods available. For consumers with these preferences and with the option of buying goods besides beer and pizza, when the price of pizza goes up, the demand curve for beer would shift left.

Chapter 10

The Core of Capitalism: The Profit-Maximizing Firm

*I*n modern, market economies like the one you live in, nearly everything you eat, drink, wear, drive, ride, fly, or use is made by some sort of business enterprise. So, naturally, economists devote a huge amount of effort to studying how businesses behave.

In this chapter, I show you how economists model a firm that's a member of a competitive industry, meaning a firm that's just one of many firms competing against each other for your business. It's important to understand how firms behave in competitive industries for two reasons:

✔ Most firms in the real world face a lot of competition because they are either members of perfectly competitive industries (which I talk about in this chapter) or monopolistically competitive industries (which I discuss in Chapter 13).

✔ All firms — even those that don't face much competition — behave in remarkably similar ways.

Above all, firms like to maximize profits. And, even more importantly, it turns out that all firms go about maximizing profits in the same way: by producing exactly the level of output at which the cost of producing one more unit just equals the increase in revenue that the firm gets from selling that unit.

In this chapter, I show you why firms behave this way. When you know that, you'll have a strong understanding of how *all* firms work, whether they face strong competition from rivals or have no rivals at all.

Maximizing Profits Is a Firm's Goal

Firms are brought into existence by people in order to produce things. That statement should make you want to ask a fundamental question: *Why* do people bother creating firms to make things? One reason could be altruism. Another could be that making things is fun. Another could be that the people who start a firm are bored doing other things. But economists think the answer is much simpler.

Economists assume that the overriding goal of all corporations is to make as big a profit as possible. Economists make this assumption for two reasons:

- ✔ If you ask around, profit maximization is near the top of every firm's "to do" list.

- ✔ No matter what other goals a firm may have, it still wants to maximize profits after taking steps to achieve those other goals.

For instance, a firm that wants to have a factory that emits no greenhouse gases still, after it builds such a factory, wants to make as much money as possible. After all, after it's taken the steps necessary to protect the environment, why not make a nice big profit?

Similarly, when the ice cream company Ben & Jerry's started, it donated a large percentage of its profits to charity. Given such a policy, the best way to help worthy causes was for Ben & Jerry's to make as big a profit as possible.

Many noneconomists object to people earning profits, but profits ensure that firms receive the crucial contributions of entrepreneurship and risk-taking. (In Chapter 4, I explain why I think entrepreneurship is a fourth factor of production, along with labor, land, and capital.) Think of someone who has the opportunity to start her own business. She could keep working for someone else and receive a steady wage. What is her incentive to strike out on her own and risk starting a business that may fail? The incentive is that she will receive the profits if the business does well. Without potential profits, no one would risk leaving a safe job in order to innovate, and consumers as a whole would be hurt because the supply of great new products and services would come to a halt.

Facing Competition

Firms may or may not face a lot of competition from other firms. At one extreme lies *monopoly,* in which a firm faces no competition because it's the only firm in its industry. At the other extreme lies what economists call *perfect competition,* a situation in which a firm competes against many other firms in an industry in which they all produce an identical good. And in between the extremes lie two situations: *oligopoly,* where there are two, three, or (at most) a few firms in an industry; and *imperfect (monopolistic) competition,* in which there are many competitors, but each produces a slightly unique good. (See Chapters 12 and 13 for details on monopolies, oligopolies, and monopolistic competition.)

In this chapter, you find out how firms behave under perfect competition because, in addition to being quite common, this situation is also the simplest case to understand. The reason it's so simple is because when there are many competitors in an industry in which every firm is producing identical products, none of them has any control over the price they charge.

Listing the requirements for perfect competition

To see why firms engaging in perfect competition have no control over the prices they charge, you have to understand that perfect competition assumes three things about the firms in an industry:

- ✔ There are many of them.

- ✔ Each of them represents a very small part of the industry.

- ✔ They all sell identical or nearly identical products.

Wheat farming is an example of an industry that satisfies each of the three criteria. There are literally tens of thousands of wheat farmers in the United States. None of them produces more than a small percentage of the total wheat produced each year. And all of their wheat is basically identical.

To see why these things together mean that individual farmers have no control over the price of wheat, start with the fact that the farmers are producing a nearly identical product. Because the wheat from one farm looks like the wheat from any other farm, the only way a Kansas wheat farmer can entice me to buy from him rather than from a Texas wheat farmer is to offer me a lower price. Because all the wheat is identical, all I care about is price, meaning that farmers have to compete on price and price alone.

With price jumping to the fore as the key factor in the wheat market, we can use supply and demand analysis to figure out what the price will be. As I describe in Chapter 8, the price is determined by where the *market demand curve* for wheat crosses the *market supply curve* for wheat. How are these curves determined?

✔ The *market demand curve* for wheat is determined by adding up the individual demand curves of all the people who want to buy wheat.

✔ The *market supply curve* for wheat comes from adding up the individual supply curves of all the individual wheat farmers.

This is where the first two assumptions of perfect competition come into play: Because there are so many wheat farmers, and because each of them produces such a very small part of the total supply of wheat, the market supply curve for wheat is basically unaffected by the presence or absence of any given individual supply curve of any particular farmer. If a trillion bushels of wheat are sold every year, the market price is unaffected by whether a small farmer with only 1,000 bushels to sell bothers showing up to the market or not. He's just too small a player to cause the market price to change.

If every player is too small to cause the market price to change, then each one has to take as given whatever price is generated by market demand interacting with market supply.

Acting as price takers but quantity makers

If the three assumptions of perfect competition are met, they produce a situation in which individual firms have no control over the prices they can charge. In fact, under perfect competition, firms are referred to by economists as *price takers* because they have to take the price as given and deal with it.

When you come right down to it, even the most powerful firm can hope to control only two things: how much of its product to make and what price to charge. Because firms have no control over their prices under perfect competition, that narrows the list to one: The only thing that price-taking firms can control is how much to produce.

Firms choose to make whatever quantity maximizes their profits. This fact is mathematically convenient because it turns out that the quantity of output that a firm chooses to produce controls each of the two things that determine profits: total revenues and total costs.

To see this fact more clearly, you have to know that a firm's profit is simply defined as its total revenue minus its total costs. Put into math,

$$Profit = TR - TC \qquad (1)$$

where *TR* stands for total revenue, and *TC* stands for total costs.

For a competitive firm, its total revenue is simply the quantity, *q,* of its output that it chooses to sell times the market price, *p,* that it can get for each unit:

$$TR = p*q \qquad (2)$$

For instance, if I can sell apples for $1 each and I sell 37 apples, my total revenue is $37.

But notice that because the price at which I can sell (*p*) is out of my hands if I'm a price taker, the only way I can control my total revenue is by deciding how many apples to sell. So a firm can determine its total revenue by its decision about how big or small to make *q*.

Much of the rest of this chapter is devoted to showing you that the firm's total costs, *TC,* are also determined by how big or small *q* is. But the interesting thing here is that while each extra unit of *q* sold brings in a revenue of *p* dollars, the cost of each unit of *q* manufactured depends on how many units of *q* have already been made. Costs tend to increase as firms produce more and more, so each successive unit costs more than the previous unit. This fact ends up limiting the number of units that a firm wants to produce.

For instance, suppose that I can sell as many apples as I want for $1 each. The first apple costs 10 cents to produce, the second one costs 20 cents, the third one costs 30 cents, and so on. In such a case, I'm willing to produce no more than ten apples. Why? Because for each of the first nine apples, I'll make a profit, but for apple ten (which costs $1 to produce), I'll break even. If I produce any more apples, I'll sustain a loss. (Apple number 11, for instance, would cost $1.10 to produce, but I'd get only $1 for selling it.)

Consequently, you can see that both the *TR* and *TC* terms in profit equation (1) are determined by the firm's choice of *q*. The only thing left to figure out is exactly how big to make *q* in order to maximize profits. It turns out that there's a ridiculously simple formula that gives the solution. Pay attention because you just may, uh, profit from reading this chapter.

But before I get to the formula, I need to clarify a major source of confusion caused by the fact that when economists say the word *profit,* they mean something slightly different than what normal people mean.

Distinguishing between accounting profits and economic profits

To an economist, the terms *profit* and *loss* refer to whether the gains from running a business are bigger or smaller than the costs involved. If the gains exceed the costs, you're said to be *running a profit,* whereas if the costs exceed the gains, you're said to be *running a loss.* If the two are just equal, you're said to be *breaking even.*

Things get complicated, however, because whereas accountants and economists agree on what counts as revenue, they disagree on what to count as costs.

Taking account of opportunity costs

Consider a business that sells lemonade. Both the accountant and the economist agree that the firm's revenues are simply how much money it makes from selling lemonade. However, they differ on what to count as costs:

> ✔ The accountant considers costs to be only actual monies spent in running the business: how much the firm pays its workers, how much it pays to buy lemons, and so on. If the firm has revenues of $10,000, and it spends $9,000 to make those revenues, the accountant concludes that the firm has a profit of $1,000. This number is the firm's *accounting profit* — the type of profit that is reported every day in financial statements and newspaper articles.

> ✔ Economists prefer a more subtle concept that they refer to as *economic profit.* Economic profit takes into account not just the money costs directly incurred by running a business but also the *opportunity costs* incurred.

As I explain in Chapter 2, opportunity costs are what you have to give up in order to do something. Think about the entrepreneur who starts this lemonade business. After paying for his materials and for his employees' wages, his accounting profits are $1,000. But is that really a good deal?

Suppose that this person left a job as a computer programmer to open up the lemonade business, and in the same amount of time that it took the lemonade business to turn a $1,000 profit, he would have made $10,000 in wages if he had stayed at his old job. That is, he gave up the opportunity to earn $10,000 in wages to open up a business that makes him only a $1,000 accounting profit. He actually sustains an *economic loss* of $9,000. When you know this fact, his decision to switch careers doesn't seem like such a good idea.

Being motivated by economic profits

Economists like to concentrate on economic profits and losses rather than accounting profits or losses because the economic profits and losses are what motivate people. In our example, you can imagine that when other computer programmers see what happened to this guy when he switched careers, they're not going to follow him.

For the rest of the chapter, whenever you see any costs listed, assume that they are *economic costs;* that is, they include not only money directly spent operating a business but also the costs of other opportunities foregone in order to operate the business. Likewise, whenever you see a profit or a loss, assume that it's an economic profit or an economic loss — the factor that motivates entrepreneurs to want to do something or to avoid doing it.

The most important application of this concept is to determine how much output a firm should produce. If producing the 12th unit of a product produces an economic profit, obviously the firm wants to produce it. But if increasing production to a 13th unit would result in an economic loss, obviously the firm doesn't want to produce it.

By taking into account economic profits and losses, you get directly at what motivates firms to produce not only the types of goods they choose to produce, but the quantities of those goods as well.

Analyzing a Firm's Cost Structure

To see how costs and revenues interact to determine economic profits or losses, economists like to break up a firm's total costs into two subcategories:

- ✔ *Fixed costs* are costs that have to be paid even if the firm isn't producing anything. For instance, once a rent contract is signed for the firm's headquarters, that rent must be paid whether the firm produces anything or not. Similarly, if the firm has taken out a loan, it's legally required to make its debt payments no matter whether it's producing zero units of output or a billion units of output.

- ✔ *Variable costs* are costs that vary with the amount of output produced. For instance, if you are in the lemonade-making business and you choose to produce nothing, you obviously don't have to buy any lemons. But the more lemonade you do produce, the more you spend buying lemons. Similarly, producing more lemonade requires more workers, so your labor costs also vary with the amount of output you produce.

Fixed costs can be represented as *FC* and variable costs as *VC*. Together, they sum up to a firm's total costs, or *TC*:

$$TC = FC + VC \tag{3}$$

As you look equation (3), keep in mind that it deals with the economic costs facing the firm and therefore captures the opportunity costs of the firm's expenditures on both fixed costs and variable costs. (All expenditures, whether they're fixed costs or variable costs, involve opportunity costs — the other things you gave up buying in order to spend the money you spent on your fixed and variable costs.)

Focusing on costs per unit of output

The reason economists distinguish between fixed and variable costs is that they have very different effects on a firm's decision regarding how much to produce. Take a look at Table 10-1, which gives data on LemonAid Corporation, our lemonade producer.

Table 10-1			The Cost Structure of LemonAid Corporation					
Workers	Output	Fixed Costs	Average Fixed Costs	Variable Costs	Average Variable Costs	Total Costs	Average Total Costs	Marginal Costs
0	0	100	---	0	---	100	---	---
1	50	100	2.00	80	1.60	180	3.60	1.60
2	140	100	0.71	160	1.14	260	1.86	0.89
3	220	100	0.45	240	1.09	340	1.55	1.00
4	290	100	0.34	320	1.10	420	1.45	1.14
5	350	100	0.29	400	1.14	500	1.43	1.33
6	400	100	0.25	480	1.20	580	1.45	1.60
7	440	100	0.23	560	1.27	660	1.50	2.00
8	470	100	0.21	640	1.36	740	1.57	2.67

When LemonAid Corporation gets started, it buys a juicer machine for $100, which gives it fixed costs of $100. It then has to decide how much to produce, which in turn determines how many workers it needs to hire. In the first column, the number of workers varies from zero to eight. If the firm hires no workers, you can see in the top entry of the second column that no output is produced. But if it hires workers, output increases as you move down the second column. More workers mean more output.

Studying increasing and decreasing returns

But pay attention to the fact that the amount of additional, or marginal, output produced by each additional worker is not constant. That is, if you go from no workers to one worker, output increases from nothing to 50 bottles of lemon-ade. However, as you go from one worker to two workers, output increases from 50 bottles to 140 bottles. Put into economic jargon, the second worker's *marginal output* is 90 bottles, whereas the first worker's marginal output is only 50 bottles.

Now look at these facts in terms of costs and benefits. If you have to pay each worker the same wage of $80 per day ($10 per hour for 8 hours of work), you're going to like the fact that while the first worker produces 50 bottles for his $80 pay, the second worker produces 90 bottles for her $80 pay.

Economists refer to situations like this as *increasing returns* because the amount of return you get for a given amount of input (one more worker) increases as you add successive units of input. But if you look further down the second column, you find that increasing returns don't last forever.

Indeed, in the case of LemonAid Corporation, increasing returns end almost immediately. Consider what happens to output when you add a third worker. Output does increase, but only by 80 units, from 140 bottles to 220 bottles. And things get even worse the more workers you add. Adding a fourth worker increases output by only 70 bottles, and adding a fifth increases output by only 60 bottles.

Economists call situations like this *diminishing returns* because each successive unit of an input, like labor, brings with it a smaller increase in output than the previous unit of input.

Determining the cause of diminishing returns

I go into detail about what causes diminishing returns in Chapter 3, but I'll briefly explain here. What's going on is that LemonAid Corporation bought only one juicer machine for squeezing the juice out of lemons.

The first worker can use the machine to squeeze enough juice for 50 bottles by carrying lemons to the machine and then operating the machine. But it turns out that two workers together can do even better by dividing up the work: One brings lemons to the machine, and the other operates it. Working together, they can produce a total of 140 bottles — more than double the 50 bottles that one worker could produce working alone.

However, a third worker doesn't increase output nearly as much as a second because the two major tasks — carrying and operating — have already been taken care of. At best, he can just help the first two workers do these tasks a little faster. The same holds true for all successive workers: Having them is helpful, but each one adds less to output than the previous one because things start getting crowded and there really isn't much room left for improvement.

Examining average variable costs

Variable costs are affected by the fact that additional workers first bring increasing returns but then decreasing returns. In the case of the LemonAid Corporation example in Table 10-1, the variable costs are all labor costs, with each worker having to be paid $80 per day. You can see these variable costs increase as you move down the fifth column.

But what's much more interesting is looking at *average variable costs* (*AVC*), which are defined as variable costs divided by quantity (*VC/q*). For instance, because one worker produces 50 bottles of output at a variable cost of $80, the average variable cost is $80/50 = $1.60 per bottle. When two workers together cost $160 in variable costs but produce 140 bottles, the average variable cost for two workers is only $160/$140 = $1.14 per bottle.

The decrease in average variable costs is the result of increasing returns: the fact that when moving from one worker to two workers, variable costs double (from $80 to $160) but output more than doubles (from 50 bottles to 140 bottles).

When diminishing returns set in, average variable costs start to rise, which you can see as you move down the sixth column of Table 10-1. This happens because while each additional worker costs an extra $80, each additional worker after the second worker brings a smaller increase in output than his predecessor. Each successive $80 wage payment brings with it fewer and fewer additional bottles produced, so the average variable cost per bottle must rise.

LemonAid Corporation's average variable costs show up as a subtle U shape when you plot them on a graph, which I do in Figure 10-1. (I also show the company's average fixed costs and average total costs.) Keep this average variable cost curve in mind because it's going to have a huge effect on how many bottles the firm's managers want to produce in order to maximize firm profits.

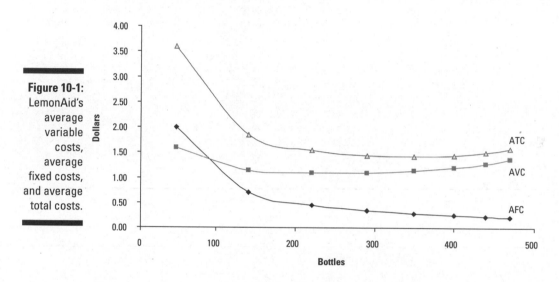

Figure 10-1: LemonAid's average variable costs, average fixed costs, and average total costs.

Watching average fixed costs fall

Average fixed costs (*AFC*) are defined as fixed costs divided by quantity (*FC/q*). The fixed costs of LemonAid Corporation are always the $100 it paid for the juicer machine, no matter what amount of output it produces. As a result, the more lemonade it produces, the less average fixed costs are. That's why *AFC* falls (see the fourth column of Table 10-1) from a value of $2.00 per bottle when 50 bottles are produced using one worker down to only $0.21 per bottle when 470 bottles are produced using eight workers.

Average fixed costs always decline, because the same fixed cost gets divided up over a greater and greater number of units of output as output increases. When you plot out average fixed costs per bottle, as in Figure 10-1, you get a downward sloping *AFC* curve. Keep this fact in mind because it helps explain the shape of the average total costs (*ATC*) curve, as I explain in the next section.

Tracking the movement of average total costs

KEY CONCEPT

In the previous two sections, I show you that average fixed costs always decline as output increases, while average variable costs first fall (due to increasing returns) and then rise (due to diminishing returns). Because total costs are the sum of fixed costs and variable costs, *average total costs* obviously depend on how average fixed costs and average variable costs sum up.

Average total costs (*ATC*) are defined as total costs divided by quantity (*TC/q*). Now, take a look back at equation (3) earlier in the chapter. If you divide every term in equation (3) by *q*, you get the following:

$$TC/q = FC/q + VC/q \qquad (4)$$

You can simplify equation (4) by realizing that $ATC = TC/q$, $AFC = FC/q$, and $AVC = VC/q$. What you get is:

$$ATC = AFC + AVC \qquad (5)$$

You can see clearly from equation (5) that average total costs depend on how average fixed costs and average variable costs interact. There are two key points to understand here:

✔ *ATC* must always be greater than *AVC*, because you have to add in *AFC*.

✔ *ATC* will reach its minimum value at a higher level of output than *AVC*.

To see that the first point is true, look at Figure 10-1, which shows that the *ATC* curve is above the *AVC* curve. The vertical distance between them at any particular level of output is equal to the *AFC* at that output level. As you move from lower output levels to higher output levels, the *ATC* and *AVC* curves converge because *AFC* becomes smaller and smaller. (In other words, the vertical distance between the *ATC* and *AVC* curves also gets smaller and smaller.)

To see that the second point is true, look at Table 10-1 again. You'll see that average variable costs reach their minimum value of $1.09 when three workers are hired and 220 bottles are produced. Average total costs, however, reach their minimum of $1.43 when five workers are hired and 350 bottles are produced.

The reason this happens is that average fixed costs are always falling, meaning that in equation (5), the *AFC* part on the right-hand side of the equation is always getting smaller and smaller. This constant decline helps to temporarily offset the increases in average variable costs that happen when diminishing returns set in. Consequently, although average variable costs bottom out at three workers, average total costs don't bottom out and start increasing until the fifth worker.

Focusing on marginal costs

What a manager of a firm wants to know is what quantity, q, of output she should produce in order to maximize profits. It turns out that to solve this problem, she needs one more cost concept: marginal cost.

Marginal cost is how much total costs increase when you produce one more unit of output. The marginal cost of one more unit of output depends on how much output has already been produced.

To see this, examine the total costs column of Table 10-1. Notice that total costs increase from $100 in the first row to $180 in the second row as output increases from 0 bottles to 50 bottles when the firm hires the first worker. In other words, costs go up $80 while output goes up 50 bottles. So each of these extra, *marginal* 50 bottles on average increases costs by $80/50 = $1.60 each. The marginal cost per bottle, *MC,* is defined as follows:

$$MC = (\text{Change in } TC)/(\text{Change in } q) \tag{6}$$

As you move down the marginal costs column of Table 10-1, you can see that marginal costs first fall and then rise. This is yet another reflection of the fact that LemonAid Corporation's production process exhibits increasing returns followed by diminishing returns. Because the second worker produces much more than the first worker but costs the same, the marginal cost falls when the second worker is added. For successive workers, costs keep increasing but marginal output keeps declining, which means marginal costs must rise.

Noticing where the MC curve crosses the AVC and ATC curves

Here's a fun fact that economists love: If you plot out marginal costs to create a marginal cost (*MC*) curve, that curve will cross both the average variable cost (*AVC*) curve and average total cost (*ATC*) curve at their minimum points — that is, at the bottom of their respective U shapes. (What, you don't see the cause for celebration? Keep reading — maybe I can boost your enjoyment quotient.)

Look at Figure 10-2, where I plot the *AVC, ATC,* and *MC* curves you get by plotting out the data in Table 10-1. The *MC* curve goes through the minimum points of both the *AVC* and *ATC* curves.

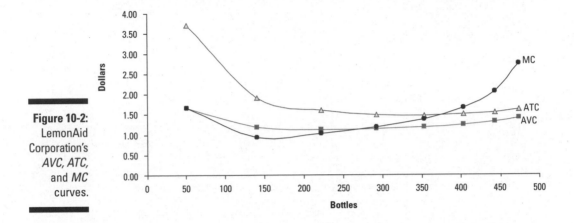

Figure 10-2:
LemonAid
Corporation's
AVC, ATC,
and *MC*
curves.

The reason this happens is because the marginal cost at each unit determines whether the *AVC* and *ATC* curves are increasing or decreasing. Huh? Let's try to simplify by changing our example for a moment; instead of thinking about costs, let's think about heights.

Think about a room with ten people in it. Suppose you determine that the average height of the people in the room is 5'6". Now think about what's going to happen to that average if another person walks into the room:

✔ If the 11th person is taller than the previous average, the average will rise.

✔ If the 11th person is shorter than average, the average will fall.

✔ If the 11th person is exactly 5'6" tall, the average will stay the same.

The same sort of reasoning applies to marginal costs and average costs. After *q* units of output, you can compute *AVC* and *ATC,* just like you can compute the average height after the first ten people enter the room. After that, *AVC* and *ATC* either rise or fall depending on the *MC* of the next unit of output, just as the average height of the people in the room increases, decreases, or stays the same depending on the height of the next person entering the room. Here's what I mean:

✔ If the *MC* is less than the previous average costs, the averages fall.

✔ If the *MC* is greater than the previous average costs, the averages rise.

✔ If the *MC* is exactly the same as the previous average costs, the averages stay the same.

You can see these effects graphically by looking at various parts of Figure 10-2. First, look at the output level of 140 bottles. At that output level, the *MC* of producing one more bottle is less than both *ATC* and *AVC,* meaning that *ATC* and *AVC* will decrease if output is increased by one more bottle. That's why the *AVC* curve and the *ATC* curve are downward sloping at that output level. The average curves are being pulled down by the low value of *MC.*

Next, look at the output level of 440 bottles. You can see that the *MC* at that output level is higher than the *ATC* and the *AVC.* Consequently, both *AVC* and *ATC* must be increasing. This is reflected geometrically by the upward slopes of both the *AVC* curve and the *ATC* curve. The curves slope upwards because the high value for *MC* is pulling them up.

Now, let's put some pieces together. Notice that the *MC* curve causes both the *AVC* curve and the *ATC* curve to be U-shaped (albeit subtly). On the left side of Figure 10-2, the fact that *MC* is less than the average curves means that the average curves slope downward. On the right side of Figure 10-2, the fact that *MC* is greater than the average curves means that the average curves slope upward.

So we've come full circle to the fact that the *MC* curve has to cross the two average curves at their respective minimum points — at the bottoms of their respective U shapes. To the left of such a crossing point, the average must be falling because *MC* is less than the average. And to the right, the average must be rising because *MC* is larger than the average. But where the curves cross, the average curve is neither rising nor falling because the *MC* of that unit of output is equal to the current average. (In other words, a 5'6" person has walked into a room that already has a 5'6" average height, so the average doesn't budge.)

Economists love to go on and on about this fact, but it's really just a reflection of the effect that increasing and then decreasing returns have on cost curves. Costs first fall and then rise. And there's some point in the middle at which they momentarily stay the same, frozen for an instant while transitioning from falling to rising. That point must be where marginal cost equals average cost, because only when *MC* equals average cost can average cost be stationary.

Comparing Marginal Revenues with Marginal Costs

In the previous section, I explain how marginal costs relate to average costs. With that info in mind, I'm finally ready to explain how managers decide how much output to produce in order to maximize profits. (You thought we'd never get here, didn't you!)

Here's a sad but true fact to keep in mind: Firms can't always make a profit. That's because a firm in a perfectly competitive industry can't control the price for which its output sells, and sometimes that price is too low for the firm to make a profit no matter what quantity it produces. When that happens, the best the firm can do is to minimize its losses and hope for the price to change. If the price drops low enough, the best thing to do may be to shut down production immediately, because that way the firm will only lose its fixed costs. (I discuss the difference between fixed and variable costs in the section "Analyzing a Firm's Cost Structure," earlier in the chapter.)

Later in the chapter, I discuss this sad situation in more detail. But first, I focus on a happier situation — one in which the market price is high enough that a firm wants to produce a positive amount of output. As you'll see, this may or may not mean that a firm is making a profit, but even if it isn't, its losses aren't great enough to halt production.

The magic formula: Finding where MR = MC

In the typical case where market prices are high enough that a firm wants to make a positive amount of output, a ridiculously simple formula is used to determine the optimal quantity of output, q, that the firm should produce. The firm wants to produce at the level of output where marginal revenue equals marginal cost ($MR = MC$).

Producing where $MR = MC$ does two things:

- ✔ It minimizes the firm's loss if it has to take a loss due to a low selling price for its output.
- ✔ It maximizes the firm's profit if it's able to make a profit because the selling price is high enough.

The idea behind $MR = MC$ is very simple and basically comes down to a cost–benefit analysis. If producing and selling a bottle brings in more revenue than it costs to make the bottle, then make it. If not, then don't make it. Easy, right?

Let's think back to our example again. Imagine that LemonAid Corporation can sell each bottle of lemonade that it produces for $2 each. Economists like to say that the *marginal revenue* of each bottle is $2, because each and every bottle when sold brings in an extra $2.

What the firm's managers must do is decide how much to produce based on whether any given bottle will cost more or less than the $2 marginal revenue that the firm would get by selling it.

TIP

Be very careful at this point. You have to remember that the relevant cost that the managers look at is an individual bottle's marginal cost, *MC*. That's because if they're deciding on making that particular bottle, they need to isolate that bottle's production cost from the costs of all previously produced bottles in order to compare it to the revenue that the bottle will bring if it's produced and sold. *MC* does just that by ignoring all previous bottles and focusing on what the next bottle will cost to make.

If the *MC* of that bottle is less than $2, obviously there is a gain to be made by making it, and the managers will choose to make it. On the other hand, if the *MC* is bigger than $2, producing the bottle would cause a loss, and the managers would choose not to produce it.

By looking at the *MC* of every possible bottle (the 1st, the 5th, the 97th, and so on) and comparing it with marginal revenue that the firm could get by selling it, the managers can determine exactly how many bottles to produce. The necessary comparisons can be done by looking at a table of costs, such as Table 10-1, but it's even easier to make the comparisons graphically.

In Figure 10-3, I've drawn in the marginal cost (*MC*), average variable cost (*AVC*), and average total cost (*ATC*) curves for LemonAid Corporation. I've also drawn in a horizontal line at $2, which is the marginal revenue for selling any and all bottles that the firm may choose to produce. I've labeled the line $p = MR = \$2$ to indicate the fact that the selling price of the bottle is $2, which is also the marginal revenue.

KEY CONCEPT

Look at the quantity q^*, which corresponds to where the horizontal $p = MR = \$2$ line crosses the *MC* curve. As you can see, $q^* = 440$ bottles. This is the level of output that the firm will choose to produce in order to maximize profits.

Figure 10-3:
The firm's optimal output level, q^*, happens where *MC* and *MR* cross.

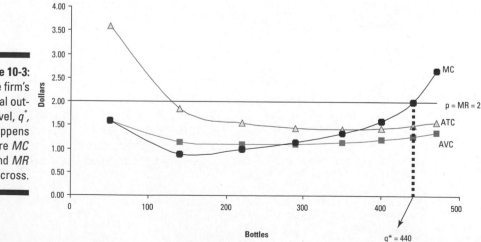

To understand why adhering to $MR = MC$ maximizes profits, look back at Table 10-1 earlier in the chapter and consider each unit of output, q, for which $q < 440$. For all these units, the marginal revenue is greater than the marginal cost ($MR > MC$), meaning that producing and selling each of these bottles brings in more money than it costs to make them. For instance, look at bottle number 140. It has a marginal cost of only $0.89 but can be sold for $2.00. Clearly, you should make such a bottle because you'll make more selling it than it costs to produce. The same is true for all the bottles for which $q < 440$; you should produce all of them because they all bring in a profit.

On the other hand, for all units above the q^* level of output ($q > 440$), the case is reversed: The marginal revenue is less than the marginal cost ($MR < MC$). You would lose money if you produced and sold those bottles. For instance, at an output level of 470 bottles, the MC is $2.67 while the MR is only $2.00. If you produced at that output level, you'd lose 67 cents on bottle number 470. Clearly, you don't want to do this.

By comparing the marginal revenues and marginal costs at all output levels, you can see that the managers of LemonAid Corporation want to produce exactly $q^* = 440$ units, the number of units where the MR and MC lines cross.

As I mention in the introduction to this section, producing where $MR = MC$ doesn't guarantee you a profit, but it does at least make sure that you only produce bottles that bring in more money than they cost to make. The reason this formula by itself can't guarantee a profit is that it doesn't take account of the fixed costs you have to pay no matter what level of output you're producing. Even though you only produce bottles for which marginal revenue is at least as great as marginal cost, you still may not make enough of a gain from these bottles to pay off your fixed costs.

Visualizing profits

Here's what we know from the previous section:

- ✔ A firm can determine its optimal output level, q^*, by producing where $MR = MC$.

- ✔ Producing at q^* doesn't guarantee a profit — rather, it guarantees that you'll either be making the biggest profit possible (if it's possible to make a profit) or the smallest loss possible (if prices are so low that there's no way to make a profit given your cost structure).

What I'm now going to show you is that there's a quick and easy way to visually use the cost curves to determine whether the firm is making a profit or a loss.

The trick to doing so it to realize that the two components of profits, total revenue (*TR*) and total costs (*TC*), can each be represented by rectangles whose areas are equivalent to their respective sizes. As a result, you can immediately tell if profits are positive or negative by looking to see if the *TR* rectangle is larger or smaller than the *TC* rectangle. If the *TR* rectangle exceeds the size of the *TC* rectangle, profits are positive. And if the *TR* rectangle is smaller than the *TC* rectangle, profits are negative — the firm is running a loss.

To see how this all works out, look at Figure 10-4, where I've drawn a generalized set of average total cost (*ATC*), average variable cost (*AVC*), and marginal cost (*MC*) curves, in addition to a horizontal line labeled *p* = *MR* to indicate that price equals marginal revenue for this competitive firm. By *generalized,* I mean this is a typical-looking set of curves; I'm no longer using the particular curves you get by plotting out LemonAid Corporation's costs. Switching to this generalized set of curves will (I hope!) convince you that the geometric way of determining the size of a firm's profits holds true for *any* set of cost curves.

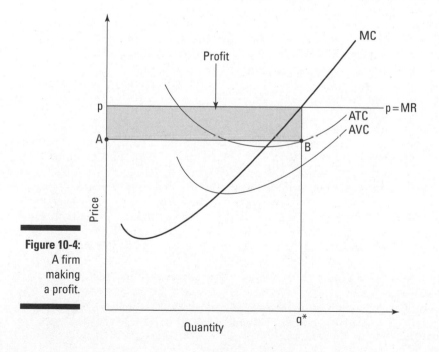

Figure 10-4:
A firm
making
a profit.

The big trick behind expressing total revenue as a rectangular area is to remember that a firm's total revenue when it's producing the profit-maximizing output level, q^*, is simply price times that quantity, or $TR = p*q^*$. Just as you can define the area of a rectangular room as length times width, you can define total revenue on a graph as a rectangle determined by price times quantity. In Figure 10-4, TR is a rectangle of height p and width q^*. Its four corners are located at the origin, at p, at the point where the $p = MR$ line crosses the MC curve, and at q^*.

You can also use a rectangle to represent the total costs that the firm incurs when producing q^* units of output. To figure out where to draw this rectangle, you have to use a little math trick to convert the information that the average total cost (ATC) curve gives you into what you want to graph, total costs (TC).

To see how to apply this math trick, first look at point B in Figure 10-4. It shows the average total cost (ATC) *per unit* when the firm is producing output level q^*. The reason the trick is handy is because it can be used to convince you that the rectangle whose width is q^* and whose height is given by the ATC at output level q^* is actually equal to the firm's total costs. That is, TC is equal to the area of the rectangle whose four corners are the origin, the point I've labeled A, the point I've labeled B, and q^*.

The heart of the math trick is realizing that when the firm is producing at q^*, $ATC = TC/q^*$. If you multiply both sides of this equation by q^*, you find that $ATC*q^* = TC$. This equation tells you that TC is indeed equal to the product of ATC and q^*, or to the area of a rectangle of height ATC and width q^* — exactly the rectangle that I just showed you!

Now that you understand how a firm's TR and TC can be represented by the areas of rectangles that are derived from the firm's cost curves, you shouldn't be surprised to learn that the firm's profits, which are by definition equal to $TR - TC$, can also be represented by the area of a specific rectangle. In fact, the profit is equal to the area of the shaded rectangle in Figure 10-4. That's because profits are simply the difference between TR and TC. Because the TR rectangle is larger than the TC rectangle in this case, the firm is making a profit whose size is equivalent to the area of the shaded rectangle that's defined by the area of the larger TR rectangle minus the area of the smaller TC rectangle.

An informative thing to do is to run a thought experiment using Figure 10-4. Imagine what would happen if the price, p, increased. First, notice that the optimal output, q^*, would increase because the place where the horizontal $p = MR$ line crosses the MC curve would move up and to the right. Simultaneously, the total revenue rectangle would increase in size, as would the total cost rectangle. But which one grows faster? Do profits rise or fall?

Go ahead and draw in some lines to convince yourself that profits will in fact increase — that is, the shaded profit rectangle will grow in size as the price increases. As you'll discover, a rising price increases the firm's profits. The next section explains how profits can go negative if the price falls far enough.

Visualizing losses

Compare the situation in the previous section to the one illustrated in Figure 10-5, where the cost curves are the same as in Figure 10-4 but the price (and therefore the marginal revenue [MR]) at which the firm can sell its product is much lower.

Following the $MR = MC$ rule for selecting the optimal output level, the firm will choose to produce at the output level q_2^* where the new lower $p = MR$ line crosses the MC curve. But because of the low price at which it is forced to sell its output, it will not be able to make a profit. (I've labeled the optimal output level for the firm in Figure 10-5 as q_2^* to make sure it's clear that the optimal output level in this case, where the price is lower, is different from the optimal output level q^* in Figure 10-4 where the price was higher.)

You can see the size of the loss geometrically by comparing the TR and the TC rectangles that occur in this situation. Because $TR = p*q_2^*$, total revenue is equal to the area of a rectangle of height p and width q_2^*. Consequently, the TR is equal to the area of the rectangle whose four corners lie at the origin, at p, at C, and at q_2^*. It's smaller than the TC rectangle defined by the origin, point A, point B, and q_2^*. Because the area of the total cost rectangle exceeds the area of the total revenue rectangle, the firm is running a loss equivalent to the size of the shaded area in Figure 10-5.

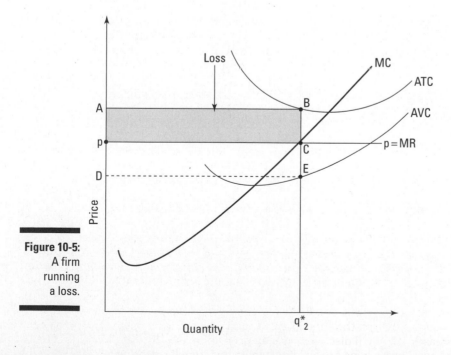

Figure 10-5:
A firm
running
a loss.

What you should gather from Figure 10-5 is that while a manager always wants to produce the level of output where $MR = MC$, doing so won't necessarily guarantee a profit. The problem is that fixed costs get in the way. For instance, suppose a firm has to pay $1,000 a month in rent. If the month has already started and the rent has already been paid, you will produce all units for which $MR > MC$. That gets you to output level q^*_2 in Figure 10-5.

Suppose that $q^*_2 = 600$ and the price at which you can sell output is $1 each. That makes for $600 in total revenue. But with $1,000 in rent costs, you still sustain a loss for the month even though the marginal revenue exceeded the marginal cost for each of the 600 units. The tricky part is that while marginal costs don't take into account fixed costs, profits do.

I'll say it again: Producing at the output level where $MR = MC$ doesn't guarantee a profit. But it does guarantee that if you have to run a loss, it will be as small as possible. While you can't do anything immediate about your fixed costs, you can make sure to produce only those units for which the marginal revenue from selling them is larger than the marginal cost of producing them.

Pulling the Plug: When Producing Nothing Is Your Best Bet

You may wonder why a firm would stay in business if it's running a loss rather than a profit. The usual answer is that it hopes that things will turn around soon. Either it expects the price at which it can sell its products to rise, or it expects that it can somehow reduce its costs of production.

Even if these expectations are well founded, a firm may still be better off completely shutting down production rather than producing some positive amount of output. The determining factor is once again fixed costs.

The short-run shutdown condition: Variable costs exceed total revenues

Suppose you're in charge of a firm that has a monthly rent of $1,000. If you produce nothing, you sustain a loss of $1,000. But that doesn't mean you should *definitely* start producing stuff in order to try to make back some of that money. Rather, you want to produce only if by doing so you are better off than if you do nothing. That is, you should choose to produce if doing so results in either an outright profit or a loss of less than the $1,000 you stand to lose by doing nothing. As I'm about to show you, sometimes the best thing to do is to produce nothing.

Consider Figure 10-6, where the price at which the firm can sell its output is so low that the marginal revenue ($p = MR$) line and the marginal cost (MC) curve intersect at a point *below* the average variable cost (AVC) curve. What does this mean? Put simply, the total revenues in this case are actually *less than* variable costs. (Total revenues are represented by the rectangle whose four corners are at the origin and points p, B, and q^*_3, where q^*_3 represents the optimal output level at this price. Variable costs are represented by the rectangle whose four corners are the origin and points C, D, and q^*_3.)

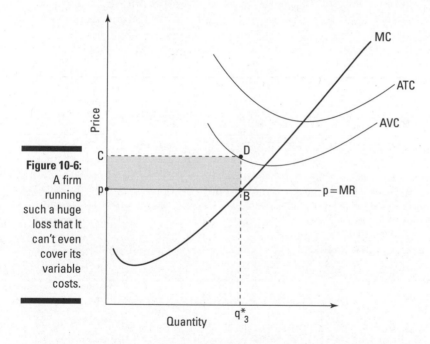

Figure 10-6: A firm running such a huge loss that It can't even cover its variable costs.

What this means is that by producing q^*_3 units, the firm doesn't even bring in enough total revenue to cover the variable costs associated with producing that many units. Not only is the firm going to lose its fixed costs, it's also losing even more money by not being able to cover the variable costs associated with producing q^*_3.

The logical thing to do in such a situation is to produce nothing. By producing zero units, you lose only your fixed costs. By producing q^*_3, you lose even more money because you can't even cover your variable costs.

For instance, suppose that fixed costs are $1,000 and that by producing q^*_3 units the firm makes total revenues of $400 and incurs variable costs of $500. Because total revenues cover only $400 of the $500 in variable costs, the firm loses $100 in variable costs by producing. Add to that the $1,000 of fixed costs it will incur no matter how much it produces, and the firm will lose a total of $1,100 by producing q^*_3 units of output. By contrast, if it shuts down and produces nothing, it loses only the $1,000 in fixed costs. Clearly, in such a situation, the firm should choose to shut down.

Economists call this situation the *short-run shutdown condition*. If a firm's total revenues at q^*_3 are less than variable costs, it's better to shut down completely. Graphically, this happens any time the horizontal $p = MR$ line intersects the *MC* curve at a point below the U-shaped *AVC* curve. In all such situations, total revenues will be less than variable costs — implying that it's better to shut down than produce.

The long-run shutdown condition: Total costs exceed total revenues

By contrast, look back at Figure 10-5. In this case, the firm is more than covering its variable costs because total revenues (represented by the box whose four corners are the origin and points *P, C,* and q^*_2) exceed variable costs (represented by the box whose four corners are the origin and points *D, E,* and q^*_2). While this firm is losing money, it's better off producing q^*_2 rather than $q = 0$ because total revenues exceed variable costs. It can take the extra money left over after paying variable costs and use it to pay off some of its fixed costs.

For instance, suppose that its fixed costs are $1,000 and that when producing output level q^*_2 it has a total revenue of $800 and variable costs of $700. The first $700 of the $800 in total revenues can go to paying off the variable costs, leaving $100 to pay off a portion of the $1,000 in fixed costs. The result is an overall loss of $900, rather than a $1,000 loss if it produces nothing.

A firm that's in the situation of Figure 10-5 will continue to operate in the short run because by doing so it's better off than if it shuts down immediately. But it's still losing money. So while it's better for it to produce output in the short run, it will eventually want to stop losing money by closing down. As soon as its fixed cost contracts expire, it will shut down permanently.

At the mercy of the market price

Because competitive firms have to take the market price as given, their decision about whether to continue operating is in some sense totally out of their hands. There are only three possibilities:

✔ If the price is high enough, the firm will be making a profit and should stay in business in order to keep collecting the profit. Graphically, this happens whenever the horizontal $p = MR$ line crosses the MC curve at a point above the bottom of the U-shaped ATC curve, as in Figure 10-4.

✔ If the horizontal $p = MR$ line crosses the MC curve at a point below the bottom of the U-shaped ATC curve, the firm is taking a loss. What it does in such situations depends on how low the price is and, consequently, how big the loss is. Two possibilities (or conditions) exist, as I explain in the previous sections:

• The *short-run shutdown condition* occurs when a firm's total revenues are less than its variable costs. Graphically, this happens when the horizontal $p = MR$ line intersects the MC curve at a point below the low point of the U-shaped AVC curve, as in Figure 10-6.

In such a situation, the firm is better off shutting down immediately and losing only its fixed costs. Producing output in such a situation would result in an even bigger loss.

• The *long-run shutdown condition* occurs when a firm's total revenues exceed its variable costs but are less than its total costs. Graphically, this happens in any situation where the horizontal $p = MR$ line intersects the MC curve at any point on the segment of the MC curve that lies above the bottom of the U-shaped AVC curve but below the bottom of the U-shaped ATC curve, as in Figure 10-5.

In such a situation, the firm is guaranteed to lose money. But as long as the firm is stuck with its current set of fixed cost commitments, it's better off producing rather than shutting down immediately. If it produces, its total revenue will exceed its variable costs, meaning that it can use the excess to pay off at least part of its fixed costs. On the other hand, if it shuts down and produces nothing, it will lose all of its fixed costs and thereby do worse.

As you can see, the perfectly competitive firm is in some sense totally at the mercy of the market price. If the price is high, it makes profits. If the price is low, it sustains losses. And even then, its decision about whether to shut down immediately or keep operating at a loss until it can get out of its fixed cost commitments depends entirely on the price. Perfectly competitive firms have no control.

In the next chapter, I discuss noncompetitive firms and how they have control over their market prices. As you can already gather from the dependency of competitive firms on the market price, having such control puts them in a far less precarious position.

Chapter 11

Why Economists Love Free Markets and Competition

*E*conomists love competitive free markets — markets in which numerous buyers freely interact with numerous competitive firms. Indeed, economists firmly believe that when they work properly, competitive free markets are the very best way to convert society's limited resources into the goods and services that people want to buy.

Why do economists place such great confidence in competitive free markets? Because the interaction of supply and demand (which I discuss in Chapter 8) leads to an outcome in which every unit of output that's produced satisfies two excellent conditions:

✔ It's produced at the minimum cost possible, meaning that there's no waste or inefficiency.

✔ Its benefits exceed its costs. That is, only output that makes the world better off gets produced.

Economists also love competitive free markets because they provide a gold standard against which all other economic institutions can be judged. In fact, many economic problems are referred to by economists as *market failures* precisely because they are instances where if markets could function properly, the problems would quickly go away.

In this chapter, I show you that competitive free markets ensure that benefits exceed costs for all the output produced. I also show you that competitive free markets produce the *socially optimal quantity* of output — the level that maximizes the benefits that society can get from its limited supply of resources. Finally, I show you how competitive industries adjust to changes in supply and demand to ensure that everything that's being produced is produced at the lowest possible cost to society.

The Beauty of Competitive Free Markets: Ensuring That Benefits Exceed Costs

Society has only a limited amount of land, labor, and capital out of which to make things. Consequently, society must be very attentive when figuring out how to best convert its limited resources into the goods and services that people most greatly desire.

Economists love competitive free markets because, if they are operating properly, they make sure that resources are allocated optimally. In particular, such markets assure that resources go toward producing only output for which the benefits exceed the costs.

This point can be easily demonstrated using nothing more complicated than a supply and demand graph such as the type I introduce in Chapter 8. But before I show you how that's done, I need to explain the conditions under which competitive free markets can function properly and thereby deliver such nice results. (Please note that for brevity, I sometimes just say "free markets" or "markets" in this chapter rather than writing out "competitive free markets" each time. I'm trying to maximize my resources here.)

Examining prerequisites for properly functioning markets

Free markets guarantee optimal outcomes only if the following conditions are met:

- ✔ Buyers and sellers all have access to the same full and complete information about the good or service in question.

- ✔ Property rights are set up so that the only way buyers can get the good or service in question is by paying sellers for it.

- ✔ Supply curves capture all the production costs that firms incur in making the good or service in question.

✔ Demand curves capture all the benefits that people derive from the good or service in question.

✔ There are both numerous buyers and numerous sellers, such that nobody is big enough to affect the market price. This is often called the *price-taking assumption* because everybody just has to take prices as given.

✔ The market price is completely free to adjust to equalize supply and demand for the good or service in question.

Basically, these six points accomplish two broad goals:

✔ They guarantee that people will want to buy and sell in a market environment.

✔ They ensure that markets will take into account all the costs and all the benefits of producing and then consuming a given amount of output.

I address each point separately in the next two sections.

Guaranteeing that people will want to participate in markets

The requirement that both buyers and sellers have access to full and complete information guarantees that both will be willing to negotiate without having to worry that the other guy has some secret information that can be used against them. (In Chapter 15, I explain how markets break down if one side or the other has more information.)

The requirement that property rights be set up in such a way that buyers *have* to pay sellers ensures there will be sellers willing to provide the product. As a counter example, consider trying to sell tickets to an outdoor fireworks display. Because everyone knows that they can see the display for free, nobody wants to pay for a ticket. But because sellers can't sell tickets, they have no incentive to put on a display. (In Chapter 15, I discuss situations like these and how society must deal with them given that markets can't.)

Capturing all costs and benefits

The requirements that supply curves capture all costs and demand curves capture all benefits ensure that a proper cost–benefit calculation can be made. For instance, if a steel factory can pollute for free, there's no way that the price of steel will correctly reflect the damage that the factory's pollution does to the environment. On the other hand, if the government forces the factory to continuously pay for cleanup costs, these costs will be reflected in the market price, thereby allowing society to properly weigh the costs and benefits of the company's output. (Chapter 14 deals with ways to help markets along if supply and demand curves don't reflect all costs and benefits.)

If the first four requirements for free markets are met, market forces can still reach a social optimum only if they are free of interference. The fifth requirement eliminates problems like monopolies, in which individual buyers or sellers are so powerful that they can manipulate the market pricing in their own favor. The sixth requirement stipulates that supply and demand must be allowed to freely determine the market price and market quantity unimpeded by government-imposed price ceilings or floors. (In Chapter 8, I explain the problems with price ceilings and floors and discuss how they hurt society.)

If all six requirements are met, an amazing thing happens. Supply and demand automatically get you to the social optimum without the government or socially conscious activists having to do anything. This insight was the basis of Adam Smith's metaphor of an invisible hand that seems to guide markets to do the right thing despite nobody being in charge — and despite the fact that each individual in the market may well be looking out only for his or her own interests.

So take this insight to heart by looking out for your own interests and reading the rest of this chapter carefully. You may just end up promoting the social optimum.

Analyzing the efficiency of free markets

Economists use supply and demand curves to demonstrate that free markets produce socially optimal levels of output. But the simple insight behind this result is that a unit of output can be socially beneficial to produce and consume only if the benefits that people derive from consuming it exceed the costs of producing it.

This simple idea is, in fact, why demand curves and supply curves are so useful in analyzing the social optimum. As I explain in Chapter 8, demand curves quantify the benefits that people get from consumption by showing what they'd be willing to pay to consume each and every particular unit of output. In a similar fashion, in Chapter 10 I explain how supply curves quantify the cost of producing each and every particular unit of output.

Using supply and demand to compare costs and benefits

By drawing the demand and supply curves for a good or service together on the same graph, you can easily compare the benefits and costs of producing each and every unit of output. To see how this is done, take a look at Figure 11-1, on which I've drawn a demand curve, *D,* and a supply curve, *S.*

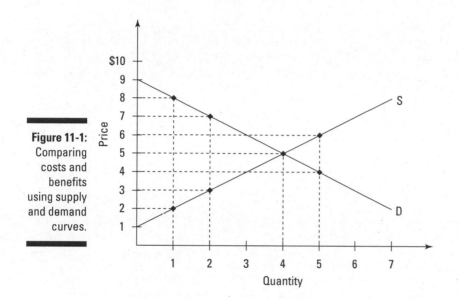

Figure 11-1:
Comparing
costs and
benefits
using supply
and demand
curves.

To start, take a look at one unit of output on the horizontal axis. At that
output level, go vertically up to the demand curve and see that people are
willing to pay $8 for one unit of output. At the same time, by going vertically
up to the supply curve, you can see that firms are willing to supply one unit
at a cost of $2.

Putting these facts together, you can see that it is socially beneficial to produce this first unit of output because it's worth more to buyers ($8) than it
costs sellers to produce ($2). Put slightly differently, while the resources that
it takes to make that unit of output cost society only $2, they bring $8 in benefits when they're converted into this particular good or service. Because the
benefits exceed the costs, this is a unit of output that *should be* produced.

Now look at the second unit of output. Going vertically up to the demand
curve tells us that people are willing to pay $7 for that unit, while going verti-
cally up to the supply curve tells us that the second unit costs $3 to produce.
Again, benefits exceed costs. Again, this unit of output *should be* produced.

By contrast, look at the fifth unit of output. By going up vertically, you can
see that the costs as given by the supply curve for producing the fifth unit
are $6, while the benefits as given by the demand curve are only $4. Because
the costs of producing this unit exceed what anyone is willing to pay for it,
this is a unit of output that *shouldn't be* produced.

In other words, producing the fifth unit of output would destroy value. Why?
Because making it involves converting $6 worth of resources into something
that's worth only $4 to consumers. Producing it would destroy wealth.

Determining the socially optimal output level

The next thing to notice about Figure 11-1 is that it can tell you precisely what quantity (q) of output should be produced. That's because the supply and demand curves let you quickly compare costs and benefits for every possible output level.

There are only three cost–benefit relationships:

- For every bit of output such that $q < 4$, benefits exceed costs.
- At exactly $q = 4$ units, benefits equal costs.
- For all output levels where $q > 4$, costs exceed benefits.

Economists look at this and conclude that the socially optimal level of output to produce is $q = 4$ units because for these units, benefits either exceed costs or are at least equal to costs. By producing the first four units of output, society either gains or is at least not made any worse off.

As you can see, the socially optimal output level is always devastatingly easy to identify on any supply and demand graph. It's just the quantity produced where the demand and supply curves cross.

Realizing that free markets produce the socially optimal output level

Adam Smith's big insight was to realize that free markets produce exactly the socially optimal output level on their own without anyone having to direct them to do the right thing.

The proof of this fact is almost trivial. All you have to do is look at Figure 11-1 and realize that the market equilibrium quantity — which happens when the market price is free to adjust so that the quantity supplied by sellers equals the quantity demanded by buyers — is determined by where the supply and demand curves cross. (To understand why, see Chapter 8.) The market equilibrium quantity is four units of output, which is exactly how many units you would want to produce if you were using the demand and supply curves to compare benefits and costs.

This is an amazing result that greatly simplifies life because it eliminates the need to have a government official or any other sort of central planner constantly checking to see if exactly the right amount of output is being produced. Free markets yield precisely the optimal level of output without anyone have to perform any sort of oversight.

Using total surplus to measure gains

Economists use a concept called *total surplus* to total up the gains that come from producing the socially optimal output level. The gain, or surplus, comes from the fact that benefits exceed costs for the units of output that are produced.

The total surplus turns out to be divided between consumers and producers. The part of the total surplus that goes to consumers is (naturally) called *consumer surplus,* while the part that goes to producers is called *producer surplus.*

In the sections that follow, I tackle consumer surplus first and then move on to producer surplus. After I explain each separately, I add them together to explain total surplus. (And I hope that when you're done with this section, you feel like you've received at least a *little* consumer surplus.)

Measuring the consumer surplus of a discrete good

Consumer surplus is the gain people receive when they can buy things for less than what they were willing to pay.

The easiest way to understand consumer surplus is by first looking at a discrete good. A *discrete good* is a good that comes only in discrete units. For instance, you can buy 1 car or 57 cars, but you can't buy 2.33 cars. You can purchase 1 horse or 13 cows but not fractional amounts of livestock (at least if you want them alive!).

Look at Figure 11-2, which shows the demand for cows. Because cows come in discrete units, you don't get a smooth, downward-sloping curve. Rather, you get what mathematicians call a *step function.* The way to understand it is that people are willing to pay $900 for the first cow, $800 for the second cow, $700 for the third cow, and so on.

Now imagine that the market price of cows is $500, which is why I've drawn a horizontal dotted line at that price. Compare that price with what people are willing to pay for each cow.

For the first cow, people are willing to pay $900. Because the market price of cows is only $500, these buyers come out ahead because they're able to purchase a cow for $400 less than they were willing to pay. Or, as economists like to say, the *consumer surplus* on the first cow is $400.

Next, look at the second cow. People are willing to pay $800 for it, but because the market price is only $500, they receive a consumer surplus for that cow of $300.

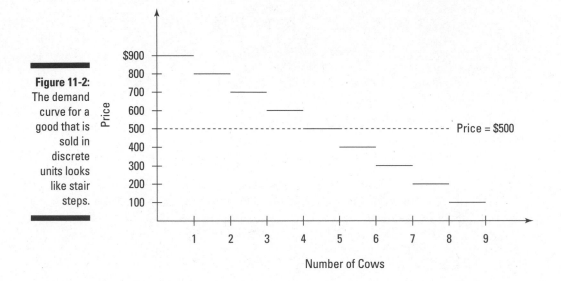

Figure 11-2:
The demand
curve for a
good that is
sold in
discrete
units looks
like stair
steps.

Similarly, for the third cow, people get a consumer surplus of $200 because they are willing to pay $700 for it but have to pay only the market price of $500.

For the first four cows, there's a positive consumer surplus, while on the fifth cow people just break even because they're willing to pay $500 and the cow costs $500. This means that people will want to buy only five cows. (Economists always assume that when the price equals your willingness to pay, you go ahead and buy.)

To calculate consumer surplus for a discrete good such as cows, we need to total the surpluses that people get on each unit that they choose to buy. In this case, the total is $1,000 ($400 for the first cow, plus $300 for the second cow, plus $200 for the third cow, plus $100 for the fourth cow, plus $0 for the fifth cow).

I show this $1,000 of consumer surplus in the graph in Figure 11-3 by shading in the area below each step and above the horizontal price line at $500. The staircase-shaped area equals $1,000.

Measuring the consumer surplus of a continuous good

Consumer surplus can also be computed for continuously measured goods and services — things like land or cooking oil or hours of music lessons, which aren't necessarily sold in discrete units. In other words, you can buy fractional amounts of continuously measured goods, such as 78.5 acres of land, 6.33 gallons of cooking oil, or 2.5 hours of music lessons.

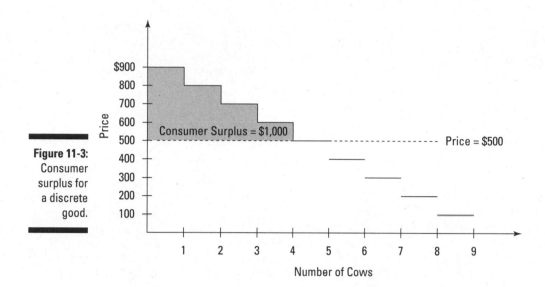

Figure 11-3:
Consumer
surplus for
a discrete
good.

The demand curves for continuously measured goods are much nicer than
the step functions that you get for discretely measured goods. In fact, the
demand curves for continuously measured goods are the smooth, downward-
sloping lines that you're used to seeing (such as in Chapter 8).

Because of the smoothness of such demand curves, when you graph consumer surplus for a continuously measured good, you get a triangular area
that lies below the demand curve and above the market price. You can see
this wedge illustrated in Figure 11-4, which depicts the cooking oil market.

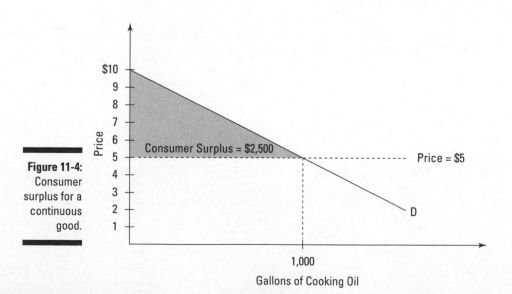

Figure 11-4:
Consumer
surplus for a
continuous
good.

In Figure 11-4, the price of cooking oil is $5 per gallon. At that price, people want to buy 1,000 gallons of cooking oil. The demand curve lies above the horizontal, $5 price line, which means that buyers are made better off by buying these 1,000 gallons because they are worth more to the buyers than the $5 per gallon that it costs to buy them.

To calculate consumer surplus for a continuous good, you total up all the gains that people receive when buying for less money than they are willing to pay — just as you would do for a discrete good. But because we're now dealing with a triangle, totaling up requires a bit of geometry. Don't worry, it's easy. You simply use the formula for the area of a triangle (1/2 times base times height) to find the total surplus. In this case, you multiply 1/2*1,000*5 = $2,500.

Measuring producer surplus

Producer surplus measures the gain that firms receive when they can sell their output for more than the minimum price that they would have been willing to accept. You can calculate producer surplus for both discrete and continuous goods, just as you can calculate consumer surplus for each. In this section, I offer an example of calculating producer surplus for a continuous good.

You can get a good handle on producer surplus by looking at Figure 11-5, which shows the supply curve, *S,* for cooking oil. This supply curve is crucial for determining producer surplus because each point on the supply curve tells you the minimum that you would have to pay suppliers for them to give you the associated amount of output. By comparing each minimum value with the higher market price that they actually receive when they sell their output, you can compute producer surplus. (For more on supply curves and how to interpret them, see Chapter 8.)

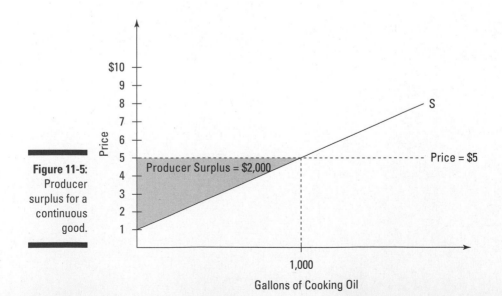

Figure 11-5: Producer surplus for a continuous good.

The price of cooking oil is still $5 per gallon. And the way I've drawn the graph, producers are going to want to supply exactly 1,000 gallons of cooking oil at that price. They want to supply this much because for each drop of oil up to and including the very last drop of the 1,000th gallon, the production costs as given by the supply curve are less than the $5 per gallon that producers get when they sell the oil.

But, crucially, producers are willing to supply almost all that cooking oil for *less than* the $5 per gallon market price. You can see this by the fact that the supply curve lies below the horizontal price line up to the very last drop of the 1,000th gallon. The fact that they receive $5 per gallon for all of it despite being willing to produce it for less is the source of the producer surplus, which is represented by the area of the shaded triangle.

Using the formula for the area of a triangle (1/2 times base times height), you can compute that the producer surplus in this example is $2,000. Producers are $2,000 better off by selling the 1,000 gallons of oil because the total cash they get from selling these 1,000 gallons exceeds the minimum amount that they would have been willing to accept by $2,000.

Computing total surplus

The *total surplus* that society receives from producing the socially optimal level of output of a certain good or service is simply the sum of the consumer surplus and producer surplus generated by that output level.

Figure 11-6 illustrates total surplus for a market in which the equilibrium price and quantity are, respectively, $p^* = \$5$ and $q^* = 4$. (If this graph looks familiar, that's because it's just like Figure 11-1.)

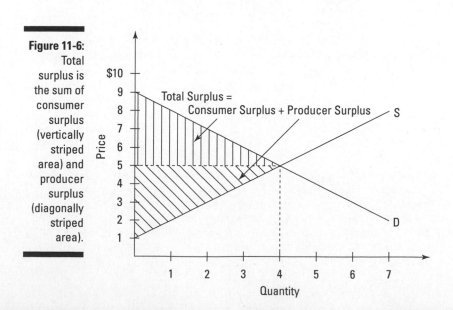

Figure 11-6: Total surplus is the sum of consumer surplus (vertically striped area) and producer surplus (diagonally striped area).

I've drawn the total surplus area so you can clearly see that it's made up of consumer surplus plus producer surplus. The two are separated by the horizontal line extending from the market equilibrium price ($5). The consumer surplus triangle is filled with vertical lines, while the producer surplus triangle is filled with diagonal lines.

By again using the formula for the area of a triangle, we multiply 1/2*4*8 to figure out that for this graph the total surplus is $16. The total gain to society of producing at this output level is $16.

Contemplating total surplus

Total surplus is very important because it puts a number on the gains that come from production and trade. Firms make things to make a profit. People spend money on things because consuming those things makes them happy. And total surplus tells you just how much better off both consumers and producers are after interacting with each other.

By putting a number on the gains made by their interaction, total surplus also provides a benchmark by which economists can measure the harm that comes from government policies that interfere with the market. It's one thing to say that, for instance, price subsidies hurt consumers. It's another thing to be able to say by exactly how many dollars consumers are harmed. And that's what I cover next.

When Free Markets Lose Their Freedom: Dealing with Deadweight Losses

As I note earlier in the chapter, economists love free markets because free markets produce only those units for which benefits exceed costs. In other words, the market equilibrium ensures that total surplus is as large as possible.

Anything that interferes with the market's ability to reach the market equilibrium and produce the market quantity reduces total surplus. Economists refer to the amount by which total surplus is reduced using the colorful term *deadweight loss*.

In the sections that follow, I give you detailed examples of deadweight losses caused by price ceilings and taxes. These types of market interference are both under the government's control, but you shouldn't think that deadweight losses are caused *only* by government policy. Anything that reduces output below the market quantity causes a deadweight loss. Monopolies and oligopolies can be to blame, as can asymmetric information and public goods problems — all things that I discuss in the next few chapters.

Dissecting the deadweight loss from a price ceiling

As an example of a deadweight loss, look at Figure 11-7 in which the government has imposed a price ceiling at P^C. As I discuss in Chapter 8, *price ceilings* are maximum prices at which sellers can legally sell their product. Generally, price ceilings are intended to help buyers obtain a low price, but, as I'm about to show you, they cause a lot of harm.

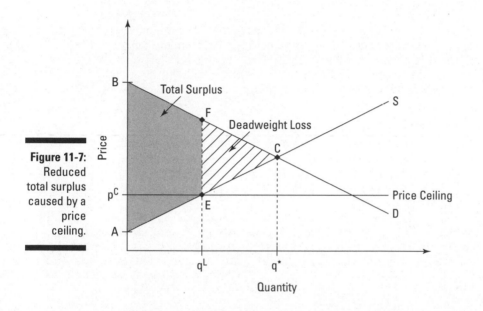

Figure 11-7: Reduced total surplus caused by a price ceiling.

To see the damage price ceilings inflict, first notice that at a maximum price of P^C, suppliers are going to want to sell only q^L units of output (the L stands for *low*). In other words, at that price, only the first q^L units of output are profitable to produce. By contrast, if no price ceiling existed and the market was left to its own devices, suppliers would choose to produce the market equilibrium quantity of output, q^*.

Consequently, if this was a free market, the total surplus would be represented graphically by the triangle defined by points *A, B,* and *C.* But because only q^L units of output can be produced, the total surplus area is reduced down to the shaded area with corners at *A, B, F,* and *E.*

The difference between the total surplus generated by producing q^* versus q^L units of output is the diagonally-striped triangle defined by points *E, F,* and *C.* The area of this triangle illustrates the deadweight loss that comes from reducing output below the socially optimal level, q^*.

The price ceiling is harmful because for all units between q^t and q^*, benefits exceed costs, meaning that such units should be produced. By tallying up the gains that should have come from producing and consuming these units, the deadweight loss triangle can precisely measure the harm that results from interfering with the market.

Analyzing the deadweight loss of a tax

Taxes on goods and services also cause deadweight losses. This happens because such taxes raise the costs of producing and consuming output. When these costs are artificially raised by the tax, people respond by producing and consuming fewer units of output than they did before the tax was imposed. Because each unit that had been consumed before the tax was imposed was a unit for which benefits had exceeded costs, the reduction in output that results from the tax necessarily reduces total surplus and causes a deadweight loss.

Seeing how taxes shift the supply curve

Before I discuss in more detail the deadweight loss that results from a tax, I have to show you that imposing a tax on the seller shifts supply curves vertically by the amount of the tax. Let's consider a concrete example — the supply of beef in a beef market in which the government is going to impose a tax of $1 per pound.

Figure 11-8 shows two curves. (Well, actually they're straight lines, but humor me here.) The lower one, *S,* is the supply curve for beef. The higher one, labeled *S + tax,* is the supply curve after the tax is imposed. The important thing to realize is that the curve *S + tax* is simply the original supply curve shifted up vertically by the amount of the tax, which in this case is $1.

The reason the supply curve shifts up vertically by the amount of the tax has to do with motivating suppliers. In Chapter 8, I explain that each point on the supply curve tells you the minimum that you would have to pay suppliers to get them to supply the relevant quantity. For instance, look at point *A.* Because point *A* is on the supply curve, you know that you have to pay $5.00 per pound if you want suppliers to provide 10 million pounds of beef. Similarly, point *E* tells you that you have to pay suppliers $4.50 per pound if you want them to supply only 9 million pounds of beef.

If the government comes in and imposes a tax of $1 per pound, it affects how much you have to pay the suppliers to motivate them. If you still want 10 million pounds of beef, you have to pay the original amount required to motivate the suppliers to give you that much beef ($5 per pound), as well as enough money to pay the taxes on that much beef ($1 per pound).

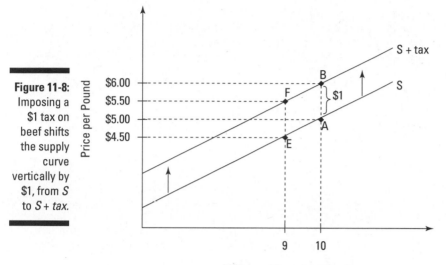

Figure 11-8:
Imposing a
$1 tax on
beef shifts
the supply
curve
vertically by
$1, from *S*
to *S* + *tax*.

Graphically, this means that point *A* on supply curve *S* shifts up by the $1 amount of the tax to become point *B* on the *S* + *tax* curve. For the same motivational reasons, point *E* on the supply curve must shift up to point *F* on the *S* + *tax* curve. That is, if you have to pay suppliers $4.50 per pound to motivate them to give you 9 million pounds of beef in a world in which $1 per pound must go to the government in taxes, you have to collect a total of $5.50 per pound. And that's exactly what happens at point *F.*

Every point on the supply curve, *S*, must shift up vertically in the same way that points *A* and *E* do, so the *S* + *tax* curve captures what the supply curve looks like after the tax is imposed. With this shift in mind, you're ready to discover how this sort of taxation causes deadweight losses.

Seeing how taxes cause deadweight losses

Figure 11-9 adds a demand curve, *D*, to Figure 11-8 so we can see what happens to total surplus when the government imposes a $1 per pound tax on the beef that's sold in the beef market.

Before the tax, the market equilibrium happens at point *A*, where supply curve *S* crosses demand curve *D*. At that point, producers supply 10 million pounds of beef at a price of $5 per pound. The total surplus in this case is given by the triangle defined by points *C, D,* and *A*.

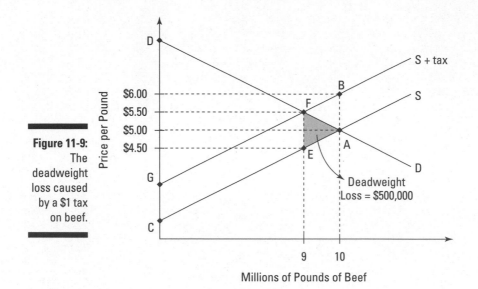

Figure 11-9:
The
deadweight
loss caused
by a $1 tax
on beef.

After the tax is imposed, however, the equilibrium happens at point *F,* where the *S + tax* curve crosses the demand curve. At that point, the price of beef is $5.50 per pound, and 9 million pounds are supplied. (Only 9 million pounds are supplied because after the government takes its $1 per pound in taxes, only $4.50 remains to motivate suppliers. You can see from the supply curve that at that much money per pound, suppliers want to supply only 9 million pounds.)

Because of the tax, the amount of beef supplied falls from 10 million pounds to 9 million pounds. Furthermore, the total surplus is reduced to the triangle whose three corners are *G, D,* and *F.*

You can immediately see that this new total surplus is much smaller than the old total surplus. But before we start ranting about the evils of government, we need to take account of the fact that taxes are being collected. Taxes (theoretically, at least) benefit society, so we need to include this amount when calculating the total surplus of this good sold at this price. At the new equilibrium, $9 million in taxes will be collected because the 9 million pounds of beef sold will be taxed $1 each.

The $9 million in tax collections are represented graphically by the parallelogram whose corners are *C, G, F,* and *E.* This area was previously contained in the old total surplus triangle whose corners were *C, D,* and *A.* Consequently, this area that used to be part of the old total surplus hasn't been destroyed; it's merely been transferred to the government.

However, part of the old total surplus *has* been destroyed. This part is shown graphically by the shaded deadweight loss triangle (with corners at *E, F,* and *A*). This area captures the fact that society has been made worse off by the reduction in beef output from 10 million pounds to 9 million pounds. (Okay, *now* you can start ranting about the evils of government.)

Measuring the size of the deadweight loss using the formula for the area of a triangle (1/2*base*height) tells us that the tax leads to a deadweight loss of $500,000. That's a big number representing a huge reduction in total surplus deriving from the fact that for each of the 1 million pounds of beef that are no longer being produced, benefits had exceeded costs. All those gains are lost when the tax is imposed.

Deadweight losses are called deadweight losses because you can't say "Your loss is my gain" in this situation. We aren't talking about something that passes from one person to another. Rather, deadweight losses are losses in the sense of annihilation. The gains that would have resulted if those million pounds of beef had been produced simply vanish; they are a dead weight that we must bear in our efforts to maximize human happiness given our limited resources.

Hallmarks of Perfect Competition: Zero Profits and Lowest Possible Costs

Earlier in this chapter, I demonstrate that free markets produce only units of output for which benefits are at least as great as costs. Another wonderful thing about free markets and competition is that output is produced at the lowest possible cost.

This fact is extremely important because it means that free markets are as efficient as possible at converting resources into the goods and services that people want to buy.

In addition, markets save society a lot of money because they produce efficiently without requiring any human intervention. We don't have to pay big salaries to experts to make sure that markets run efficiently; markets do the job for free.

Understanding the causes and consequences of perfect competition

To ensure that markets function efficiently, you need really strong competition between firms, a situation that economists refer to as *perfect competition*.

As I explain in Chapter 10, perfect competition exists when there are many firms within a given industry that are all producing identical (or nearly identical) products. The following things are also true when perfect competition exists:

- ✔ Every firm is a *price taker* — it has to accept the market equilibrium price for what it produces — because its output is a very small fraction of the industry's total output (see Chapter 10).
- ✔ Every firm has identical production technology.
- ✔ Firms are free to enter or leave the industry as they please.

When these requirements are met, perfect competition leads to two very excellent outcomes:

- ✔ Every firm in the industry makes zero economic profits.
- ✔ Every firm produces output at the minimum possible cost.

The first outcome does not mean that businesses earn no money above the costs of doing business; if that was true, no one would go into business. Firms must earn enough money to keep entrepreneurs motivated to stay in business (and to attract other entrepreneurs to open new firms).

So what does the first outcome mean? In Chapter 10, I explain that the *economic profits* earned by a firm are any monies collected above and beyond what is required to keep an entrepreneur owner interested in continuing in business. So the fact that perfect competition leads to zero economic profits means that firms just barely want to stay in their industry.

It also means that nobody in the industry is getting filthy rich at anyone else's expense. Rather, they're doing just well enough to keep on supplying the output that society wants them to supply. This situation is great for society, because it would be wasteful to pay entrepreneurs more than necessary to get them to do what society wants.

I discuss the second outcome of perfect competition — the fact that firms all end up producing output at the lowest cost possible — in the upcoming section "Graphing how profits guide firm entry and exit." This outcome is also good for society because it means that the least possible amount of resources are consumed while making the output that society wants produced.

Peering into the process of perfect competition

The previous section gives you an idea of how perfectly competitive markets emerge and how they benefit society. But how does perfect competition actually work? The following four steps explain:

1. **The market price of the output sold by every firm in the industry is determined by the interaction of the industry's overall supply and demand curves.**

2. **Each of the firms takes the market price as given and produces whatever quantity of output will maximize its own profit (or minimize its own loss if the price is so low that it's not possible to make a profit).**

3. **Because each firm has an identical production technology, each will choose to produce the same quantity and will consequently make the same profit or loss as every other firm in the industry.**

4. **Depending on whether firms in the industry are making profits or losses, firms will either enter or leave the industry until the market price adjusts to the level where all remaining firms are making zero economic profit.**

The fourth point in this process — firm entry and exit — is very important. To understand it clearly, let me break it into two cases, one where every firm in the industry is making a profit because the market price is high, and another where every firm in the industry is making a loss because the market price is low:

✔ **Attracting new firms by making profits:** If every firm in an industry is making a profit, new firms are attracted to enter the industry, too, in hopes of sharing the profits. But when they enter, total industry output increases so much that the market price begins to fall. As the price falls, profits fall, thereby lowering the incentive for further firms to enter the industry.

The process of new firms entering the industry continues until the market price falls so low that profits drop to zero. When that happens, the incentive to enter the industry disappears, and no more firms enter.

✔ **Losing existing firms when making losses:** If every firm in an industry starts out making losses because the market price is low, some of the existing firms exit the industry because they can't stand losing money. When they do, total industry output falls. That reduction in total supply, in turn, causes the market price to rise. And as the market price rises, firms' losses decrease.

The process of firms leaving and prices rising continues until the remaining firms are no longer losing money.

As I explain in the previous section, the fact that firms can freely enter or leave the industry means that after all adjustments are made, firms always make a zero economic profit. In other words, if there is perfect competition, you don't have to worry about firms exploiting anyone; they just barely make enough money to stay in business.

The other important result of perfect competition — that competitive firms produce at minimum cost — becomes apparent if we flesh out the four-stage process of perfect competition by using the cost curves that I explain in Chapter 10. If you haven't read that chapter, this section may cause your eyes to cross (and you know what your mother said about the dangers of crossing your eyes). I encourage you to take a look at Chapter 10 before moving on to the next section.

Graphing how profits guide firm entry and exit

In this section, I use the firm cost curves that I introduce in Chapter 10 to demonstrate how market forces automatically cause firms to produce output at the lowest possible cost. To make this process clear, I present two cases. In the first, firms begin by making profits. In the second, firms begin by making losses. Either way, adjustments happen so that they end up making zero economic profits and producing at minimum costs.

Visualizing firm entry when there are profits

To see how an industry adjusts when it starts off making profits, look at Figure 11-10, which consists of two graphs. The one on the left gives the market demand curve, *D,* and the initial market supply curve, *S$_o$,* for tennis balls. The one on the right gives the cost curves for one of the many identical firms that make tennis balls.

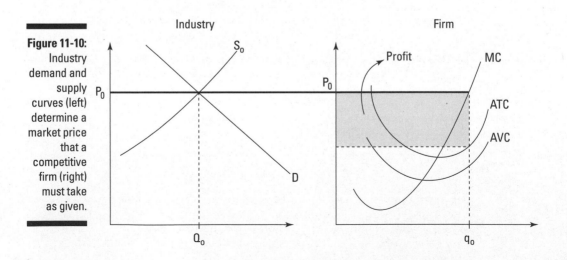

Figure 11-10: Industry demand and supply curves (left) determine a market price that a competitive firm (right) must take as given.

Industry

Firm

Because the firms in this industry are identical, they all have the same cost structures. In particular, they all have the same marginal cost curve (*MC*). This point is important because, as I show in Chapter 10, a competitive firm's marginal cost curve is its supply curve.

The firm in our example takes the market price, P_o, that's determined by supply and demand in the left graph and uses it to figure out its profit-maximizing output level in the right graph. (To emphasize that P_o is the same in both graphs, I've drawn a solid horizontal line that goes all the way across both graphs.)

As I show in Chapter 10, each firm chooses to produce the output level at which the horizontal price line intersects the *MC* curve. In the right-hand graph, I label the output level q_o. In the left-hand graph, you can see that the industry's total supply is Q_o. The industry's total supply is simply each individual firm's output, q_o, times the total number of firms in the industry.

Next, focus on the fact that each firm runs a profit when the market price is P_o. The profit is shown by the shaded rectangle in the right graph. (I explain these profit rectangles in — where else? — Chapter 10.)

This profit is important because it attracts entrepreneurs to enter the industry. They realize that they can set up yet more identical firms and make some nice profits. As economists like to say, profits attract entrants.

Seeing how new entry reduces profits

Figure 11-11 shows what happens when the new entrants to the industry arrive. Their new production increases overall production so that the total supply curve shifts from S_o to S_1 in the left-hand graph. That lowers the market equilibrium price from P_o to P_1.

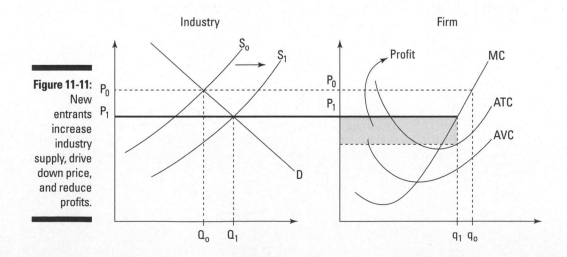

Figure 11-11: New entrants increase industry supply, drive down price, and reduce profits.

Each of the price-taking firms reacts to the lower price by producing a lower output level, q_1, which you can see illustrated in the right-hand graph. More importantly, the firms' profits decrease, which you can see by comparing the shaded profit rectangles in Figures 11-10 and 11-11.

The new entry results in smaller profits. The smaller profits are less attractive to entrepreneurs. So while there will still be new entry caused by the fact that some profits are still available, there won't be as much new entry as when profits were larger.

Seeing how enough entry drives profits to zero

What ends up happening, in fact, is that entry continues until prices fall so far that all profits are driven away. This situation is illustrated in Figure 11-12, in which new entry has increased supply still more, to S_2. The result is that the market price falls to P_2, which results in zero profits. (Note that there's no shaded profit rectangle in the right-hand graph.) Because profits fall to zero, entry ceases.

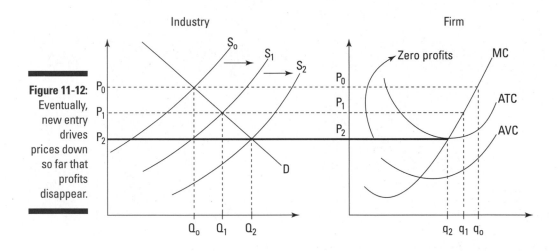

Figure 11-12:
Eventually, new entry drives prices down so far that profits disappear.

Realizing that zero profits also means minimum cost production

When profits are driven to zero by the entry of new firms, the cost per unit at which output is produced is minimized. You can see this fact in the right-hand graph of Figure 11-12 by noticing that when faced with price P_2, firms choose to produce at the quantity that minimizes per-unit production costs.

You can tell this is true because the output that firms choose to produce, q_2, lies exactly at the minimum point of the U-shaped average total cost curve (*ATC*). When output is produced at that level, the average cost per unit is lower than at any other output level. (In other words, any other output level results in a higher average total cost.)

This is an astonishingly wonderful thing because it means that each firm is being as efficient as possible, producing output at the lowest possible cost per unit. Moreover, each firm is voluntarily choosing to produce at that level without any need for coercion.

What's going on here is that profits serve as a self-correcting feedback mechanism. High profits automatically attract new entrants who automatically increase supply and drive prices down. That process continues until there are no more profits and no more new entrants. But more importantly, it continues until each and every firm is producing output at the most efficient, least-cost output level. This is truly Adam Smith's invisible hand at work.

Visualizing firm exit when there are losses

A similar feedback mechanism leads to zero profits and efficient production if the industry starts out making losses. To see this, take a look at Figure 11-13, where the initial supply curve, S_3, interacts with the demand curve, *D,* to produce a very low market price of P_3.

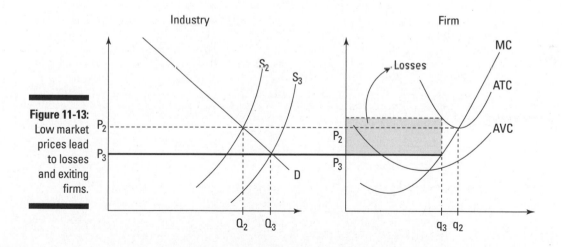

Figure 11-13: Low market prices lead to losses and exiting firms.

At this market price, you can see in the right-hand graph that each firm in the industry is making a loss, which is shown by the shaded rectangle.

This loss discourages all the firms in the industry, and those in the weakest financial condition begin to exit. As that happens, the industry supply curve in the left-hand graph shifts left (because supply decreases). That shift raises the market price and reduces the losses made by firms remaining in the industry. But as long as there are losses, firms continue to exit until the supply curve moves all the way back to S_2, at which point the market price is P_2, and firms are making zero profits as in Figure 11-12.

When the market price reaches P_2 and firms are making zero profits, firm exits stop and, more importantly, each firm is producing at the least-cost output level, q_2.

Understanding that entry and exit don't happen instantly

You've now seen that market pressures always push perfectly competitive firms to produce at the lowest possible per-unit cost. Keep in mind that this nice result doesn't happen overnight. When firms are making profits or sustaining losses, it takes time for new firms to enter (if there are profits) or for existing firms to leave (if there are losses).

Depending on the industry, these adjustment processes may take anywhere from a few weeks to a few years. For example, setting up new power plants takes a while because building a new power plant takes at least a year. Similarly, even if agricultural prices fall and farmers are making losses, those farmers who drop out of the industry won't do so until the next growing season. On the other hand, if producing U.S. flags suddenly becomes really popular, you can be sure that scores of new firms will pour into the industry within weeks.

The wonderful thing about perfect competition is that there are always market forces acting to drive firms to produce at the minimum possible cost. As I show you in the next few chapters, this lovely result falls apart when monopolies, oligopolies, public goods, and other problems prevent or preclude perfect competition.

Chapter 12

Monopolies: How Badly Would *You* Behave If *You* Had No Competition?

A firm that has no competitors in its industry is called a *monopoly*. Monopolies are much maligned because their profit incentive leads them to raise prices and lower output in order to squeeze more money out of consumers. As a result, governments typically go out of their way to break up monopolies and replace them with competitive industries that generate lower prices and higher output.

At the same time, however, governments also very intentionally create monopolies in other situations. For instance, governments issue patents, which give monopoly rights to inventors to sell and market their inventions. Similarly, many local services like cable television and trash collection are also monopolies created and enforced by local government.

In this chapter, I explain why society forbids monopolies in some situations and promotes them in others. First, I show you that profit-maximizing monopolies compare unfavorably with competitive firms because they set higher prices and produce less output than competitive firms. Then, I explain how these problems may, in certain cases, be outweighed by other factors — the need to promote innovation, for example, and the odd fact that in some cases having a lot of competitors is just too annoying.

This is interesting stuff, so I expect to have a monopoly on your attention! (You have my permission to groan now.)

Examining Profit-Maximizing Monopolies

Essentially, this chapter is one big exercise in cost–benefit analysis. Monopolies aren't all evil. Neither are they utterly good. Whether you want to have one in any particular instance depends on whether, in that situation, the benefits outweigh the costs.

This section goes into detail about the costs associated with monopolies. When we finish our cost analysis, we move on to the benefits of monopolies. By the end of the chapter you'll understand why society ruthlessly forbids monopolies in some industries while enthusiastically endorsing them in others.

Zeroing in on the problems monopolies cause

In an industry that has only one monopoly firm rather than lots of small competitive firms, three socially harmful things occur:

- ✔ The monopoly firm produces less output than firms in a competitive industry would.

- ✔ The monopoly firm sells its output at a higher price than the market price would be if the industry was competitive.

- ✔ The monopoly's output is produced less efficiently and at a higher cost than the output produced by firms in a competitive industry.

While all these things are harmful to consumers, it's important to keep in mind that monopolies don't do these things to be jerks. Rather, these outcomes are simply the result of monopolies acting to maximize their profits — which is, of course, the very same thing that competitive firms try to do.

Consequently, the difference in outcomes between a competitive industry and a monopoly industry doesn't have anything to do with bad intentions. Rather, it results from the fact that monopolies are free from the pressures that lead competitive industries to produce the socially optimal output level (see Chapter 11). Without these pressures, monopoly firms can increase prices and restrict output to increase their profits — things that competitive firms would also love to do but can't.

The lack of competitive pressure also means that monopoly firms can get away with costly, inefficient production. This is a real problem that you should take seriously when considering whether the benefits of a monopoly outweigh its costs. I talk more about this issue later in the chapter.

Identifying the source of the problem: Decreasing marginal revenues

All the bad outcomes generated by a monopoly derive from the same source: Unlike a competitive firm that faces a horizontal marginal revenue curve, the monopolist faces a downward-sloping marginal revenue curve. (*Marginal revenue* is the increase in total revenue that comes from selling each successive unit of a product; see Chapter 10.) This simple fact causes monopolies to charge more, produce less, and produce at higher costs than competitive firms.

How could one little curve cause such mayhem? A downward-sloping marginal revenue curve implies that each additional unit that the monopoly sells brings less revenue than the previous unit. For instance, while the 10th unit sold may bring in $8, the 11th brings in only $3. Obviously, such a situation reduces the incentive to produce a lot of output.

This situation also stands in stark contrast to the marginal revenue situation facing competitive firms. As I explain in Chapter 11, competitive firms face horizontal marginal revenue curves, meaning that whether they sell 11 units or 11,000, each unit brings in the same amount of money. Naturally, that's much more of an inducement to produce a lot of output.

Facing down demand

Why is there such a difference between the marginal revenue curves facing monopolists and competitive firms? A monopoly is free to choose the price it wants to charge along the demand curve it faces for its product. A competitive firm, on the other hand, has to take the market price as given (as I explain in Chapter 11).

A monopoly firm can choose its price because, by being the only firm in its industry, it controls all the output in that industry. As a result, it can create a relatively high price by producing only a few units, or it can induce a relatively low price by flooding the market. By contrast, each firm in a competitive industry is such a small part of its industry that its choice of output makes too small a difference in total output to cause price changes. (See Chapter 11 for more on why competitive firms can't affect prices.)

The monopolist's ability to control the price by altering its output level means that it has to step back and consider what output level to produce. Obviously, because its goal is profit maximization, it has to figure out what level of output will maximize its profits.

It turns out that a monopolist's profit-maximizing output level is defined by the same condition as that of a competitive firm: Produce at the output level where the marginal revenue curve crosses the marginal cost curve.

So the first step in figuring out how much a monopoly will produce is to figure out what its marginal revenue curve looks like. When you do, you can see where that curve crosses the monopoly's marginal cost curve to figure out how much it will produce.

Deriving marginal revenue from the demand curve

A monopoly's marginal revenue curve has a precise relationship with the demand curve for the monopoly's output. The marginal revenue of each successive unit of output is less than the marginal revenue of the previous unit of output because demand curves slope downward. If the demand curve is a straight line, the slope of the marginal revenue curve is twice as steep as the slope of the demand curve, meaning that marginal revenue falls quite quickly as output increases.

To see how this works, take a look at Figure 12-1, which draws out a demand curve and its associated marginal revenue curve.

Figure 12-1:
The *MR*
curve for a
monopolist
facing a
straight-line
demand
curve has a
slope twice
as steep as
that of the
demand
curve.

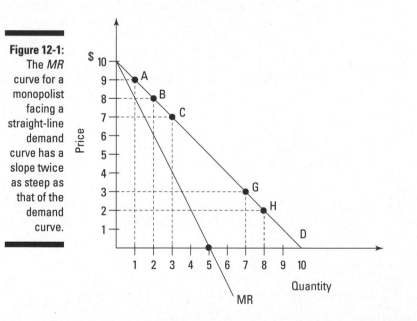

I provide the data needed to draw these two curves in Table 12-1. The first column contains different output levels ranging from zero to ten units. The second column shows the price per unit that can be charged at each output level. The third column shows the total revenue that the monopoly would get for producing and selling each output level — the price per unit times the number of units. And the final column gives the marginal revenue — the change in total revenue — that happens as you increase output by one unit.

Table 12-1	Price and *MR* for Various Output Levels on the Figure 12-1 Demand Curve		
Output	**Selling Price**	**Total Revenue**	**Marginal Revenue**
0	10	0	
			9
1	9	9	
			7
2	8	16	
			5
3	7	21	
			3
4	6	24	
			1
5	5	25	
			−1
6	4	24	
			−3
7	3	21	
			−5
8	2	16	
			−7
9	1	9	
			−9
10	0	0	

To make it clear that marginal revenue represents the change in total revenue, the entries in the marginal revenue column are displayed between the two total revenue figures to which they correspond. For instance, total revenue increases from $0 to $9 as you move from producing no output to one unit of output. That's why I place the marginal revenue of $9 at the top of the marginal revenue column, between the total revenue entries of $0 and $9.

As you see in Figure 12-1, the marginal revenue (*MR*) curve starts at the same point as the demand curve, but it falls with twice the slope. It hits the horizontal axis at an output level of $q = 5$ instead of the $q = 10$ output level at which demand hits the horizontal axis (where q stands for quantity produced).

Relating marginal revenue to total revenue

You can get a handle on why the marginal revenue curve falls so quickly if you first examine total revenue, or *TR*. The total revenue that the monopolist can get is simply the output it produces times the price at which it can sell its output. That is, $TR = p*q$. However, the price at which a monopolist can sell depends on how much it produces.

The relationship between output produced and the price at which it can be sold depends on the demand curve. For instance, consider point *A* on the demand curve in Figure 12-1. At that point, one unit is being produced, and it can be sold for $9. Consequently, the total revenue at that point is $9. Next, look at point *B,* at which two units of output are being sold. At that output level, each unit can be sold for $8. Consequently, total revenue is $8*2 = $16. And at point *C,* where three units can be sold for $7 each, total revenue is $21.

The important thing to notice is how total revenue changes as you move from *A* to *B* to *C* and output increases from one to two to three units. Total revenue goes from $9 to $16 to $21. Obviously, total revenue increases.

But look more deeply. Moving from *A* to *B, TR* increases by $7 (from $9 to $16). But moving from *B* to *C,* it increases by only $5 (from $16 to $21). Each successive increase in total revenue is smaller than the previous increase.

Increasing production, decreasing marginal revenue

Because marginal revenue is defined as the change in total revenue that happens as you increase production by one unit, the phenomenon I describe in the previous section is the same thing as saying that marginal revenue declines as the monopoly increases production.

If you look at Table 12-1, you can see that marginal revenue continues to fall for each successive unit. In fact, it becomes negative for all units after the fifth. You can see why by looking at points *G* and *H* in Figure 12-1 as examples. At point *G,* the monopolist can sell seven units of output for $3 each. That makes for a total revenue of $21. But if he increases output to eight units at point *H,* he can sell these units for only $2 each, implying a total revenue of $16.

Increasing output from seven units to eight units means decreasing total revenue from $21 to $16. That's the same thing as saying that marginal revenue is *negative* $5 as you move from seven to eight units of output.

Sliding down the demand curve: Higher output, lower prices

The reason marginal revenue keeps declining and even becomes negative is that the demand curve slopes downward, meaning that the only way to get people to buy more stuff is to offer them a lower price. You have to offer them a lower price not just on additional units, but on all previous units as well.

In other words, if the monopolist wants to sell only one unit (see point *A*), he can get $9 for it. But if the monopolist wants to sell two units (see point *B*), he has to lower the price down to $8 per unit for *both* the first unit *and* the second unit.

Because total revenue equals price times quantity ($TR = p*q$), you can see that the monopolist faces a tradeoff as he increases production and slides down the demand curve. As he produces more, q obviously goes up, but p must fall. What happens to TR depends on whether the increases in q (output effects) are bigger than the decreases in p (price effects).

You can see from Table 12-1 that as the monopoly increases production through the first four units, total revenue keeps increasing, meaning that the gains from selling more units more than offset the declines from getting less money per unit. At an output of five units, the two effects cancel each other. And for higher outputs, total revenue falls because the negative effect of less money per unit overwhelms the positive effect of selling more units.

Because marginal revenue tells you how total revenue changes as you increase output, the changes in TR caused by increasing output show up in MR as well. If you look at Figure 12-1, you can see that MR is always declining. That's because the negative price effect of getting less per unit keeps getting stronger and stronger relative to the positive quantity effect of selling more units.

As I note earlier in the chapter, for straight-line demand curves like the one you see in Figure 12-1, the MR curve is a straight line that has twice as steep a slope as the demand curve. If you know calculus, you can prove that the MR curve falls twice as fast as the demand curve by taking the equation of the demand curve shown in Figure 12-1, $p = 10 - q$; substituting it into the total revenue equation, $TR = p*q$; and then taking the first derivative with respect to output, q. Because marginal revenue is dTR/dq, you'll find that $MR = 10 - 2q$, meaning that MR has the same vertical intercept as the demand curve but twice as steep a slope.

Now that you've seen the marginal revenue situation facing a monopolist, you can combine it with his marginal cost curve to figure out his profit-maximizing output level. As I'm going to show you, this level is less than that chosen by a competitive firm — a behavior that leads to a social harm that can be quantified using the method of deadweight losses that I explain in detail in Chapter 11.

Choosing an output level to maximize profits

A monopoly is no different than a competitive firm when it comes to the costs of producing output. Just like a competitive firm, a monopoly has fixed costs, variable costs, and marginal costs (see Chapter 10). More importantly, these costs all behave in exactly the same way whether a firm is competitive or a monopoly. This means you can use costs to help analyze the decision-making process of a monopoly in the same way that you use them to analyze the decision-making process of competitive firms.

The key difference, however, is that the monopoly faces a downward-sloping marginal revenue curve. As I'm about to show you, this factor causes a profit-maximizing monopoly to produce less output than would a profit-maximizing competitive firm.

Setting MR = MC for a monopoly

The monopoly goes about maximizing profits in much the same way as a competitive firm. To see this, take a look at Figure 12-2, which draws a monopoly's average total cost (*ATC*) and marginal cost (*MC*) curves on the same graph as the monopoly's demand curve and marginal revenue (*MR*) curve.

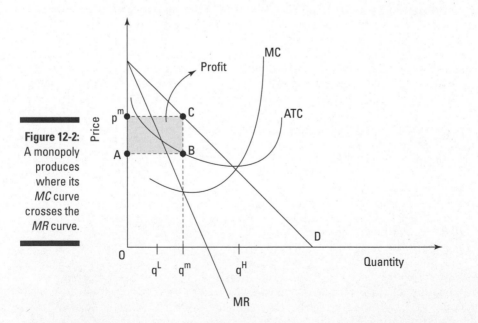

Figure 12-2:
A monopoly produces where its *MC* curve crosses the *MR* curve.

As I explain in Chapter 10, for every output level, *q,* the *ATC* curve gives the average total cost per unit of producing *q* units of output. This curve is U-shaped because average total costs first fall due to increasing returns and then increase due to diminishing returns. The marginal cost curve gives the cost of producing one more unit of output; that is, it tells you how much total costs rise if you increase output by one unit.

As Figure 12-2 illustrates, the profit-maximizing monopolist's optimal output level, q^m, is determined by where the *MR* and *MC* curves cross. As with a competitive firm, choosing to produce where marginal revenues equal marginal costs (*MR* = *MC*) either maximizes profits or minimizes losses, depending on whether demand is strong enough for the firm to be able to make a profit (see Chapter 10).

The reason that q^m is optimal can be seen by looking at two different output levels, q^L and q^H, where *L* stands for low and *H* stands for high:

- **Low output:** At output level q^L, you can go up vertically to see that *MR* at that output exceeds *MC*, meaning that if you produce and sell that unit, it will bring in more in revenue than it costs to produce. Clearly, this is a good unit to produce. Because a similar relationship holds true for all output levels less than q^m, the monopolist should keep increasing output until it reaches q^m.

- **High output:** On the other hand, the monopolist does not want to increase output beyond q^m. To see why, examine output level q^H. At that output level, marginal costs are much bigger than marginal revenues, meaning that if you produce that unit of output, the cost of producing it will exceed the money you could get selling it. In other words, if you produce that unit, you'll lose money.

So, as you can see, the monopolist wants to produce exactly q^m units because for all units up to q^m, marginal revenues exceed marginal costs, meaning that you receive more money selling such units than you spend producing them.

Figuring out what price to charge

To figure out what the price of each unit of output should be, use the demand curve. Move up vertically from the monopolist's profit-maximizing output level to the demand curve, and then head sideways. In Figure 12-2, you can see that at output level q^m, the monopolist can charge price p^m.

Eyeing the monopoly's profit

In Figure 12-2, the profit that the monopolist makes is shown by the shaded rectangle with corners at *A*, p^m, *C*, and *B*. As I discuss in Chapter 10, such profit rectangles are derived by comparing the two rectangles that give, respectively, total revenues and total costs.

The basic trick is to remember that the area of a rectangle is defined as a product — the product of its length times its width. For the monopolist maximizing profits by producing q^m units and selling them for p^m dollars, total revenue is price times quantity ($TR = p^m * q^m$). Consequently, total revenue is the area of the rectangle whose length is equal to the price and whose width is equal to the quantity. That is, *TR* is the area of the rectangle that has corners *O, p^m, C,* and *q^m*.

You can derive a total cost rectangle by first realizing that total costs are also a product — a product of the average cost per unit times the number of units. If you go up vertically from point *q^m* until you hit the *ATC* curve, you get to point *B*. The vertical distance up to point *B* gives the average cost per unit of producing output *q^m*. So if you multiply that amount by the output *q^m*, you get total costs. Geometrically, that means that total costs are given by the rectangle whose corners are *O, A, B,* and *q^m*.

In Figure 12-2, the total revenue rectangle (*O, p^m, C, q^m*) is bigger than the total cost rectangle (*O, A, B, q^m*), meaning that the monopoly is earning a profit. That profit is given by the shaded rectangle whose points are *A, p^m, C,* and *B*, which represents the difference in areas between the total revenue and total cost rectangles.

Understanding that monopoly doesn't guarantee profitability

Just because a firm has a monopoly doesn't mean that it's guaranteed a profit. If demand is too weak, prices will be too low to make any money.

To see an example of this situation, look at Figure 12-3, where I've drawn a situation where there is very low demand. The new demand curve, *D₁*, leads to a lower marginal revenue curve, *MR₁*.

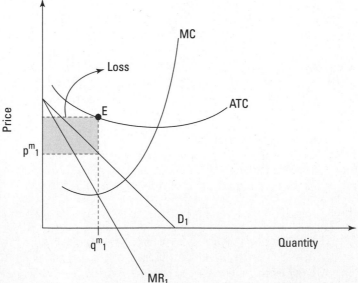

Figure 12-3:
A monopoly facing weak demand can sustain a loss. Being a monopoly does not guarantee a profit.

The monopoly again sets marginal revenue equal to marginal cost to find the optimal output level, $q^m{}_1$. But because of weaker demand, the monopoly operates at a loss represented by the area of the shaded rectangle.

One way to see that the shaded rectangle gives a loss is to compare the total revenue rectangle with the total cost rectangle, as I do for Figure 12-2 in the previous section. In this case, the total cost rectangle exceeds the total revenue rectangle by the amount of the shaded rectangle.

A different way to understand where the loss comes from is by comparing the monopoly's average total cost per unit with the price per unit it gets when producing and selling at output level $q^m{}_1$. At that output level, the price per unit, $p^m{}_1$, is found by starting on the horizontal axis at $q^m{}_1$ and then going up vertically to the demand curve. As you can see, you have to go up even farther to get to the *ATC* curve, meaning that the average total cost per unit to make $q^m{}_1$ units exceeds the price per unit you get from selling these units. This fact implies that the firm will lose money producing at output level $q^m{}_1$.

As I show in Chapter 10, a firm in such a situation can't do any better. That is, any other output level besides $q^m{}_1$ would produce an even bigger loss. If the monopoly can't figure out a way to either reduce costs or increase demand, it will quickly go bankrupt.

So keep in mind that even if you're the only seller in an industry, low demand may mean that you cannot cover your production costs and make a profit.

Comparing Monopolies with Competitive Firms

So far in this chapter, we've examined how a monopoly acts in order to maximize its profits. I now want to compare a profit-maximizing monopoly with a profit-maximizing competitive firm. This comparison comes off very badly for the monopoly because, as I explain in Chapter 11, competitive firms deliver socially optimal output levels. Because monopolies always end up producing less than competitive firms, their output levels are always less than socially optimal.

Looking at output and price levels

Monopolies produce less than competitive firms because they have different marginal revenue curves. As I show earlier in the chapter, monopolies face downward-sloping marginal revenue curves. By contrast, competitive firms face horizontal marginal revenue curves.

You can see the comparison in Figure 12-4, where I've drawn in both the downward-sloping marginal revenue curve of a monopoly, MR^m, and the horizontal marginal revenue curve of a competitive firm, MR^C. The graph also has an average total cost curve, ATC, as well as a marginal cost curve, MC.

Figure 12-4:
If a monopoly and a competitive firm have the same cost structure, the monopoly produces less, which causes a deadweight loss.

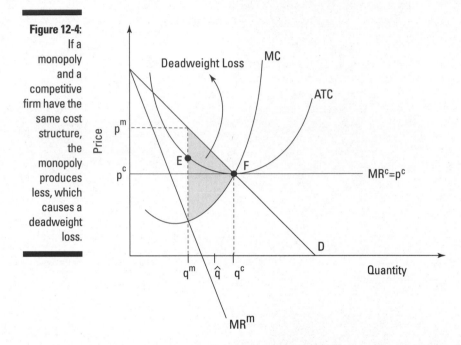

Figure 12-4 assumes that the competitive firm and the monopoly have the same cost structure, which is why I show only one MC curve and one ATC curve. By assuming that both firms have the same cost structure, I can isolate the effect that the difference in marginal revenue curves has on each firm's output decisions.

Maximizing profits for each firm

As I explain in Chapter 11, the marginal revenue curve for a competitive firm, MR^C, is a horizontal line set at the market price, p^C. This is the case because a competitive firm is such a small part of its industry that it can't affect the market price. As a result, it can sell as many or as few units as it wants at p^C, meaning that the marginal revenue it gets for every unit it chooses to produce is p^C. As I show in Figure 12-4, $MR^C = p^C$ for a competitive firm.

In addition, I show in Chapter 11 that market forces adjust supply and demand until the market price is equal to the minimum average total cost at which a firm could produce. Geometrically, this means that the horizontal $MR^C = p^C$ line just touches the bottom of the U-shaped ATC curve.

As I note earlier in the chapter, monopolies and competitive firms follow the same basic rule to maximize profits: They each produce where their marginal revenue curve intersects their marginal cost curve. But because they have different marginal revenue curves in Figure 12-4, they produce different outputs. The competitive firm produces q^C, while the monopoly produces q^m.

Understanding why the monopoly produces less

As you can see, the competitive firm produces more than the monopolist. This happens because the competitive firm doesn't have to worry about reducing its revenue per unit if it increases output. No matter how much it produces, it always receives $MR^C = p^C$ on every unit sold because its output is too small relative to total output to affect the market price.

By contrast, the monopolist faces the market demand curve, meaning that every additional unit it sells lowers the price per unit it receives on all units sold. Geometrically, this implies the downward-sloping MR^m that leads the monopoly to restrict output because it knows that the more it produces, the less money per unit it gets.

Because the monopoly restricts output compared to the competitive firm, the monopoly price, p^m, is also higher than the competitive price, p^C. This fact really irks consumers, but, as I'm going to show you, the real harm comes from the reduction in output.

Deadweight losses: <u>Quantifying</u> the harm caused by monopolies

Monopolies cause harm because they reduce output below the socially optimal level produced by competitive firms. Take another look at Figure 12-4, and consider whether it would be good for society if all the units of output between the monopoly output level, q^m, and the competitive output level, q^C, were produced.

For instance, look at unit $\hat{q}$. At that level of output, the demand curve is above the marginal cost curve. That implies that people are willing to pay more for that unit of output than it costs to make it. In other words, benefits exceed costs for that unit of output. Because this is true for all units between q^m and q^C, monopolies hurt society by failing to produce units of output for which benefits exceed costs.

The harm caused to society when the monopoly fails to produce output level $\hat{q}$ can be quantified by the vertical distance between the demand curve and the marginal revenue curve above output level $\hat{q}$. That vertical distance is a dollar amount — the number of dollars by which benefits would exceed costs for that unit if it was produced and consumed.

If we go through the same exercise for each and every unit between q^m and q^C, we can total up the harm caused by the failure of the monopoly to produce all of those units. Graphically, the total harm measured in dollars is equal to the area of the shaded deadweight loss triangle in Figure 12-4.

As I explain in Chapter 11, you get this triangle by thinking of all the vertical distances between the demand curve and marginal cost curve that lie above all the units of output between q^m and q^C. All these little vertical distances shade in the deadweight loss triangle, which sums up the dollar losses that result when the monopoly restricts output.

The deadweight loss triangle demonstrates that when monopolies restrict output in order to maximize their profits, they fail to produce units for which benefits exceed costs. That harms society. The next section shows that the decision to restrict output also drives up production costs.

Focusing on efficiency

Another problem with monopolies is that they are not efficient producers. You can see this by again looking at Figure 12-4.

Competitive firms produce at output level q^C. If you go up vertically from that output level to the *ATC* curve, you end up at point *F,* which happens to lie at the very bottom of the U-shaped *ATC* curve. As I explain in Chapter 10, competition leads competitive firms to produce at the output level that puts them at the bottom of the U-shaped *ATC* curve.

That output level minimizes production costs per unit of output, which you can see by comparing q^C with any other output level. Whether you produce more or less than q^C, average costs per unit will be higher due to the U shape of the *ATC* curve.

In particular, look at the monopoly output level, q^m. If you go up vertically from that output level to the *ATC* curve, you get to point *E.* Because the vertical distance between the horizontal axis and *E* is longer than the vertical distance between the horizontal axis and point *F,* you know for certain that total costs per unit when producing the monopoly output level, q^m, are higher than those when producing the competitive output level, q^C. Consequently, a monopoly firm produces output at a more costly output level than does a competitive firm.

This bad result is yet another manifestation of the fact that monopolists face downward-sloping marginal revenue curves. A competitive firm has an incentive to increase output all the way to q^C because doing so lowers per-unit production costs and can thereby increase profits. The same incentive exists for a monopolist, but it's more than offset by the reduction in revenue that would happen if the monopoly firm increased its output. As a result, the monopolist's profits are maximized at q^m even though q^C is the lowest-cost output level.

Considering Examples of Good Monopolies

So far in this chapter, I have shown you that compared to a competitive firm, a monopoly produces too little at too high a cost and turns around and sells it for too much money. Given these three bad things, you may simply want to say, "Three strikes — you're out!" and get rid of monopolies altogether. But if you did, you'd be acting a bit too hastily. In some cases, the benefits of monopolies outweigh their costs.

Encouraging innovation and investment with patents

The most obvious place where monopolies do society a lot of good is patents. Patents give inventors the exclusive right to market their inventions for 20 years, after which time their inventions become public property. That is, patents given inventors the right to run a monopoly for 20 years.

The reason monopolies are so important in this context is that without them, an inventor is unlikely to ever see any financial reward for her hard work because copycats will steal her idea and flood the market with rip-offs, thereby collapsing the price. Consequently, in a world without patents, far fewer people would bother to put in the time, effort, and money required to come up with new inventions.

To remedy this situation, nations all over the world offer patent monopolies to inventors. The result is faster innovation, much more rapid economic growth, and much faster increases in living standards. Indeed, it's hard to think of any more socially beneficial monopoly than patents.

Reducing annoyingly redundant competitors

Societies have also stepped in to create monopolies in situations where competition means annoying redundancies. Consider the following examples:

- **Trash hauling:** Garbage trucks are extremely loud and annoying. If one company has a monopoly on hauling trash, you have to endure a loud, annoying truck only once per week. But if, say, seven different trash-hauling companies compete, you may have to endure one each day if you and six of your neighbors each choose to use a different company that picks up on a different day of the week.

- **Cable television:** If ten different cable TV companies compete for your business, neighborhoods must have ten different sets of cable TV wires running through them — at much greater expense than running just one set of wires.

✔ **Natural gas:** Laying the pipes that deliver natural gas is expensive, and laying down multiple grids of gas pipe in one area would be wasteful.

Consequently, most towns and cities have decided that there will be only one trash-hauling company, one cable TV company, and one natural gas company. Each company is given a monopoly and is then regulated to make sure that it doesn't exploit customers. (See the upcoming "Regulating Monopolies" section.)

Keeping costs low with natural monopolies

Another place where society may decide it's better to have a monopoly rather than competition is in the case of what economists refer to as *natural monopoly industries,* or *natural monopolies.*

An industry is a natural monopoly if one large producer can produce output at a lower cost than many small producers. A good example is electric power generation. Due to engineering constraints, a ten-megawatt power plant can produce energy for far less than a one-megawatt power plant.

To see how this leads to a natural monopoly, imagine a situation in which a town that needs ten megawatts of power is initially served by ten of the small, one-megawatt power plants. But then a big corporation comes along and builds a ten-megawatt power plant. Because it can produce at a lower cost than the smaller, less efficient plants, the big plant offers lower prices and steals all the customers — meaning that the smaller plants quickly go bankrupt.

Such an industry is called a *natural monopoly* because it naturally becomes dominated by a single, low-cost producer. The perplexing problem here for policymakers is what to do with a natural monopoly.

On one hand, everyone welcomes the fact that the big plant is much more efficient: It burns less fuel and causes less environmental damage. But because it has crushed all competition, people now have to worry about the new monopoly charging high prices and producing less than the socially optimal output level.

These conflicting good and bad points typically mean that governments allow the natural monopoly to stay in business as the only firm in its industry, but at the same time they regulate it so that people don't have to worry about high prices or low output levels. By doing so, society gets the benefits brought by the most efficient production method without having to worry about the problems that would otherwise result if the monopoly was left unregulated.

Regulating Monopolies

Governments have to decide when to support and when to suppress monopolies. For instance, patents support an inventor's monopoly right to produce and sell her invention for 20 years. After that, the production and sale of the invention is thrown open to competition.

In other situations, various regulatory institutions have been developed either to destroy a monopoly by breaking it apart or to regulate it after deciding to let it continue to be the only firm in its industry. In this section, I present several of these regulatory schemes and explore what they do to improve the behavior of monopolies.

Subsidizing a monopoly to increase output

I establish earlier in the chapter that a profit-maximizing monopoly produces less than the socially optimal level. In particular, the profit-maximizing monopoly in Figure 12-4 produces where its downward-sloping marginal revenue curve, MR^m, intersects its upward-sloping marginal cost curve, MC. This output level, q^m, is less than the socially optimal output level that would be produced by a competitive firm, q^C.

One way to get the monopoly to produce more is to subsidize its production costs so that the marginal cost curve in effect shifts down vertically. Doing so causes the marginal cost and marginal revenue curves to meet at a higher level of output. And if the subsidy is big enough, the monopoly can be induced to increase output all the way to q^C.

Some governments use this type of subsidy to get gas, electric, and phone companies to serve more people, especially poor people. If the monopoly firms' costs of hooking up customers are subsidized, the firms are willing to hook up more customers than they would without the subsidy.

Some people object to subsidizing a monopolist, so this sort of solution isn't necessarily the most popular politically. But it is effective in increasing output.

Imposing minimum output requirements

Another way to get a monopoly to produce more is simply to order it to produce more. For instance, in many areas telephone companies are required to provide basic telephone service to everyone — even to people who cannot pay for it themselves. (The idea is to make sure that everyone is able to call for help if they have an emergency.) The same is often true of companies that provide heating in the winter; in some jurisdictions, you can't turn off someone's heat for nonpayment of bills.

Minimum output requirements can force a monopoly to produce the socially optimal output level. They are often very politically popular because many people think of monopolists as evil and exploitative and don't mind seeing them ordered to produce more.

Any forced increase in output also means a reduction in the monopoly's profit. Therefore, such programs are also popular because many people consider a monopoly's profits to be ill-gotten given the fact that the firm doesn't have to compete to earn them.

Regulators have to be careful, however, not to bankrupt the monopolies that they are regulating. Depending on a monopoly's cost curves, it's quite possible to force a monopoly to produce at an output level where it loses money. Because regulators don't want to bankrupt monopolies and thereby deny consumers access to the goods or services they produce, regulators are careful to take a monopoly's cost structure into account when considering minimum output requirements.

Regulating monopoly pricing

Perhaps the most common way to regulate a monopoly is to set the price at which it can sell each and every unit of output that it produces. This approach works because it changes the monopoly firm's marginal revenue curve from sloping downward to being horizontal. Therefore, it eliminates the monopoly's usual problem that the more it sells, the less it can charge per unit.

However, as with quantity requirements, regulators have to pay close attention to a monopoly's cost structure when choosing the regulated price so they don't bankrupt the monopoly.

To see the problem facing the regulator, consider the monopoly whose cost curves are given in Figure 12-5. Left unregulated, the monopoly will choose to produce the profit-maximizing output level q^m, defined by where MR crosses MC. From the demand curve, you can see that it will be able to charge price p^m per unit for that amount of output. (For more on the behavior of an unregulated monopoly, see the earlier section "Choosing an output level to maximize profits.")

Next, think about how a regulator might want to modify the monopoly's behavior. For instance, a well-intentioned regulator might want to get the monopoly to produce every single unit of output for which benefits exceed costs. Looking at Figure 12-5, you can see that she would want to get the monopoly to produce output level q^{mc}, defined by where the downward-sloping demand curve intersects the MC curve.

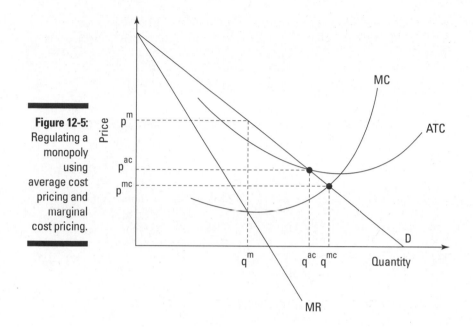

Figure 12-5:
Regulating a
monopoly
using
average cost
pricing and
marginal
cost pricing.

As I explain in the earlier section "Deadweight losses: Quantifying the harm caused by monopolies," it's socially beneficial to produce each unit up to and including q^{mc}. That's true because, for each unit, what people want to pay to consume it (given by the vertical distance from the horizontal axis up to the demand curve) exceeds the marginal cost of producing it (given by the vertical distance from the horizontal axis up to the MC curve).

As a result, the regulator will set the price at p^{mc}. At that price, the demand curve tells us that consumers will want to purchase q^{mc} units of output. Better yet, the monopoly will want to supply that level of output because the marginal revenue from selling each unit exceeds the marginal cost of producing it.

There is, however, a big problem with this policy given this particular monopoly's cost structure: The monopoly will go bankrupt. That's because at output level q^{mc}, the firm's total costs will exceed its total revenues.

You can see this problem on a per-unit basis by noting that the average total cost per unit at output level q^{mc} (given by the vertical distance from the horizontal axis up to the ATC curve) is more than the regulator-imposed revenue of p^{mc} per unit. Because average total costs per unit exceed revenues per unit, the monopoly will be operating at a loss. And unless the regulator relents and allows a higher price, the monopoly will eventually go bankrupt unless the government steps in to subsidize the firm by giving it a cash grant equal to the amount of its loss.

The method of regulation I just described is called *marginal cost pricing* because the regulated price, p^{mc}, is set where the marginal cost curve crosses the demand curve. But because this method can cause a monopoly to lose money, a more common alternative is *average cost pricing,* which sets the regulated price where the average total cost curve (*ATC*) intersects the demand curve.

In Figure 12-5, a regulator using average cost pricing would set the price at p^{ac}. At that price, you can see from the demand curve that consumers demand q^{ac} units of output. The monopoly is happy to supply that output level because for each and every unit up to q^{ac}, marginal revenue (the regulated price per unit, p^{ac}) exceeds marginal cost — meaning that the monopoly gains financially by producing each and every one of these units.

The main benefit of this system is that you don't have to worry about the monopoly going bankrupt (or where to get the money to subsidize a monopoly that would go bankrupt under marginal cost pricing). Average cost pricing guarantees that the monopoly will break even.

You can see this fact by comparing the average total costs per unit at output level q^{ac} with the revenue per unit at that output level. You get the average total cost per unit by going up vertically until you hit the average total cost curve. Because that vertical distance is equal to the regulated price per unit, p^{ac}, you know that the average total costs per unit are equal to the regulated price per unit — so the firm must be breaking even.

The downside to average cost pricing for this monopoly is that all the socially beneficial units between q^{ac} and q^{mc} don't get produced. On the other hand, the only way to keep this monopoly in business to produce those units if you imposed marginal cost pricing would be to subsidize it. Using average cost pricing eliminates any worries associated with providing subsidies. In particular, you don't have to worry about any potential harm that you may cause when raising the taxes that have to be imposed somewhere else in the economy in order to subsidize the monopoly.

Breaking up a monopoly into several competing firms

Finally, another solution to the problem of a monopoly is to destroy it by breaking it up into many competing firms. In the United States, the most famous case of this solution was the division of American Telephone and Telegraph Corporation (AT&T) into a bunch of smaller competitors in 1984.

Before 1984, AT&T was a nationwide monopoly. If you wanted to make a telephone call anywhere in the United States, you had to use AT&T because it was the only telephone company in the country. It was highly regulated, with both quantity requirements to provide everyone a phone and price requirements that encouraged it to provide a high quantity of telecommunication services. But it was still a monopoly, and a judge ruled in 1984 that it should be broken up into numerous local firms in order to foster competition.

The policy change worked extremely well. There was soon a very competitive market for telephone services between firms that had been part of AT&T. And more recently, the telephone service industry has become even more competitive due to the arrival of cellphone companies, Internet telephony companies, and even cable TV companies offering phone services. This robust competition eliminates the problems associated with monopolies and ensures that telecommunication services are provided at low cost and in large quantity.

Creating competition is also a handy way to deal with a monopoly because it eliminates the costs associated with having to continually monitor a regulated monopoly. As I explain in Chapter 11, competition gets you to the socially optimal output level without any sort of central control. That stands in stark contrast to regulated monopolies, which typically require expensive bureaucracies to develop and enforce laws and regulations.

Chapter 13

Oligopoly and Monopolistic Competition: Middle Grounds

Chapters 10 and 12 examine in detail the two most extreme forms that an industry can take: perfect competition with many small competitive firms, and monopoly where there's only one firm (and hence no competition). This chapter concentrates on two interesting intermediate cases.

The first possibility is an oligopoly, an industry in which there are only a small number of firms — two, three, or a handful. The word itself is Greek for "few sellers." A diverse group of industries looks like this, including soft drinks, oil production, and video game machines. For instance, Coke and Pepsi dominate the soft drink market, vastly outselling other carbonated beverages. Similarly, just three or four countries produce the majority of the world's oil. And just three companies produce and sell virtually all the video game consoles used in the world.

Oligopoly industries are interesting because, depending on specific circumstances, the firms can either compete ruthlessly with each other or unite to behave almost exactly like a monopoly would. This means that in some cases oligopolies can be left alone because competition ensures that they produce socially optimal output levels, while in other cases government regulation is needed to prevent them from acting like monopolies and behaving in socially undesirable ways.

The second type of intermediate industry is one where you find *monopolistic competition* — a sort of hybrid between perfect competition and monopoly. The key thing that sets firms in this type of industry apart from firms in a perfectly competitive industry is *product differentiation* — the fact that each firm produces a slightly different product than the others.

This chapter starts with a detailed look at oligopolies and the decisions that firms in this type of industry have to make. I then move on to monopolistic competition and show why product differentiation doesn't necessarily translate into tidy profits.

Choosing to Compete or Collude

In industries where only a few firms operate, firms have a choice about whether to compete or cooperate. This situation is very different from perfect competition, which I discuss in Chapter 11.

In perfectly competitive markets, there are so many firms, and each firm is such a small part of the market, that their individual outputs don't have any effect on the market price. As a result, competitive firms just take the market price as given and adjust their output levels accordingly to make as large a profit as possible.

Realizing that oligopoly firms interact strategically

However, in a market in which there are only a few sellers, each one produces enough of the total output to be able to affect the market price. For instance, two major producers of cola-flavored sodas operate in the United States: Coke and Pepsi. These two corporations produce such large fractions of the total output that if either one were to suddenly increase supply, the market price of cola-flavored soda would drop dramatically. An increase in output made by one company will cause the price to decrease for other companies in the market as well.

In other words, if Pepsi produces twice as much of its product and literally floods the market, the price of Pepsi will drop dramatically. But because most people aren't 100 percent loyal to one brand or the other, if the price of Pepsi drops dramatically, a lot of regular Coke drinkers are going to switch brands and drink Pepsi. In turn, the price of Coke will drop, too.

Pepsi and Coke are involved in a situation where each of their supply decisions affects not only their own sales but those of their competitor as well. Economists refer to such situations as *strategic situations* because the firms involved have to decide what type of strategy to pursue. In particular, they have to decide whether to compete or collude:

- ✔ If they collude, they will jointly cut back on production in order to drive up prices and increase their profits.

- ✔ If they compete, they will both try to increase production in order to undercut each other on price and capture as many customers as possible.

Comparing the outcomes of competition and collusion

These two strategies, compete or collude, lead to hugely different outcomes for both producers and consumers:

- ✔ For producers, collusion is better than competition because it leads to profits that last as long as the firms keep colluding.

- ✔ For consumers, collusion is worse than competition because it leads to higher prices and lower output.

Seeing these results, you may assume that government intervention is called for in order to protect consumers from collusion. But such intervention is needed only if firms actually collude.

A fascinating thing about the real world is that collusion doesn't happen in a lot of industries where you would expect it to. For instance, Coke and Pepsi are fierce competitors that spend hundreds of millions of dollars a year on advertising to try to steal each other's customers.

Similarly, most cities have only a handful of competing cellphone companies. But instead of colluding, they compete so ruthlessly that many of them are constantly flirting with bankruptcy. The same holds true for the airline industry, where bankruptcies are routine.

The big question that economists have to answer is, "Why do we see so little collusion in industries where you would expect more of it?" The next few sections show you how economists respond.

Cartel Behavior: Trying to Imitate Monopolists

A group of firms that colludes and acts as a single coordinated whole is known as a *cartel*. Because a cartel acts essentially as one gigantic firm, it effectively turns a bunch of individual firms into a single big monopoly.

This fact makes understanding the profit-maximizing behavior of a cartel easy, because it's just like that of a monopoly. In fact, you can see what a cartel wants to do by looking at the figures in Chapter 12, which illustrate what a monopoly likes to do.

In particular, a profit-maximizing cartel will choose to produce the monopoly's profit-maximizing output level of q^m units shown in Figure 12-2. Producing that output level maximizes the cartel's collective profit, which is shown as the shaded area of Figure 12-2. And better yet for the cartel, that monopoly profit will persist as long as the participating companies keep cooperating and producing a combined output of q^m.

Coordinating a cartel is hard work

Unfortunately for the firms in the cartel, it's often very difficult to get all the firms to coordinate so they are collectively producing the monopoly output level, q^m. To get the individual firms to cooperate and produce exactly q^m units of combined output, you have to get them to agree about two related things:

- **How to share the profits:** Obviously, every firm wants as large a share as possible.

- **Output quotas:** The firms must agree, and abide by, how much of the total output (q^m) each firm will produce. Each firm will constantly be tempted to produce more than its quota because doing so would bring higher revenues.

Examining OPEC to see the difficulties of collusion

The difficulties of meeting these two requirements are illustrated by the OPEC oil cartel. OPEC stands for *Oil Producing and Exporting Countries*. Although OPEC is a dull name, it's a very lively group that includes Saudi Arabia, Iraq, Venezuela, Nigeria, Kuwait, Indonesia, and several other key oil exporting nations.

Together, these nations control the vast majority of the world's oil supply, meaning that they occupy an oligopoly industry with only a few firms. Because there are only a few firms, they have a chance to form a cartel and try to produce the monopoly output and make monopoly profits. Do they succeed?

On the whole, no. I say "on the whole" because while it's true that they do negotiate agreements about oil production, these agreements are constantly broken. For instance, suppose that the monopoly output level that would maximize OPEC's collective profit is 20 million barrels per day, and at that output level the price of oil would be $60 per barrel.

To achieve that combined output, OPEC has to agree on each country's production quota. For instance, Saudi Arabia may get to produce 4 million barrels per day while Venezuela may have a quota of only 2 million barrels per day, leaving the other 14 million barrels per day to be split up among the other member countries.

Unfortunately for OPEC, there's no way to enforce the quotas. In particular, there's no way to stop Venezuela from pumping more than its 2 million barrels per day and selling the excess onto the world oil markets. Nearly all the OPEC countries cheat and overproduce.

The reason they do so is because the high price of oil is just too tempting. For instance, if all the other countries obey the agreement and drive up the price of oil, Venezuela will find it very tempting to produce more than its quota because each additional barrel it produces will bring in lots of money.

Unfortunately, this same temptation faces each country, so nearly all of them overproduce their quotas. The increase in supply caused by all their cheating floods the market and reduces the price to well below what the countries could have received if they had stuck to their respective quotas.

Put slightly differently, cartels have self-destructing incentives. To the extent that they work and create monopoly profits, they create temptations for cartel members to cheat. In the case of OPEC, these temptations are so strong that OPEC has only occasionally been able to act as an effective cartel.

In the next section, I go over a game theory model called the *Prisoner's Dilemma,* which gets to the heart of why firms in cartels cheat and why, in many cases, it's nearly impossible to stop them from doing so.

Understanding the Prisoner's Dilemma Model

The behavior of cartels and their incentive to cheat is best understood by applying to cartels a very famous game theory model known as the *Prisoner's Dilemma*.

Game theory is a branch of mathematics that studies how people behave in strategic situations — situations in which their actions or anticipated actions are taken account of by other people who then modify their own actions accordingly.

For instance, chess and checkers are strategic situations because what I do on my current move changes what my opponent does in subsequent moves. Even more important, what I *think* my opponent will do in response to each of the moves that I may make right now helps me to choose the best thing to do. That is, I take into account how he will react to each of my possible actions before I decide the best thing to do.

Cartels are strategic situations, too, because each firm has to take into account what it thinks all the other firms are going to do before deciding what it should do. Consequently, game theory models are the best way to understand the motivations and temptations that guide the behavior of cartel members.

To keep matters simple, let's examine a *duopoly,* an industry in which there are only two firms. They have the opportunity to form a cartel, act as a monopoly would, and generate a monopoly profit which can then be shared. But will they? That all depends on whether either firm (or both) will cheat on the cartel agreement.

The best way to understand each firm's temptations is to first study the Prisoner's Dilemma, a game in which two criminal partners have to individually decide whether or not to cheat on an agreement they had previously made with each other to remain silent and not talk to the police about their illicit activities.

Fleshing out the Prisoner's Dilemma

Imagine that two criminals named Jesse and James have just robbed a bank. The police know this but don't have any hard evidence against them. Rather, their only way of getting a conviction is to get one or both of the bank robbers to confess to the crime and give evidence against the other.

Fortunately for the police, they do have some leverage because they managed to catch Jesse and James committing other unrelated, minor crimes. These other crimes carry with them a one-year jail sentence. The police are hoping to use the threat of a year in jail to get one or both of the bank robbers to implicate his partner in exchange for immunity from prosecution.

Jesse and James had both sworn to each other several days before that they'd never rat on each other, but let's see what happens when push comes to shove.

Comparing the payoffs of confessing or remaining silent

Following standard procedures, the police separate Jesse and James, questioning them in separate interrogation rooms. The police offer each of them the chance to give evidence against the other in exchange for immunity.

The problem for each man is that what happens to him depends not only on what he does but on what his partner does as well. Each man can trade a confession for immunity, but he gets the deal only if his partner doesn't confess at the same time in the other interrogation room.

Four outcomes are possible:

- ✔ If the men both keep their pact not to talk and neither confesses to robbing banks, each man will get only a year in jail for the minor offense.

- ✔ If Jesse confesses and agrees to give evidence against James while James remains silent, Jesse will go free because he cooperated with police, but James will get ten years for bank robbery.

- ✔ If James gives evidence while Jesse remains silent, James will go free while Jesse goes to jail for ten years.

- ✔ If both men admit to the crime, both will get five years in jail. Why five years each? If both confess, the police don't need to make such a generous deal; they don't need to give either man immunity in order to get evidence against the other. On the other hand, the police want to give each criminal an incentive to confess, so they send each man to jail for only five years instead of the ten years he'd get if he remained silent while his partner gave evidence.

Putting the payoffs into a matrix for easy comparison

Figure 13-1 contains a payoff matrix. It illustrates the outcomes in terms of jail time that each bank robber will receive depending on the decision that each man makes about whether to remain silent or confess.

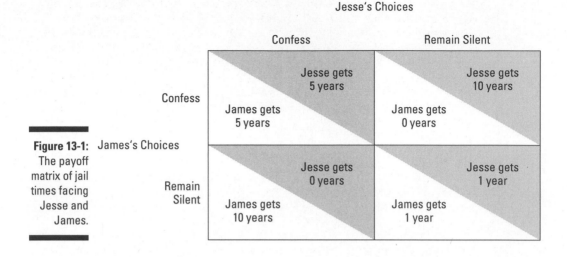

Figure 13-1: The payoff matrix of jail times facing Jesse and James.

The columns give each of Jesse's options, Confess or Remain Silent. The rows give each of James's options, which are the same. Each of the four rectangles in the grid shows the jail times that result from each of the four possible combinations of their individual decisions about whether or not to confess.

For instance, the upper-left rectangle represents what happens if both of them confess. It's divided diagonally in half, with Jesse's payoff of five years in jail given in the upper shaded triangle and James's payoff of five years given in the lower triangle. Similarly, the upper-right rectangle gives each of their payoffs if Jesse remains silent while James confesses: Jesse gets ten years in jail while James gets zero years because he gave evidence against Jesse.

Determining the dominant strategy for each prisoner

The Prisoner's Dilemma is famous because it illustrates the fact that the way the police have set up the potential payoffs, each criminal has an incentive to confess — no matter what the other criminal does.

For instance, concentrate on James. Should he confess or remain silent? Well, first examine which is the better option for him if his partner in the other interrogation room confesses. Looking at the left column of payoffs, you can see from the upper-left rectangle that if James confesses while Jesse confesses, James gets five years. On the other hand, the bottom-left rectangle tells you that if James remains silent while Jesse confesses, James gets ten years.

Clearly, the best thing for James to do if Jesse confesses is to also confess. But let's consider whether it's better for James to confess or remain silent when Jesse remains silent in the other interrogation room. Begin with the upper-right rectangle, which shows that if James confesses while Jesse remains silent, James will get zero years in jail. By contrast, the bottom-right rectangle tells you that if James remains silent while Jesse is also silent, James will get one year in jail. Clearly, if Jesse remains silent, the best thing for James to do is confess and get zero years in jail rather than one year.

In other words, it's *always* better for James to confess. If James confesses when Jesse confesses, James gets five years rather than ten. And if James confesses when Jesse remains silent, James gets zero years rather than one. So James should *always* confess no matter what Jesse is saying or not saying to the police in the other room.

Because the payoffs of confessing are always better for James than the payoffs of not confessing, confessing is referred to by game theorists as being James's *dominant strategy,* by which they mean superior strategy.

If you go through the payoffs from Jesse's perspective, you'll find that confessing is also Jesse's dominant strategy, because no matter what James is doing, the payoffs to Jesse if he confesses are always better than those from remaining silent.

Confessing is thus a dominant strategy for both players, meaning that you should expect both of them to separately confess. If they do so, they end up in the upper-left box of the payoff matrix, where they both get five years in jail.

Realizing that the dominant strategy leads to a lousy outcome for both players

The police, of course, want each criminal to separately confess and go to jail for five years, which is why they keep the prisoners apart and set up the payoffs in the way they do.

Jesse and James previously promised each other not to talk to the police, but the fact that payoffs are structured so that confessing is the dominant strategy puts them in a bind. Each man either keeps his promise and risks huge jail time if his partner confesses, or he breaks his promise in an effort to reduce his own potential jail time. This hard choice is why this situation is known as the Prisoner's Dilemma.

Typically, both men go with their dominant strategy and confess. But because both separately decide to confess, they each end up getting five years in jail — a much worse outcome than if they had both kept their promise to each other to remain silent. If they had both kept their promise, they each would have gone to jail for only a year. The logic of the dominant strategy is so compelling, though, that they each break the agreement and end up going to jail for five years rather than one.

As I show you later in the chapter, cartel members also face a Prisoner's Dilemma because they must decide whether to obey the cartel agreement (to reduce output to the monopoly level) or to cheat and overproduce. As you'll see, the temptation for cartel members to overproduce and break their cartel output agreement is just as strong as the temptation for prisoners to confess and break their agreement not to talk to the police.

Using omerta to resolve the Prisoner's Dilemma

I love the *Godfather* movies, but not for the acting or the scripts or the fact that I once got to meet their director, Francis Ford Coppola, while getting on a plane in Paris. Rather, my sick, geeky reason is because mafia movies illustrate a bloodthirsty but effective system that mobsters developed to prevent people from confessing.

The system is called *omerta,* which is Sicilian for "silence." Basically, what the mafia does is change the payoffs to the Prisoner's Dilemma so that the dominant strategy switches from confessing to remaining silent. The mob does this by explaining to their criminal members that if anybody talks to the police and confesses to anything or implicates anyone else, they're going to die.

This threat totally rearranges the payoffs to the Prisoner's Dilemma. Instead of just comparing jail times, as in Figure 13-1, prisoners now have to factor in death, as in Figure 13-2. If you look at Figure 13-2 carefully, you find that the dominant strategy for both players is now to remain silent because if either talks, the mafia will hunt him down and kill him no matter what the other guy does. The result is that both Jesse and James will go to jail for only one year each because they'll both keep their mouths shut.

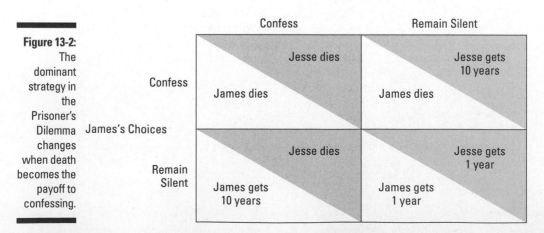

Figure 13-2: The dominant strategy in the Prisoner's Dilemma changes when death becomes the payoff to confessing.

Jesse's Choices

	Confess	Remain Silent
Confess	Jesse dies / James dies	Jesse gets 10 years / James dies
Remain Silent	Jesse dies / James gets 10 years	Jesse gets 1 year / James gets 1 year

James's Choices

Paradoxically, the death threat benefits the two criminals. Even though the threat of death is scary for both Jesse and James, it actually serves their individual interests because it means that they'll go to jail for only one year instead of five. If you're going to be a criminal, you want to be part of a criminal organization that has enough power to bully you around and keep you from defecting on your agreements with your fellow criminals.

This idea of a strong enforcer is crucial. You'll see in the following sections that one way to get a bunch of firms to stick to a cartel agreement is if the cartel sets up a strong threat against cheaters in the same way that the mafia threatens to kill anyone who breaks with the *omerta* agreement to never talk to the police.

Applying the Prisoner's Dilemma to Cartels

To see how the Prisoner's Dilemma applies to cartels, imagine a duopoly industry — an industry in which there are only two firms. Suppose the industry in question is the snack market in a town called South Park, and the only two makers of snacks are Cheezy Poofs, Ltd. and Snacky Smores, Inc.

The firms can either compete against each other aggressively or restrict supply to keep prices high and make big monopoly profits. To keep things simple, imagine that the managers of both firms think of their situation in terms of two prices that they could charge, $3 per bag or $2 per bag.

Figure 13-3 shows a payoff matrix for both firms depending on the choices each makes about which price to charge. The payoffs are given in terms of each firm's profits per day, with those of Snacky Smores given in the shaded areas.

Snacky Smores's Choices

	Charge $3	Charge $2
Charge $3	$1,000 per day for Snacky Smores $1,000 per day for Cheezy Poofs	$2,000 per day for Snacky Smores $500 per day for Cheezy Poofs
Charge $2	$500 per day for Snacky Smores $2,000 per day for Cheezy Poofs	$800 per day for Snacky Smores $800 per day for Cheezy Poofs

Cheezy Poofs's Choices

Figure 13-3: Each firm's profit depends not only on its own pricing decision but on that of the other firm.

For instance, in the upper-left rectangle, where both firms charge $3 per bag, they each earn a daily profit of $1,000. By contrast, if they both charge $2 per bag, their individual daily profits fall to only $800, as you can see in the bottom-right rectangle.

Obviously, if these two firms collude and charge $3 instead of $2 per bag, they can raise profits by $200 per day each. The joint monopoly profit that they can earn totals $400 per day ($200 each). Their problem is to effectively form a cartel that will, in fact, get them this monopoly profit.

Such a cartel will be hard to maintain because there will always be a temptation to cheat. For instance, the other two rectangles (the upper-right and bottom-left) show what happens if one firm charges $3 while the other charges $2. The firm charging $2 steals business away from the $3 firm and earns a much higher profit. Indeed, the firm charging $2 per day earns a profit of $2,000 per day while the firm charging $3 per day earns a profit of only $500 because it's losing business to its more cheaply priced competitor.

If you look at each firm's incentives, you notice that the dominant strategy for each firm is to charge the lower price, $2 per bag. To see this, look at Cheezy Poofs's payoffs. If Snacky Smores charges $3 per bag, the better thing for Cheezy Poofs to do is to charge $2 per bag. You can see this by comparing Cheezy Poofs's payoff of $1,000 per day in profits in the upper-left rectangle with its payoff of $2,000 per day in the bottom-left rectangle.

Similarly, if you look at the upper-right and bottom-right rectangles, you see that the best thing for Cheezy Poofs to do if Snacky Smores charges $2 per bag is to also charge $2 per bag. That's because Cheezy Poofs's profit will be $500 per day if it charges $3 per bag, while it will be $800 per day if it also charges $2 per bag.

What all this means for Cheezy Poofs is that no matter what Snacky Smores decides to charge, it's always better for Cheezy Poofs to charge only $2 per bag.

If you go through the rectangles, you find that charging $2 per bag is also Snacky Smores's dominant strategy no matter what Cheezy Poofs charges. The result is that both firms will always decide to charge $2 per bag — and they'll lose out on their chance to join forces, reduce output, drive up prices, and earn monopoly profits.

If both firms could somehow figure out a way to truly commit to selling at $3 per bag, they could end up in the upper-left rectangle and earn $1,000 per day each in profits. But without a way to commit, they're each going to follow their dominant strategy, charge $2 per bag, and end up in the bottom-right rectangle earning only $800 per day in profits. By failing to work together, they each lose $200 per day in profits.

Of course, this situation is great for South Park's consumers, who would much rather pay only $2 per bag for their snacks. So keep in mind that the dominant strategy of charging the lower price works toward the benefit of consumers and society at large. This fact is why society often doesn't have to bother regulating oligopoly industries. Thanks to the Prisoner's Dilemma, cartels very often fail to raise prices.

Seeing that OPEC is trapped in a Prisoner's Dilemma

The basic version of the Prisoner's Dilemma that I show you in previous sections is set up for just two people or two firms. But mathematicians have developed more advanced versions of the Prisoner's Dilemma that can be used to analyze the behavior of larger numbers of participants. These models are invaluable for understanding oligopoly industries with several firms and the incentives faced by firms in such industries when they try to form cartels. The basic conclusion of these multifirm models is that the dominant strategy is usually to cheat on cartel agreements.

This result goes a long way toward explaining why the OPEC oil cartel has a hard time when it tries to achieve its goal of raising oil prices by reducing oil production. Quite simply, cheating on OPEC cartel agreements is a dominant strategy for OPEC member countries.

To see how this works, you have to first understand that OPEC has meetings where it decides how much total oil should be produced and what fraction of that overall production should be done by each country. At the meetings, each country is given a *quota* — a maximum amount that it's supposed to produce. For instance, Saudi Arabia may be given a quota of 10 million barrels per day, while Venezuela may be given a quota of 1 million barrels per day.

The problems start after the meetings when all the oil ministers go home. Each country realizes that producing more than its quota is the best strategy no matter what the other countries do. For instance, Venezuela is better off producing more than its 1 million barrels a day quota no matter what the other countries do:

✔ If the other countries obey their quotas, Venezuela is better off producing more than its quota because it can sell lots of oil at a high price. (The high price is caused by the fact that the other countries are obeying their quotas.)

✔ If the other countries break their quotas and overproduce, the price of oil will be low, meaning that Venezuela should also overproduce its quota. There is no reason to obey the quota if prices are low due to everyone else's cheating.

Because each country faces the same temptation to overproduce its quota, the OPEC cartel doesn't typically work very well. Overproducing is a dominant strategy and is simply too tempting to resist given the payoffs.

Using an enforcer to help OPEC members stick to quotas

In the earlier section "Using omerta to resolve the Prisoner's Dilemma," I explain how the mafia uses death threats to get its members to never speak to the police. The death threats change the payoffs so much that the dominant strategy in the Prisoner's Dilemma switches from confessing to remaining silent.

In a similar fashion, OPEC could also benefit if it had some way of threatening its members if they violated their quotas. Because the member countries are sovereign nations, death threats aren't an option. Rather, Saudi Arabia has sometimes tried to provide an economic threat against quota violators.

The economic threat comes in the form of super low oil prices. Saudi Arabia is in the best position to make such a threat for two reasons:

- **It's the world's largest oil producer.** Saudi Arabia produces around 25 percent of the world's oil.

- **It's the world's lowest cost oil producer.** Saudi Arabia can produce profitably even if the price of oil falls down to $3 per barrel. (It's typically priced at around $30 to $40 per barrel, and other countries need a price of at least $10 per barrel to break even.)

These two facts mean that if other countries cheat on their quotas, Saudi Arabia could potentially increase its production so much that the price of oil would fall very low. For instance, suppose the price fell to $3 per barrel. Saudi Arabia would be the only OPEC member making a profit at that price; everyone else would be losing money.

As a result, Saudi Arabia appears to be in a position to threaten other OPEC members with bankruptcy if they violate their quotas. Unfortunately, the threat doesn't work that well in the real world.

The problem is that Saudi Arabia has limited pumping capacity. While Saudi Arabia may be able to produce an extra 10 or 20 percent more oil per day than it normally does, that much of an increase wouldn't be enough to drive the price down to $3 per barrel and bankrupt the other OPEC nations.

As a result, the Saudi Arabian threat isn't nearly strong enough to switch the dominant strategy from cheating on the quota to obeying the quota. And because OPEC has never figured out a way to effectively threaten quota violators, the cartel doesn't work very well.

Regulating Oligopolies

In previous sections, I explain why the Prisoner's Dilemma means that firms in many oligopoly industries have a hard time forming effective cartels. In some industries, however, cartels *are* effective at reducing output and raising prices. Typically, these are industries where one firm is large enough and powerful enough to truly threaten other firms with bankruptcy.

Dealing with dominant firms

In U.S. history, the Standard Oil Company run by John D. Rockefeller during the 19th century dominated an oligopoly industry. It controlled something like 90 percent of the oil sold in the United States, and if a competitor didn't do what Rockefeller wanted, he would simply bankrupt the other firm by offering oil at a ridiculously low price that the competitor couldn't match.

Rockefeller would lose money temporarily while taking this action, but by bankrupting the competitors who disobeyed him, he was able to convince the remaining firms to help him restrain output and make huge profits. Indeed, because Standard Oil exerted so much control, its industry was much more like a monopoly than an oligopoly.

Rockefeller's effectiveness, however, soon brought a governmental response. Standard Oil was broken up into dozens of smaller, independent oil companies, none of which was large enough and powerful enough to dominate its industry and enforce collusion the way that Standard Oil had.

Applying antitrust laws

In the 19th century, cartels were called *trusts* — for example, the Sugar Trust, the Steel Trust, the Railroad Trust, and so on. Therefore, laws that broke up monopolies and cartels were called *antitrust laws*. The most famous such law in the United States was the Sherman Anti-Trust Act, and most other countries have now passed similar legislation to break up monopolies and cartels.

A big problem with antitrust laws is deciding when to regulate oligopolies or break them up to promote competition. The first sign that there may potentially be a cartel is, of course, when you see only a few firms in an industry. But, because of the Prisoner's Dilemma, in some cases even a two-firm industry won't be able to form an effective cartel. Consequently, prosecutors typically have to do more than just show that there aren't many firms in an industry.

Typically, there has to be concrete proof of collusion. In other words, if one day every firm in an oligopoly decides without coordination to cut its output in half and thereby raise prices, that may not be illegal. But if even one e-mail from a manager of one firm to a manager of another firm is found saying that the firms should enter into a cartel, that is illegal and enough for a prosecutor to hang a case on.

In some cases, the industry will be broken up into even more firms to promote competition, but in others regulations may be installed that regulate the prices firms can charge or the quantities they can produce. The specific policy often depends intimately on the circumstances of the firms in the industry and what policymakers think will best promote the general welfare.

Studying a Hybrid: Monopolistic Competition

An interesting form of competition that's found in some industries has the odd name of *monopolistic competition*. In such industries, you find characteristics of both monopolies (see Chapter 12) and competitive firms (see Chapter 11).

Benefiting from product differentiation

Like competitive firms operating in free markets, industries featuring monopolistic competition have lots of firms competing against each other. But unlike the situation in competitive free markets where all the firms sell an identical product, in monopolistic competition each firm's product is slightly different.

Think of the market for gasoline. Any large city has dozens, if not hundreds, of gas stations — all selling gasoline that is pretty much the same. But if you look at each gas station with a little wider scope, you notice that each one provides a product that is at least slightly different from the product provided by the others.

For instance, some stations provide gas pumps that take credit cards, while others have free air pumps to fill car tires or soapy water to wash windows. And, crucially, each gas station is clearly differentiated from all the others because it has a unique location — something that's very important to people who live nearby.

Economists use the term *product differentiation* to describe the things that make each firm's product a little bit different from its competitors' products. The overall result of these differences is that they slightly decrease the intensity of competition. Your local gas station, for instance, may be able to get away with charging you one or two cents more per gallon than its competitors if it has nice facilities and the next closest competitor is several miles away.

On the other hand, there's still a lot of competitive pressure in the industry. While your local station may be able to use its unique characteristics to get away with charging you a little more, it couldn't charge you a lot more — if it tried to do that, you'd take your business to one of its competitors.

In a similar way, all the restaurants in your neighborhood have to worry about what the other restaurants are charging even if the others specialize in completely different cuisines. While you may be willing to pay 20 percent more for something exotic, you wouldn't likely be willing to pay 90 percent more. Product differentiation lessens, but does not eliminate, price competition.

Facing profit limits

You may think that because monopolistically competitive firms can use their unique characteristics to raise prices, they're guaranteed nice profit margins. After all, in pure competition where firms all sell the same product and have no way of differentiating themselves from their competitors, prices fall so low that firms end up earning zero economic profits (see Chapter 11). If monopolistically competitive firms can raise prices above the competitive price, it seems like a no-brainer that they should be guaranteed to make profits.

Unfortunately for them, this isn't the case.

As pointed out by Cambridge economist Joan Robinson during the 1930s, monopolistically competitive firms still face competition. In particular, they face the prospect that if they're making tidy profits, those profits attract new entrants to their industry. When the new entrants begin producing, they take business away from the established firms and ruin their previously tidy profits. In fact, new entrants continue to arrive until profits have been driven all the way back to zero.

Dealing with downward sloping demand

Robinson was able to show how this process works by slightly modifying the monopoly model that I introduce in Chapter 12. To see what she did, look at Figure 13-4, which shows a single monopolistically competitive firm initially making a profit. The figure shows the firm's marginal cost curve, *MC,* and average total cost curve, *ATC,* along with its demand curve, D_1, and the associated marginal revenue curve, MR_1.

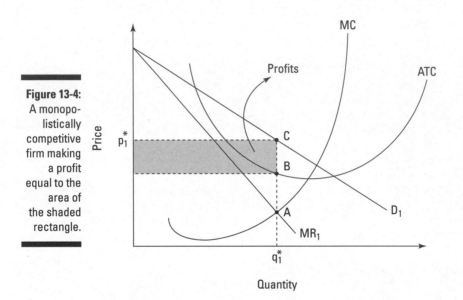

Figure 13-4:
A monopolistically competitive firm making a profit equal to the area of the shaded rectangle.

Because of product differentiation, the firm in Figure 13-4 faces the downward sloping demand curve, D_1. Its demand curve is downward sloping because, like a monopoly, it has some control over its price. Product differentiation means that it can choose whether to set a higher or lower price. At a higher price, the quantity demanded of its product falls because some customers will not think that the unique characteristics of the firm's product are worth the extra money. At a lower price, the quantity demanded increases because the lower price steals customers away from the firm's competitors.

By contrast, competitive firms that sell identical products have no control over the prices they set. As I explain in Chapter 11, because competitive firms sell identical products, the only thing that matters to consumers when choosing among them is who offers the lowest price. The result is that all firms have to sell at the same price, the *market price,* which is determined by where the overall industry supply curve crosses the industry demand curve. The demand curve for an individual competitive firm's product is a horizontal line at the market price (see Chapter 11). This stands in sharp contrast to the downward sloping demand curve facing the monopolistically competitive firm in Figure 13-4.

An important consequence of the downward sloping demand curve, D_1, is that the marginal revenue curve, MR_1, associated with demand curve D_1 is also downward sloping. Why is this so? The additional, or marginal, revenue that the firm can get from selling an additional unit of output is less than the marginal revenue it gets from selling the previous unit.

As I explain in Chapter 12, declining marginal revenue is a natural consequence of a downward sloping demand curve. Because the only way to get consumers to buy more of your product is to entice them with a lower price, the marginal revenue you get has to fall with every additional unit you sell.

The monopolistically competitive firm optimizes profits by choosing to produce at point *A,* where the downward sloping marginal revenue curve, MR_1, crosses the upward sloping marginal cost curve, *MC.* Producing the associated quantity, q^*_1, will either maximize the firm's profit (if it's possible to make a profit) or minimize its loss. Whether making a profit is possible depends on the position of the firm's demand curve — on how much demand there is for the firm's product.

In Figure 13-4, demand is strong enough that the firm makes a profit. You can see this by comparing the firm's average total cost per unit at output level q^*_1 with its selling price per unit at that output level. The average total cost per unit is found by going up vertically from the horizontal axis at output level q^*_1 until you hit the *ATC* curve at point *B.* The price per unit that the firm can charge at output level q^*_1 is found by going up vertically until you hit the demand curve at point *C.*

Because the vertical distance up to point *C* exceeds the vertical distance up to point *B,* you can immediately determine that the firm's selling price per unit exceeds the total cost of production per unit — meaning that the firm must be making a profit on each unit sold. The size of the firm's total profit on all units is the profit per unit times the total number of units sold, so its total profit is equivalent to the area of the shaded rectangle in Figure 13-4. The area of the shaded rectangle is the width of q^*_1 units times the height of the profit per unit — the vertical distance between points *B* and *C.*

Finding equilibrium: Firm entry and exit

What Joan Robinson realized was that this profit attracts new entrants to the monopolistically competitive industry. Each new entrant steals some business away from existing firms. Graphically, this means that the demand curve for any existing firm, like that of Figure 13-4, shifts down and to the left. At each possible price that the firm might charge, it sells fewer units than before because some of its old business has been stolen away by new entrants.

Furthermore, new entrants continue to enter the industry and move demand curves down and to the left until profits are driven all the way down to zero. Only then does the entry of new firms come to a halt.

You can see this sort of equilibrium in Figure 13-5. There, the demand curve has shifted left all the way to D_2, where it is just tangent to the *ATC* curve at point *B*. As the demand curve moves left, so does the marginal revenue curve, which now lies at MR_2. Consequently, when the firm optimizes its production level by producing where the *MC* curve crosses MR_2, it now produces at output level q^*_2.

Figure 13-5:
A monopolistically competitive firm makes zero profits after entry (or exit) has shifted its demand curve until it's tangent with its *ATC* curve.

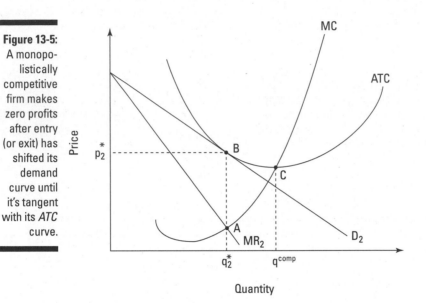

At this output level, profits are zero. You can see this by using the graph to show that the average total cost per unit of producing output level q^*_2 is equal to the price per unit that the firm can get selling those units. Go up vertically from the horizontal axis at point q^*_2 to point *B*. Because point *B* lies both on the demand curve, D_2, and the average total cost curve, *ATC,* the vertical distance from the horizontal axis at point q^*_2 to point *B* represents both the average total cost per unit as well as the price per unit that the firm can charge. They are equal, so the firm is making zero profits.

If for some reason the firms in a monopolistically competitive industry are making losses, some firms will exit the industry. As each of them exits, the remaining firms gain more business, and the demand curves for firms still in the industry shift up and to the right. Exit continues until you reach an equilibrium like that of Figure 13-5, in which all firms are making zero profits.

Producing inefficiently

A key thing to notice about the equilibrium in Figure 13-5 is that it implies that each firm produces less efficiently than would firms in a competitive industry. The best way to see this fact is to compare the monopolistically

Communism, Wendy's hamburgers, and product differentiation

One of the funniest TV commercials ever produced made its debut in 1987, at the height of Soviet communist power. It depicts a communist fashion show. A woman walks down the runway in a drab gray factory worker's uniform, and the announcer shouts out, "Day wear!" Then she marches down the runway again in the same outfit but this time holding a flashlight. The announcer shouts out, "Evening wear!" Next, she marches down the runway again — still in the same uniform — holding an inflatable beach ball. "Swimwear!"

The commercial made fun of the fact that the central planners who ran communist countries didn't care much about product differentiation.

They typically made only one design of any given product in order to be able to mass produce it at the lowest possible cost. The result was a society in which there was so much sameness that the Wendy's commercial was only a modest exaggeration.

The commercial helped to hammer home to U.S. consumers the idea that they should embrace the fact that the food produced by Wendy's was different from that produced by its main rivals, McDonald's and Burger King. Unlike the rigidly planned Soviet economy, free market U.S. capitalism allows for huge amounts of product differentiation.

competitive firm's output level when the industry is in equilibrium, q^*_2, with the output level that would be produced by a firm with the same cost curves that was operating in a fully competitive industry in which all firms sold an identical product. I've labeled this output level as q^{comp} in Figure 13-5.

In Chapter 11, I explain how market forces push competitive firms to produce at q^{comp}, and why it ends up being exactly the level of output at which the *ATC* curve hits its minimum — that is, q^{comp} is the output level at the bottom of the U-shaped *ATC* curve. The socially significant implication of this fact is that competitive firms produce at the lowest possible average total cost per unit. That makes them as efficient as possible in terms of production costs per unit.

By contrast, a monopolistically competitive firm operating in an industry where product differentiation allows it to have some control over the prices it charges ends up producing at a higher average total cost per unit. This is clearly the case in Figure 13-5 because the vertical distance from the horizontal axis up to point *B* is longer than the vertical distance from the horizontal axis up to point *C*. This fact means that firms in monopolistically competitive industries are not efficient in the way that firms in competitive industries are.

Some people look at this result and conclude that society would be better off if it could transform monopolistically competitive industries into competitive industries. But the cost savings may not be worth the loss of product differentiation.

After all, variety is the spice of life. Would you really want every single restaurant to be identical in every way, to serve the same food in the same type of room, under the same lights, with identical furniture? I certainly wouldn't want that. And if the cost of variety is that firms in monopolistically competitive firms produce their output at a higher cost than firms in competitive industries, I would typically be willing to endure those higher costs for the sake of having some variety.

But you have to decide for yourself whether you think the high costs of variety are worthwhile — and in what situations. While they may be worth it to you for restaurants, you may have a different feeling about the product differentiation found among gas stations.

Chapter 14

Property Rights and Wrongs

*I*n Chapter 11, I explain Adam Smith's *invisible hand* — the idea that even though individuals pursue their own interests, if you allow markets to allocate resources, the common good is achieved. Adam Smith was quite aware, however, that you achieve this nice result only if society's property rights are set up correctly before people start to trade goods and services in markets. In fact, he spent a good deal of his famous book, *The Wealth of Nations,* talking about how governments must properly define property rights if they want markets to yield to socially beneficial outcomes.

The gist of the problem is that if property rights are not set up correctly, a person won't fully take into account how his or her actions affect other people. For instance, consider two pieces of land. One is privately owned, while the other is wilderness land that nobody owns and everyone is free to use as they please. If you want to dump your trash on the privately owned land, you have to pay the owner for the right to do so. (In other words, the owner is running a trash dump.) But, like everyone else, you can dump trash for free on the wilderness land because nobody has the right to stop you.

Naturally, the difference in property rights with respect to the two pieces of land leads people to dump a lot more on the wilderness land because it's less costly personally to do so. But the problem is that while it's less costly personally, lots of costs are imposed on others because of the decision to dump on the wilderness land. For example, what could have been a very nice park is now a heap of rotting garbage. Bad property rights lead to bad outcomes.

In this chapter, I talk about positive and negative *externalities* — situations where one person's behavior results in either benefits or costs to other people, but where the property rights are so badly defined that the costs and benefits aren't properly accounted for. (Negative externalities result in such serious problems as pollution and global warming.) I also show you how most cases of endangered or extinct species are the result of nonexistent property rights, and how redefining property rights can save species from oblivion.

Allowing Markets to Reach Socially Optimal Outcomes

For markets to achieve socially optimal outcomes, they must take into account all the costs and benefits involved in any activity, regardless of who feels the effects of those costs and benefits. If markets do this, the demand curve captures all benefits, the supply curve captures all costs, and the market equilibrium quantity ensures that only units of output for which benefits exceed costs are produced.

Chapter 11 contains all the details about how supply and demand create socially optimal outcomes, but I want to offer a quick review here. Look at Figure 14-1, which shows a demand curve and a supply curve for ice cream. The market equilibrium quantity is q^*, and the market equilibrium price is P^*.

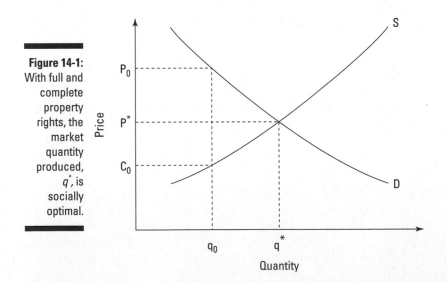

Figure 14-1: With full and complete property rights, the market quantity produced, q^*, is socially optimal.

The important thing to realize is that it's socially beneficial to produce every unit up to and including q^*. The reason for this can be seen by examining unit q_o. You can see from the demand curve that buyers are willing to pay price P_o for unit q_o, but it costs suppliers only C_o to produce unit q_o.

What does this mean? The overall happiness of society is improved by making unit q_o because it's clearly worth more to people to have it than the cost of the resources used in making it. Because the demand curve is above the supply curve for all units up to and including q^*, all those units are socially beneficial to produce.

As I explain in Chapter 11, the wonderful thing about markets is that supply and demand just happen to cause the socially optimal level of output, q^*, to be produced. The fact that this happens entirely as the result of people pursuing their own selfish interests is, of course, why markets are so amazing. It's as though the invisible hand of some kindly deity magically turns the pursuit of individual goals into a socially optimal outcome.

What I show you next is that this nice result happens only if property rights are *full and complete,* meaning that the demand curve captures all benefits that people are willing to pay for and the supply curve captures all costs associated with production. As you'll see, if property rights aren't full and complete, markets won't generate socially optimal output levels like q^*. In such cases, the invisible hand turns out to be *really* invisible — because it isn't there!

Examining Externalities: The Costs and Benefits Others Feel from Our Actions

Property rights give owners control over their property. For instance, I can paint my car any color I want. I can modify the engine or the tailpipe. I can even install big, shiny 19-inch wheels to try to disguise the fact that, like most economists, I'm not actually very hip.

On the other hand, property rights aren't totally unlimited. Society does restrict what I can do with my car. For instance, I can't be a source of noise pollution by removing the muffler. I can't drive it 90 miles per hour past an elementary school. And it's also illegal for me to play my 2,000-watt stereo at full volume late at night.

The reason I'm not legally allowed to do these things is because I don't live on an island by myself. Rather, I live in a community with many other people, and making lots of noise or driving really fast affects their quality of life. The way economists describe this situation is by saying that my actions cause *externalities*.

Defining positive and negative externalities

An *externality* is a cost or a benefit that falls not on the person(s) directly involved in an activity, but on others. Externalities can be positive or negative:

- ✔ A *positive externality* is a benefit that falls on a person not directly involved in an activity. Think of a beekeeper. She raises bees to sell the honey, but the bees also happen to fly around pollinating flowers for local farmers, thereby increasing their crop yields and providing them with a positive externality.

- ✔ A *negative externality* is a cost that falls on a person not directly involved in an activity. Think of a steel mill that, as a byproduct of producing steel, puts out lots of soot and smoke. The pollution is a negative externality that causes smog and pollutes the air breathed by everyone living near the factory.

Noting the effects of negative externalities

The key thing to understand about negative externalities is that goods and services that impose negative externalities on third parties end up being overproduced. The reason this happens is because negative externalities and the costs that they impose on others aren't taken into account when people make decisions about how much to produce.

Failing to take account of costs imposed on others

In the case of a polluting steel mill, the mill's managers take into account only their private costs of raw materials and running the plant. This happens because of the poor property rights regime that's in place.

If someone owned the atmosphere, the mill's managers would have to pay for the right to emit pollution. And if the atmosphere was owned by the people who would have to breathe in the mill's pollution, the firm would be forced to pay those people for the right to pollute and would be forced to take into account the harm that the pollution causes them.

But because nobody owns the atmosphere, and firms don't have to pay to pollute into it, there's no mechanism for making the mill's managers take into account the costs of pollution that fall onto members of the broader community. The result is that the firm overproduces steel.

Why does overproduction happen? In Chapter 10, I explain that a competitive firm's supply curve is equal to its marginal cost curve. Because the mill doesn't take into account the marginal costs that its production of steel imposes on others, its marginal cost curve (its supply curve) is too low and leads to an overproduction of steel.

You can see this situation in Figure 14-2, where I have drawn in two supply curves. The lower one is labeled *Private MC* because the firm's supply curve is its private marginal cost curve, which takes into account only the firm's own costs of producing steel.

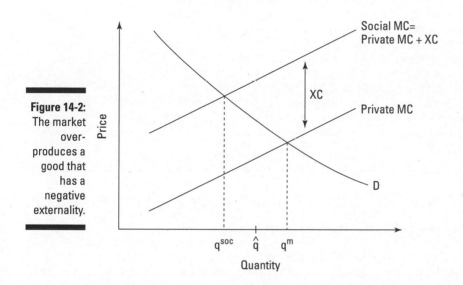

Figure 14-2: The market over-produces a good that has a negative externality.

The higher curve, however, takes into account not only the firm's private costs, but the external pollution costs, which I have labeled *XC* (for external costs). This higher curve is called the *Social MC* curve and is useful because it captures all costs associated with producing steel — both the firm's costs of making it and the costs imposed on others as negative externalities.

Overproducing things that impose negative externalities

So why is too much steel produced? The market equilibrium is where the demand curve, *D*, crosses the *private MC* curve. That equilibrium results in a quantity q^m of steel being produced, where *m* stands for market.

On the other hand, the socially optimal amount of steel to produce is q^{soc}, where *soc* stands for social. The socially optimal quantity is determined by where the *Social MC* curve crosses the demand curve. You can tell that q^{soc} is socially optimal because for every unit up to and including q^{soc}, the demand curve is above the *Social MC* curve, meaning that the benefits of producing these units exceed the costs of producing them. That's true when taking into account not only private costs but the external costs that fall on third parties as well.

The problem with producing all the units from q^{soc} up to q^m is that while the benefits do exceed the firm's private production costs, they don't exceed the total costs when you take into account XC, the cost of the negative externality.

For instance, look at output level $\hat{q}$, which lies between q^{soc} and q^m. You can see by going vertically up from $\hat{q}$ to the demand curve that the market price that people are willing to pay for that level of output does exceed the private marginal cost of producing it. (That is, the demand curve is above the *Private MC* curve at output level $\hat{q}$.) But if you go up even farther, you see that what people are willing to pay for that level of output is actually less than the total, social cost of producing that much output. (That is, the *Social MC* curve is higher than the demand curve at output level $\hat{q}$.)

Output level $\hat{q}$ shouldn't be produced because the total cost of producing it exceeds what anyone is willing to pay for it. That's why it's unfortunate that output level q^m is, in fact, produced in a market economy. Every unit of output produced in excess of output level q^{soc} is a unit for which the total costs exceed the benefits.

Realizing that you want positive amounts of negative externalities

A very important thing to realize is that the common reaction to negative externalities — Outlaw Them! — is almost never socially optimal. Look back at Figure 14-2 and note that the socially optimal output level q^{soc} is a positive number. That is, it's socially optimal to produce steel even though some pollution will be produced along with it.

To understand the intuition behind this fact, think about automobiles. Cars pollute. And the only way to totally get rid of their pollution is for society to totally ban cars. But do you really want to do that?

While it's true that big, gas-guzzling cars produce prodigious amounts of pollution without justifiable benefits, do you really want to get rid of all cars, including ambulances and fire trucks? Not at all, because while these vehicles do emit pollution, the costs imposed on society by the pollution are more than compensated for by their social benefits — the lifesaving activities in which the vehicles are engaged.

The same holds true for the pollution being produced by the steel factory at output level q^{soc}. The only way to totally eliminate the pollution from the steel factory is to shut it down. But that means removing from society all the benefits that steel can provide, such as earthquake-proof buildings and crash-resistant safety cages in automobiles.

The goal isn't to eliminate negative externalities. Rather, the goal is to ensure that when *all* costs and *all* benefits are weighed, the benefits from the units of output that are produced outweigh the costs of producing them — including the costs of the negative externalities. In Figure 14-2, for all units of output up to and including q^{soc}, the total benefits are at least as great as the total costs, meaning that society as a whole benefits if these units are produced.

The next thing to consider is how to make sure that only q^{soc} units are produced when, as I show you in the previous section, the market wants to over-produce goods with negative externalities.

Dealing with negative externalities

There are basically three ways to deal with negative externalities:

- ✔ Pass laws banning or restricting activities that generate negative externalities. For instance, most cities now forbid you to dispose of your trash by burning it.

- ✔ Pass laws that directly target the negative externality itself (rather than the underlying activity that leads to the externality). For instance, steel mills are now required to install smokestack scrubbers that filter out most of the pollution before it goes into the atmosphere.

- ✔ Impose costs, such as taxes, on people or firms generating negative externalities. For instance, governments can charge companies for each ton of pollution they emit.

The last of these three solutions is appealing to economists because it's the one that is most likely to lead to the production of the socially optimal output level.

You can see why economists like pollution taxes by looking back at Figure 14-2. Recall that *XC* is the external cost of the steel mill's pollution on others. If the government imposes a tax of *XC* dollars on every unit of steel produced by the firm, the tax raises the firm's cost curve up vertically from *Private MC* to *Social MC*.

Setting the pollution tax at exactly *XC* dollars causes the firm's marginal cost curve to lie exactly where the *Social MC* curve lies. Because a firm's marginal cost curve is its supply curve, the result is that when demand and supply now interact, the socially optimal output level q^{soc} is produced.

That is, by imposing exactly the right tax on steel, the government can sit back and let the market do the rest. That makes this sort of pollution-reducing policy attractive compared to other potential solutions.

Compare this solution with a system where firms are ordered to install smokestack scrubbers to reduce pollution. In such a system, you need to hire inspectors to constantly monitor factories to make sure they aren't cheating. This sort of system is much more costly to implement than simply imposing a tax on the mill's easily measured steel output and then letting supply and demand set the socially optimal output level.

On the other hand, it may be difficult to figure out exactly how big the tax XC should be, so the pollution tax solution isn't without problems, either.

Calculating the consequences of positive externalities

Externalities can be positive as well as negative. The key thing to understand about positive externalities is that goods and services that provide positive externalities to third parties end up being underproduced.

Underproducing things that provide positive externalities

To see why goods that have positive externalities are underproduced, consider a beekeeper named Sally. Sally raises bees so she can sell the honey and make some money. The people who buy her honey do so because the honey brings them utility when they eat it. But because Sally's bees go around pollinating the flowers of local farmers, these farmers also benefit from her beekeeping activities.

But — and here's the crucial point — the farmers don't pay Sally for the benefits that her bees bring them; the bees just fly in and out of their fields, and there's no way to keep track of them. The result is that Sally is going to raise fewer hives of bees than she would if the farmers were paying her for the benefits that her bees bring them.

You can see how this situation works in Figure 14-3. Sally's supply curve is her marginal cost curve, and I've labeled it $S = MC$. I've labeled the demand for her honey by the customers who pay for it as *Private Demand*. Where the supply curve and the *Private Demand* curve intersect gives the market equilibrium quantity of honey, q^m.

But this output level doesn't take into account the benefits that bees bring to farmers. Suppose that these benefits have a dollar value of XB, which stands for external benefits. Then the total social demand for Sally's honey is given by the *Social Demand* curve, which is the *Private Demand* curve shifted up vertically by XB dollars to take account of the fact that honey production benefits the farmers as well as Sally's honey-loving customers.

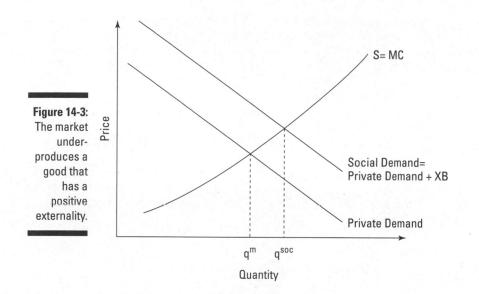

Figure 14-3:
The market under-produces a good that has a positive externality.

The socially optimal output level, q^{soc}, would be where the *Social Demand* curve crosses Sally's supply curve because for each unit of output up to and including q^{soc}, the total social benefit is at least as great as Sally's cost of production.

As you can see, the market equilibrium quantity produced, q^m, is less than the socially optimal output level, q^{soc}. In other words, because the market mechanism has no way of taking account of the positive externality, Sally produces less honey than is socially optimal.

Underproduction is typical for goods that generate positive externalities. Because property rights are set up in such a way that the recipients of the positive externalities don't have to pay for them, the producer of the good that generates the positive externalities has no incentive to provide extra units of output for the benefit of those receiving the externalities. Rather, she produces output only for people who can directly pay her for her product.

Subsidizing things that provide positive externalities

Because markets tend to underproduce goods and services that have positive externalities, people have come up with ways to encourage higher levels of production.

The most common way to encourage higher production of goods that generate positive externalities is with a subsidy. In the case of Sally's beekeeping business, the government may actually pay her a honey subsidy of, say, 20 cents per pound to encourage her to keep more hives. The result is more bees pollinating more flowers leading to higher output levels for the farmers. In fact, the government may even tax the farmers to get the money to subsidize Sally's honey. Doing so would make the program pay for itself.

Similarly, governments also often subsidize the planting of trees in and around cities. They must do so because many of the benefits of trees — shade, cooling, cleaner air, less soil erosion, and so on — are positive externalities that aren't taken into account by the markets. Without the subsidy, fewer trees would be planted than is socially optimal.

Taking in the Tragedy of the Commons

An important economic problem that results from poorly defined property rights that don't take account of negative externalities is referred to by economists as the *Tragedy of the Commons*. The following sections examine this problem in detail.

Having a cow: Overgrazing on a commonly owned field

To understand the Tragedy of the Commons, think of a farming town in which most of the land is privately owned. However, there is one large field of *common land* — land on which anyone can graze their cattle. We want to consider the difference between the number of cattle grazed on private land and the number grazed on common land.

In a private field, the owner has an incentive to limit the number of cattle that he puts out to graze. That's because if you put too many beasts in the field, they quickly eat up all the grass and ruin the field for later grazers. Consequently, the owner of a private field puts only a few cattle out to graze. Doing so reduces his short-run profits (because he restricts the current number of cows) but maximizes his long-run profits (because the field stays in good shape, and he can keep grazing cattle well into the future).

On the other hand, think about the incentives that people face when considering the publicly held field on which anyone can graze their cattle. Because the field is commonly owned, you don't have to pay for the right to put a cow out to graze. So everyone is going to want to put some cattle out there because the personal cost of doing so is nothing.

But because everyone is thinking the same thing, the field is soon overrun with cattle and ruined as they eat all the grass and turn it into a big, muddy mess. So while there's no personal cost to putting a cow out to graze on a common field, there *is* a social cost. Each additional cow causes damage to the field — damage that reduces the future productivity of the field.

The difference between what happens to the private field versus the common field is totally the result of the different property rights governing the two types of land. In the case of privately owned fields, farmers have an incentive to weigh the costs as well as the benefits of putting more cattle out to graze. In particular, they take into account how much future profits will be reduced if current overgrazing ruins the future usability of the field.

With the commonly held field, however, nobody has a personal incentive to preserve its future usability. In fact, the incentives are actually horribly perverse because if the common field is currently lush with grass, your incentive is to put as many of your own cattle out there as quickly as possible to eat up all the grass before the field is ruined. And because everyone else sees things the same way, there is a mad rush to put as many cattle out to graze as quickly as possible. The result, of course, is that the field is rapidly ruined — for everyone.

You can view the Tragedy of the Commons as a case of negative externalities. If I see lush grass on the common field, I rush to put out as many of my own cattle as possible without considering the damage that overgrazing will cause to the field. The same is true of everyone else. Nobody cares about the negative externality of a ruined field because no individual owns the field and personally suffers when it's ruined.

The nice thing about a privately owned field is that the owner does take into account the costs of ruining the field by overgrazing. And because he does, he won't overgraze.

Sleeping with the fishes: Extinctions caused by poor property rights

Many environmental problems are caused by Tragedy of the Commons situations in which nobody owns the property rights to a given resource. Notably, most animal extinctions are the result of an absence of property rights.

For instance, think of tuna swimming in the open ocean. By international treaty, nobody owns the open ocean. Hence nobody owns the tuna swimming in the open ocean.

On the other hand, if you catch a tuna and pull it up onto your boat, you then have a property right over it and can sell it for money. That is, the only way to economically benefit from a tuna is to kill it.

The result is that tuna and many other fish species are hugely over-fished, and many are near extinction. That's because each fisherman has the incentive to harvest as many fish as quickly as possible before anyone else can get to them. This quickly leads to an extinct species, and fishermen are very aware of the problem.

But because of the way that property rights are set up in this case, no individual fisherman can do anything to prevent the calamity. That's because if one guy decides to hold back and take fewer fish with the hope that by doing so the species will survive, someone else just comes in and catches the fish that he spared. The species will go extinct anyway. As a result, nobody has an incentive to hold back.

Economists look at problems like these and conclude that the only way to stop them is to change the property rights so that people can own a living fish as well as a dead fish. In particular, if you own a school of living tuna, your incentives are very different. You want to preserve the species rather than kill it off, because by preserving it and harvesting fish at a sustainable rate, you benefit not just this year but forever.

Consequently, when an economist sees a Tragedy of the Commons situation, his first instinct is to change the property rights system governing the resource in question. Instead of commonly held property rights in which each person has an incentive to take as much of the resource as possible before anyone else does, economists suggest private ownership so there will be an incentive to preserve the resource.

In the case of over-fishing, one solution has been to give fishermen private property rights to an entire fishing ground — that is, to all the fish in an area while they're still alive. That gives the new owners the proper incentive to manage the stock on a sustainable basis. Furthermore, because only one person has the right to fish in a given area, there's no longer a mad rush between competing fishermen to harvest as many fish as possible before anyone else can get to them.

For fish species that migrate freely between different areas, a different solution has been developed. In such cases, biologists first determine the maximum number of fish that can be sustainably harvested each year. The government then auctions off fishing permits for exactly that amount of fish.

This method prevents the Tragedy of the Commons by creating a new sort of property right — the fishing permit. It also has the nice benefit of creating a self-sufficient government program. The money raised from auctioning off the fishing permits can be used to hire game wardens to prevent unlicensed fishing, as well as for conservation and wildlife management programs.

Chapter 15

Market Failure: Asymmetric Information and Public Goods

· ·

· ·

Markets provide nearly everything that we consume. But markets also fail to provide many things that we'd *like* to consume. Economists refer to such situations as cases of market failure, and in this chapter, I discuss two of the most interesting and common causes of market failure: asymmetric information and public goods.

Asymmetric information is a situation in which either the buyer or the seller knows more about the thing they're bargaining over than the other party knows. The classic example is a high-quality used car: The owner who's trying to sell the vehicle knows all about the car's high quality and reliability, but the potential buyer can only take the owner's word for it.

Because the potential buyer has no reason to trust the seller's assertions that the car is really good, he assumes the worst and offers a low price just in case the car turns out to be a lemon. But because the owner knows that the car is of high quality, he rejects the low offer and the car goes unsold — all because there's no cheap and easy way to prove the car's high quality to the potential buyer.

Public goods kill off markets in a different way. That's because the very nature of a public good makes it extremely difficult for private sellers to charge users. The classic example is a lighthouse. Once it's up and running, it benefits all nearby ships, regardless of whether they pay for the service.

That being the case, each and every ship owner tries to avoid paying for the service in the hopes that somebody else will pay for it. But with everybody not paying in the hopes that somebody else will, the lighthouse soon goes bankrupt and society is denied a valuable service.

In the remainder of the chapter, I discuss these two causes of market failure further, show you how pervasive they are, and describe some of the clever solutions that people have come up with to remedy them. So don't expect any asymmetric information here — I'm going to make sure that you end up knowing everything I do.

Facing Up to Asymmetric Information

There are many situations in real life in which buyers and sellers don't share the same information. Depending on the situation, it may be the buyers or the sellers who are better informed.

For instance, when it comes to selling used cars, sellers are much more knowledgeable about the true quality of the vehicles than the buyers are. On the other hand, when it comes to health insurance, the buyers of the insurance policies are much better informed because they know all about their own bodies and how healthy they are.

Regardless of which party is better informed, situations such as these are referred to by economists as cases of *asymmetric information* because one side has more information than the other.

Realizing that asymmetric information limits trade

Asymmetric information is very important in the real world because it limits what markets can do. The fundamental reason is that if you know that the other guy is better informed, you're afraid that he'll use his information to take advantage of you.

In the case of used cars, buyers are afraid that sellers who know their cars are bad will keep that fact to themselves and try to negotiate high prices as if their cars were good. In the case of insurance, insurance companies are afraid that people who know they are high insurance risks will pretend to be low insurance risks so they can get lower rates.

Depending on how bad the asymmetric information gap is, markets may even collapse completely. That is, if you have huge worries that the seller of the used car may be exaggerating the value of the vehicle he's trying to sell you, you probably won't buy. That sounds like a reasonable thing to do, but it prevents the sale of good cars because everybody's worried about bad cars. Similarly, if insurance companies can't figure out a way to tell the good insurance risks from the bad insurance risks, they may charge high rates to everybody as though everyone is a high risk. And that, typically, causes the low risk people to not buy insurance because they know they're being overcharged.

So keep in mind that asymmetric information can lead to what economists call *market failure* — situations in which there's no market for a good or service. In this case, there's no market because people have been scared off by the fact that other market participants are better informed and may use that information to take advantage of them.

Souring on the lemons problem: The used car market

Berkeley economist George Akerlof got the Nobel Prize in Economics in 2002 for a famous paper he wrote called "The Market for Lemons." The paper is all about asymmetric information and market failure, and it was especially memorable because Professor Akerlof used the market for used cars as his primary example. (I hope you didn't think I was bright enough to come up with that example on my own. But if you did, bless you.)

The used car market is interesting because it suffers from an interesting form of market failure: Almost all the used cars for sale are lousy. What Akerlof correctly explained was that poor-quality vehicles, or lemons, dominate the market because asymmetric information drives away almost all sellers who want to part with high-quality used cars.

To make the intuition behind the result clear, imagine that there are only three kinds of used cars for sale: good, okay, and bad. They all look the same on the outside and even test-drive pretty much the same, but they have major differences in terms of how much longer they're going to last before the engine gives out. Because of the difference in engine quality and how long the cars are likely to last, the good cars are worth $15,000, the okay cars are worth $10,000, and the bad ones are worth only $5,000.

The problem that leads to market failure is the asymmetric information that exists between buyers and sellers. In particular, while each seller knows how good her own car's engine is, the buyers have no way of knowing.

Buyers could, of course, ask sellers to be truthful about the quality of their cars, and no doubt many sellers — probably most — would tell the truth. But there's no way to *know* if they're telling the truth. Consequently, when a particular seller tells you that her car is good, you're still going to be nervous about being cheated.

As I'm about to show you, this very reasonable fear causes nearly all good and okay cars to be withdrawn from the market. The result is a used car market that's dominated by bad cars; as Akerlof put it, the used car market ends up becoming "a market for lemons."

Seeing how quality used cars are driven from the market

Imagine that you want to buy a used car, but you don't want to overpay for it. You know that there are only three types of cars: good, okay, and bad. In addition, you happen to know that one-third of all used cars on the road are good, one-third are okay, and one-third are bad. How much would you be willing to pay for a used car?

Well, given the fact that good cars are worth $15,000, okay cars are worth $10,000, and bad cars are worth $5,000, and also given the fact that you don't know which cars are which, imagine that you'd be willing to pay no more than $10,000.

Why $10,000? Because that's what the okay used car — the car of average quality — is worth.

Because sellers have no way of proving to you how good their cars are, a sensible thing to do when presented with a used car is to assume that it's of average quality and, therefore, worth $10,000. So you offer $10,000. And so do all the other buyers presented with used cars because they, like you, can't tell the quality of used cars apart.

Now look at how different sellers react to the $10,000 offer depending on the true quality of their vehicles:

- ✔ If a seller knows his car is bad and worth only $5,000, he happily accepts your offer.

- ✔ If a seller knows his car is okay, he also accepts because you're offering what the car's actually worth.

- ✔ If a seller has a good car, he won't accept unless he's in some sort of dire circumstance. He knows the car is worth $15,000, so he won't accept your $10,000 offer unless he's really desperate to raise cash in a hurry (perhaps to pay off some gambling debts to a guy named Machete Bob).

The result is that nearly all the good cars on the market are withdrawn, leaving only bad and okay cars. Now consider how that situation changes what buyers are willing to offer.

If all the good cars are withdrawn from the market, there's now a 50/50 chance that a car is okay or bad. In such a case, how much would you offer to pay if you were a buyer? Well, with a 50/50 chance of the car being worth either $10,000 or $5,000, you'll probably offer the average of these two values: $7,500. But when you do, the market becomes even more dysfunctional.

After all, how are the sellers of okay cars going to react to being offered $7,500? They're going to reject the offer and withdraw their vehicles from the market, too.

The sad result is that with the good cars and then the okay cars withdrawn from the market, the only cars left are the bad ones, the lemons. Because of the asymmetric information problem, the used car market ends up being a market for lemons.

Buyers know this, so they offer only $5,000 for any car on the market. And because only bad cars are offered, sellers accept the $5,000. So while it's true that bad cars end up being priced correctly in the used car market, no market exists for good or even okay used cars.

That's a problem because people — both buyers and sellers — want to trade good and okay cars, and they would be much happier if they could. But unless some solution can be found to the asymmetric information problem, they're all left out in the cold.

Making lemonade: Solutions to the lemons problem

The fundamental issue driving the lemons problem is that the sellers of good and okay cars have no way of convincing buyers that their cars are as good as the sellers know them to be. The whole problem could be resolved if some way could be found to convince buyers that a good car was, in fact, a good car and an okay car was, in fact, an okay car.

In the next three sections, I discuss ways to achieve this goal. These methods don't work perfectly, but because they offer some reassurance to buyers, buyers are willing to offer enough to get sellers to part with higher quality automobiles.

Offering a warranty

One way a seller can convince a buyer that she's really got a good car is to offer the buyer a warranty. The reason that a warranty is convincing is because only the seller of a good car is willing to offer a warranty. The seller knows that her good car won't break down after you buy it, meaning that she'll never have to pay for any repairs.

On the other hand, the seller of a bad car would never offer a warranty because he knows that his car will probably break down and that he'll have to pay for the repairs.

Consequently, if someone is willing to offer you a warranty, she almost certainly has a good car. That's why you see so many used car dealers offering warranties on the vehicles they sell. If they didn't offer warranties, the lemons problem would quickly take over, and prices would fall so low that only bad cars would be bought and sold on the used car market.

Building a reputation

Another way to solve the lemons problem is to reassure buyers by setting up a market in such a way that sellers can build a reputation for honesty and fair dealing. This is why most good used cars are sold through used car dealers rather than directly between individuals.

Compare a used car dealership with an individual selling her used car online. Who has more of an incentive to tell you the truth about car quality?

The used car dealer makes his living selling used cars, so if he overcharges one customer by pretending a bad car is good, he soon gets in trouble. When that car starts to break down, the buyer becomes angry and tells all his friends that the dealer cheated him. And that loss of reputation cuts into the dealer's future sales. In fact, he'll quickly go bankrupt if he develops a reputation for lying.

By contrast, an individual selling her used car doesn't have to worry about developing a reputation for lying. Her main source of income isn't selling cars. If she cheats you and you get mad and tell all your friends, it won't affect her much because she's not in the business of selling used cars.

The result is that she has much more of an incentive to lie than does the used car dealer who has to worry about his reputation. As a result, most good used cars are sold through used car dealers. (But even at used car dealers, people still need some reassurance, which is why most used car dealers also offer warranties.)

Getting an expert opinion

Because the heart of the lemons problem is asymmetric information, another method of resolving the problem is for skeptical buyers to hire an expert who can give them the information they need to distinguish good, okay, and bad cars. Many car buyers employ this strategy when they have doubts about a seller's honesty.

For a relatively small fee, a buyer can hire a disinterested third party expert — for instance, a professional mechanic — to inspect the vehicle and make a list of repairs that will most likely be needed in the near future. In this way, the buyer can get a better picture of the car's quality and what a fair price would be.

However, this method may not be able to fully resolve the asymmetric information problem because the expert probably can't discover *everything* that may be wrong with the car. To the extent that this is true, buyers may still be suspicious, and there may still be some potential for market failure. That's why you often see buyer-initiated inspections used in conjunction with other methods of resolving asymmetric information, such as warranties and sales by dealers who have a reputation to protect.

Issuing insurance when you can't tell individuals apart

An insurance company faces an asymmetric information problem of its own. Its problem is that the people buying insurance know more than the company does about the risks they face.

Consider automobile insurance. Who needs it more: good drivers who hardly ever get into accidents, or bad drivers who get into lots of accidents? Now, clearly, even good drivers want insurance because they're sometimes involved in accidents for which they're not to blame. But bad drivers want insurance even more to help pay for all the accidents they know they're going to cause because of their poor driving.

An asymmetric information problem faces the insurance companies because while individual drivers know whether they're good or bad, the insurance companies can't easily tell them apart. If they *could* tell them apart, insurance companies would simply charge the good drivers a low rate for insurance and the bad drivers a high rate.

But because they can't tell the good and bad drivers apart, the insurance companies run a serious risk of going bankrupt. To see why, imagine that insurance companies offered the same low rate to everyone, as though they were *all* good drivers. This would soon lead to bankruptcy because the insurance companies wouldn't be collecting enough in premiums to pay off all the damage caused by the bad drivers.

To avoid bankruptcy, the insurance companies could go to the other extreme, charging everyone as though they were bad drivers. But then the good drivers wouldn't bother buying insurance because for them it would be overpriced. The result would be that only bad drivers would sign up for insurance.

This is a very poor result socially because you want everyone to be able to buy insurance at a rate that fairly reflects their driving ability. Good drivers should be able to get insurance at a fair rate. And because good drivers make up most of the drivers in the real world, insurance companies lose out on lots of potential profits unless they can figure out a way to separate the good drivers from the bad drivers.

Grouping individuals to help tell them apart

Insurance companies have come up with a paradoxical way of dealing with the fact that they can't tell whether an individual is a good or bad driver. Instead of focusing on the individual, they look for clues about the individual based on the groups to which he or she belongs. Doing so often gives the insurance companies a pretty good idea about whether the individual is a good or bad driver.

For instance, it's a well-known fact that males under 25 get into many more accidents than females under 25. So if two people walk into an insurance company and one of them is a 23-year-old male and the other is a 22-year-old female, chances are that the male is a much worse driver than the female. Consequently, you charge the male a higher insurance rate.

This situation has the nice result of making sure that everybody can get insurance at what is *likely* to be a fair price given the fact that, on average, males under 25 get into many more accidents than females under 25.

In reality, this nice result isn't the compelling reason behind insurance companies' decisions to intuit as much as possible about their customers by looking at what groups they belong to. These companies really have no choice; competition *forces* them to do so.

Why is this true? Consider two insurance companies, only one of which uses group membership information to help set rates. The company that doesn't use group information has to sets very high rates because it's afraid that all its customers may be bad drivers. Doing so drives away all the good drivers who don't want to pay bad-driver rates for their insurance.

But the company that uses group information can offer multiple rates, such as high ones to young men and low ones to young women. Doing so allows it to capture the business of many good drivers who don't want to deal with the first insurance company that set only one high rate for everyone. The result is that insurance companies are always looking for ways to try to estimate an individual's unknown risk profile based on the well-known risk profiles of the groups to which he or she belongs.

This process can lead to some rather unfair conclusions. The oddest is that good-driving young males end up paying higher rates than bad-driving young females because the only thing insurance companies have to go on is gender.

But such a system is still better than the even more unfair alternative in which *all* good drivers would have to pay bad-driver rates, which is what would happen if insurance companies were banned from using group membership information to try to distinguish their customers. The closer insurance companies can get to fully distinguishing good and bad drivers using group membership information, the more fair rates will be.

Keep in mind that the drivers for whom insurance companies have the greatest need to use group membership information are new drivers. Because insurance companies don't have any accident or violation records for new drivers, there's a pressing need to try to separate the good from the bad drivers using group membership information. As drivers get more experience, the insurance companies can get increasingly accurate accident and violation information that distinguishes the good from the bad.

Avoiding adverse selection

Using the groups to which a person belongs to estimate his or her individual insurance risk goes only part of the way to resolving the asymmetric information problem that exists between insurance companies and their customers.

Obviously, there's still a lot of individual variation within any group. For instance, even if young women are, on average, better drivers than young men, some young women are bad drivers. This leads to a very difficult problem known as *adverse selection*.

If an insurance company sets a premium for young women on the basis of how often young women *on average* get into accidents, insurance will be more attractive to young women who are really bad drivers than to young women who are really good drivers.

As a result, bad-driving young women will be more prone to sign up for insurance than good-driving young women. This tendency is known as adverse selection because it's as though the bad, or adverse, insurance risks self-select into buying insurance policies. The result is a customer pool that contains a disproportionately high number of bad drivers.

Adverse selection is a difficult problem because it feeds on itself. The insurance company has to raise rates to take account of the fact that bad drivers are more likely to sign up than good drivers. But when it raises rates, the problem just gets worse because the higher rates make insurance even less attractive to good drivers, meaning that the pool of applicants is going to be even more disproportionately dominated by bad drivers.

One solution to adverse selection is for an insurance company to offer a large group of people one rate — on the condition that nobody can opt out. For instance, at the school where I teach, our health insurance company offers the school one low rate for every employee on the condition that every employee must be enrolled. By enrolling everyone, there's no chance that the insurance pool is dominated by the sickly because all the healthy have declined to be enrolled.

Mitigating moral hazard

The other big problem facing insurance companies is called *moral hazard*. Moral hazard arises because buying insurance tends to change people's behavior. For instance, if I didn't have car insurance, I would drive much more slowly, knowing that I would have to use my own money to pay for any damage I cause. But because I do have insurance, I drive faster and more recklessly knowing that if something goes wrong, the insurance company is going to be stuck with the bill. (Please know that when I say "I" in examples like this one, I don't actually mean me. You see, *I* am above moral hazard.)

The way car insurance companies deal with moral hazard is by offering discounts in exchange for high deductibles. For instance, if I get into an accident, the $1,000 deductible that I've chosen means that of any bills that ensue from the accident, I have to pay the first $1,000.

The deductible serves as a strong inducement for me not to give into moral hazard and drive recklessly. And because the insurance company knows that my high deductible gets rid of most of my moral hazard problem, they're willing to offer me insurance at a lower rate than if I'd opted for only a $100 deductible.

Deductibles are a clever way of reducing moral hazard problems and helping to make insurance more affordable for responsible drivers.

Group discrimination, individual identification

The idea of grouping individuals to help sort them extends beyond insurance. For instance, companies want hard-working employees but can't tell when you walk in for an interview if you are, in fact, hard-working. So they try to estimate the chances that you are by seeing what groups you belong to.

For instance, nearly all straight-A students are hard-working. Therefore, if you're a straight-A student, a company is going to be much more likely to hire you. You may actually be lazy, but by seeing what group you belong to, the firm improves its odds that you're not.

The practice of using information about the groups to which an individual belongs to try to figure out personal characteristics is referred to as *statistical discrimination.* While this practice typically improves economic outcomes, you have to decide for yourself whether — and in what cases — you think it's fair or unfair.

Providing Public Goods

Public goods are things that can't be profitably produced by private firms because there's no way to exclude nonpayers from using them. The inability of private firms to profitably produce public goods derives from the fact that they have two very special characteristics. Public goods are nonrival and nonexcludable:

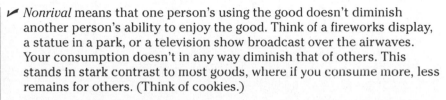

✔ *Nonrival* means that one person's using the good doesn't diminish another person's ability to enjoy the good. Think of a fireworks display, a statue in a park, or a television show broadcast over the airwaves. Your consumption doesn't in any way diminish that of others. This stands in stark contrast to most goods, where if you consume more, less remains for others. (Think of cookies.)

✔ *Nonexcludable* means that it's hard to prevent nonpayers from consuming a good or service. For instance, when you produce a fireworks display, everyone in the vicinity gets to see it for free no matter how much you'd like to charge them for it. A more serious example is an army: When it's in place to provide national defense, it provides national defense for everybody, including those who don't want to contribute to the cost of maintaining it.

The nonrival and nonexcludable characteristics of public goods make it very hard for private firms to make any money producing them. Think about trying to get people to buy tickets to an outdoor fireworks display. Because people know that they're going to be able to see it for free, they won't buy tickets. Because they won't buy tickets, there's no way to raise the money needed to put on the display.

This sort of chicken-and-egg problem is frustrating, because while people don't want to pay for something they can get for free, they actually do like firework displays — meaning that they're fundamentally willing to pay something to see them. The problem is figuring out how to get them to pay.

Taxing to provide public goods

The most common solution to the problem of how to provide public goods has been for governments to step in and use tax money to pay for them. In the case of fireworks, because nearly everybody likes fireworks, there's no problem getting enough political support for spending tax money on displays. And after they've been funded by the taxpayer, everyone can enjoy them.

National defense has historically been provided for by the government because it, too, is very much a nonexcludable, nonrival public good. For instance, because protection from foreign invaders is nonexcludable, there's always a temptation to not help pay for it because you know that if someone else does pay, you get to enjoy safety from foreign invaders for free. And because national defense is nonrival, you know that the safety you enjoy is of just as high a quality as the safety everyone else enjoys. This fact, too, lessens your incentive to pay. As a result, governments force people to share the expense for national defense by levying taxes.

Taxes and a good portion of government spending are often derided as wasteful (and often are wasteful), but keep in mind that in many cases taxes are the only way to fund the wide variety of public goods we enjoy. While nobody likes taxes, you'd probably not want to trade a reduced tax burden for no public parks, no national army, no public fireworks displays, no public roads, no public sewers, and so on. Without the government's ability to force people to pay for these things, we'd likely not have them — at least not in the quantity and variety that we currently enjoy.

Enlisting philanthropy to provide public goods

While most public goods are paid for through taxation by the government, some are paid for privately. In the middle of Los Angeles, where I grew up, there's a huge and beautiful mountain park called Griffith Park. The land for it was donated by a millionaire named Griffith J. Griffith. That is, he provided a public good at personal expense.

In ancient Greece and Rome, public philanthropy went even further, with rich aristocrats building roads, aqueducts, and temples for public use. In some cases, rich men even paid for entire armies to be sent out to defend the country in times of war.

So please don't think that governments are absolutely necessary to provide public goods. They aren't. But they are a much more reliable way to provide public goods because you don't have to rely upon the philanthropic largess of the rich, who are under no obligation to spend their wealth on public rather than private goods.

Along the same lines, don't make the common mistake of thinking that public goods are called public because they're typically provided by the government rather than the private sector. Economists call them public goods because private firms can't profitably produce them, not because they have to be produced by the government. Private philanthropy can produce public goods without any help at all from the government.

Providing a public good by selling a related private good

Broadcast television is a public good. After a TV program's signal has been sent out over the airways, it's nonrival: My watching the program doesn't reduce anyone else's ability to tune in. It's also nonexcludable: There's no way to stop anyone with a TV set from tuning in. So given that TV programming is very much a public good, why are lots of TV programs produced by privately owned and operated TV stations?

The answer is that the broadcast industry figured out that while TV itself is a public good, the commercials that accompany TV programs are very much private goods for which they can charge a lot of money. That is, if a car maker or beer maker or the publisher of a revolutionary new economics book with a yellow and black cover wants its commercial to be shown to the millions of viewers who tune in for free to the public good known as TV, the company has to pay for commercial air time.

The trick behind TV is that the privately sold good called advertising pays for the freely provided public good called television. To a more limited extent, newspapers work the same way. While they raise some money from subscriber fees or the newsstand price, a huge chunk of their revenue comes from the advertising they sell.

Ranking new technology as a public good

We live in an age of rapidly rising living standards. Why is this the case? Because institutions are fostering the creation of new and better technologies that allow us to produce more goods and services from the same old resources, or to produce entirely new goods and services that were previously impossible to produce.

Technological progress is a public good. And because it is, society has had to come up with ways to make sure that technological progress happens given the fact that private individuals and firms have little incentive to invent new technology.

To understand how new technologies are public goods, consider the invention of the moveable-type printing press by Gutenberg in 1435. Before Gutenberg, books were copied by hand. But after he invented the printing press, it was much cheaper to make new copies by printing them.

Furthermore, think about how simple the technology really is. The printing press is basically just a big version of the rubber stamps that little kids like to play with. The invention was immediately understandable to anyone and everyone who heard about it, which meant that they could make their own printing presses as soon as they heard about it.

So how does this invention satisfy the characteristics of a public good?

- ✔ It's nonrival because my building and using a printing press doesn't in any way lessen your ability to build and use a printing press.

- ✔ It's basically nonexcludable because the cost of communicating the new idea to another person is so low — just a short conversation does the trick.

The result is that unless society creates some sort of an institution to reward the creation of new ideas, there's not going to be much of a profit incentive to go into the invention business. In fact, what happened to Gutenberg was that everyone copied his idea and didn't pay him for it. So unless you can come up with a way to financially reward the creation of new inventions, you're not likely to get many of them.

Patenting to turn public goods into private goods

The solution has been the creation of patents. By giving inventors the exclusive right to market and sell their inventions for 20 years, patents provide a financial incentive to get people to invest the time and energy necessary to come up with new technologies that benefit everyone. It's no coincidence that economic growth took off only after government-enforced patents became widely available in western Europe in the 18th century.

Subsidizing research into technologies that can't be patented

But even today, not every new innovation can be patented. That's because you can patent only something you invent, not something you discover. For instance, if you think up a chemical that's never existed before and then synthesize it, you can patent it. But if you merely discover an existing chemical that's been floating around the sea or lying in the soil, you can't patent it.

This is a big problem for things like cancer research because many potential cures are chemicals derived from plants and animals, chemicals that have existed in nature for eons. These chemicals have huge potential benefits, but because they can't be patented, nobody has a strong financial incentive to try to discover them.

As a result, the government and many private philanthropic groups fund research into areas of science where the public goods problem would otherwise limit research.

This solution is very important to an economist because providing public goods is an economic problem that markets and the invisible hand can't fix. Other types of market failure, like asymmetric information, have pretty decent private sector solutions (as I discuss in the section "Making lemonade: Solutions to the lemons problem," earlier in the chapter).

But unless a society can come up with good ways of providing public goods, it is permanently deprived of their benefits. For public goods like fireworks displays, this hardly matters. But for technological innovations like curing cancer, it's literally a matter of life and death.

Part IV
The Part of Tens

The 5th Wave   By Rich Tennant

In this part . . .

The chapters in this part offer some fun, fast reading. Chapter 16 covers the lives and ideas of some great economists. Chapter 17 debunks ten very common but very incorrect pieces of economic thinking — the kind of stuff you hear on radio talk shows and in politicians' speeches all the time. Chapter 18 features ten correct and truly great economic ideas that should guide your thinking about public policy and how to best run an economy.

Chapter 16

Ten (Or So) Famous Economists

*I*n this short chapter, I give you brief descriptions of the ideas put forth by 12 of the very best and most influential economists. (Ten just wasn't enough.) Each one either radically changed the way that economics conceptualizes the world or radically changed the way that politicians and government officials formulate public policy.

But don't for a second think that these guys did it all on their own. As with any science, in economics a single person's breakthrough is built on the foundation of hundreds of contributions made by scores of researchers.

In other words, there are a whole lot more than 10 — or even 12 — great economists. With any luck, this book has sparked your interest to learn more about economics, so you can come to know the stellar ideas of the many great economists who didn't happen to make this list.

Adam Smith

Adam Smith (1723–1790) developed the intuition that as long as firms are constrained by robust competition, their self-interested profit seeking inadvertently causes them to act in ways that are socially optimal — as though they are guided by an *invisible hand* to do the right thing.

But Smith was not naive. He believed that businessmen prefer to collude rather than compete whenever possible, and that governments have a very important economic role to play in fostering the robust competition needed for the invisible hand to work its magic. He also believed that governments must provide many essential public goods, like national defense, that aren't readily produced by the private sector.

David Ricardo

David Ricardo (1772–1823) discovered comparative advantage and argued correctly that international trade is a win-win situation for the countries involved. Comparative advantage destroyed the intellectual respectability of *mercantilism,* the mistaken theory behind colonialism that viewed trade as being one-sided and consequently argued that trade should be set up to benefit the mother country at the expense of its colony.

In addition, Ricardo correctly analyzed the economic phenomenon of diminishing returns, which explains why costs tend to increase as you increase production levels. He was also a strong early proponent of the quantity theory of money, the idea that increasing the money supply will increase prices.

Karl Marx

Karl Marx (1818–1883) was the foremost economist among 19th-century socialists. None of his major economic theories is now believed to be true, but because proponents of his Marxist ideas came to power in dozens of countries during the 20th century, he is surely one of the most influential economists who ever lived. (Marx gets the most space here not because he's the most important economist on this list, but because I have to take the time to explain his ideas before discrediting them. The ideas of the other economists on this list are already explained in detail in other places in this book.)

Marx's most important intellectual contribution is his idea that capitalism is a historically unique form of social and productive organization. In *Capital,* he analyzed capitalism as a brand-new form of social and economic organization based on capital accumulation and factory production. He called the owners of the factories "capitalists" and argued that they would be forced to exploit the workers who labored in their factories.

In particular, he believed that the only capitalists who would survive and whose businesses would grow were those who paid workers the minimum salaries necessary for the workers to survive. Thus, even as productivity and output rose rapidly, workers would endure permanent, grinding poverty out of which they could never rise except by means of a violent overthrow of the capitalists — an overthrow in which the workers would gain control over the factories.

Marx argued that this violent overthrow would be facilitated by what he saw as an inevitable tendency toward concentration and monopoly. When there was only one monopoly firm in each industry, it would be much easier for the workers to revolt and take over the system.

With a century and a quarter of hindsight, we know that Marx was wrong in his economic thinking. In particular, workers' wages *do* rise over time — in fact, they rise on average as fast as technological innovation increases productivity levels. That's because capitalists compete over the limited supply of workers, and wages get bid up as quickly as productivity improvements allow one capitalist to bid higher wages to steal workers away from other capitalists.

In addition, competition does *not* lead to each industry being dominated by a single monopoly firm. Rather, competition remains robust in most industries and consequently delivers all the benefits of Adam Smith's invisible hand.

Alfred Marshall

Alfred Marshall (1842–1924) invented the supply-and-demand method for analyzing markets. Applying mathematics to economic theory, he clearly differentiated between *shifts* of demand and supply curves and movements *along* demand and supply curves. In doing so, he cleared up 2,000 years of faulty reasoning. He also made the revolutionary prediction that the market price would be where the demand and supply curves cross.

Marshall then went one step farther and realized that by comparing points along demand and supply curves with the market price, you could quantify the benefits that consumers and producers derive from market transactions. These benefits are, respectively, consumer surplus and producer surplus, and their sum is the total economic surplus.

This method of quantifying the benefits of production and consumption is still used today and forms the basis of *welfare economics,* which studies the costs and benefits of economic activities. This method also just happens to illustrate in a very simple graph the intuition behind Adam Smith's invisible hand. The free market equilibrium, where demand and supply cross, is exactly the same as what a benevolent social planner would choose to do if she were trying to maximize social welfare by maximizing total economic surplus. In other words, a free market does indeed act "as if moved by an invisible hand" to promote the common good.

John Maynard Keynes

John Maynard Keynes (1883–1946) invented modern macroeconomics and the idea of using government-provided economic stimuli to overcome recessions. Much of the rest of 20th-century macroeconomics was a series of responses to his seminal ideas.

His most famous ideas were developed in response to the long agony of the Great Depression of the 1930s. He first asserted that the Great Depression was the result of a collapse in the expenditures being made on goods and services. He then asserted that monetary policy had been ineffective in combating the decline in expenditures. And he finally concluded, given his dismay about monetary policy, that fiscal policy was the only remaining source of salvation. In particular, Keynes believed that the best way to increase expenditures in such dire circumstances was for the government to spend heavily to pay for programs that would buy up lots of goods and services in order to get the economy moving again.

Keynes's policy prescriptions were adopted during the Great Depression in many countries, including the United States. And while many of his specific ideas about the cause of the Great Depression and the best policies for dealing with recessions are no longer embraced, his underlying idea that governments are responsible for taming the business cycle remains very much with us today.

Kenneth Arrow and Gerard Debreu

Kenneth Arrow (b. 1921) and Gerard Debreu (b. 1921) mathematically proved that Adam Smith's intuition about the invisible hand was, in fact, correct. Not only do competitive firms provide society with the utility-maximizing combination of goods and services, they do so efficiently, at minimum cost. Since this proof came in the 1950s, it served to disprove the assertions of totalitarians and communists that centrally planned economies were more productive or more efficient than market economies.

Milton Friedman

Milton Friedman (b. 1912) convinced economists that the quantity theory of money is, in fact, true: Sustained inflations are the result of sustained increases in the money supply (printing too much money). This insight put limits on using monetary policy to stimulate the economy.

Friedman also argued that the Great Depression was chiefly a monetary disaster and that its severity was the result of a gruesomely tight money supply that kept real interest rates much too high. This diagnosis of the cause of the Great Depression is now the standard explanation, meaning that the intellectual ammunition for Keynes's solution to recessions — large increases in government spending — has lost much of the sway that it once had. It has also led economists to conclude that monetary policy is more important than fiscal policy for regulating the economy and preventing recessions.

Paul Samuelson

Paul Samuelson (b. 1915) has made many contributions to economics. Perhaps the most important was crystallizing the idea that all economic behavior can be thought of as consumers and firms maximizing either utility or profits subject to a set of constraints. This idea of *constrained maximization* has become the dominant paradigm that governs how economists conceive of economic behavior.

Samuelson also developed a judicious blending of Keynesian and classical ideas about the proper use of government intervention in the economy. Keynes argued for large government interventions to mitigate recessions. Classical economists like Smith and Ricardo argued for minimal government interventions, fearing that government interventions tend to make things worse.

Samuelson's *neoclassical synthesis* states that during recessions the government should be willing to make large interventions in the economy to get it moving again, but when the economy is operating at full potential, the proper role of government is to provide public goods and take care of externalities. Many economists embrace this view of the government's place in the economy.

Robert Solow

Robert Solow (b. 1924) has made huge contributions to the understanding of economic growth and rising living standards. In addition to developing innovative models of how economies grow over time, he also showed that the dominant long-run force propelling economic growth is technological innovation.

Before Solow, the economic profession believed that increases in output were the result of increases in inputs. In particular, increases in output were solely the result of either using more workers or more capital (such as bigger factories). What Solow demonstrated was that *at most* 50 percent of the long-run growth of living standards can be explained by increases in labor and capital. The rest has to be the result of technological innovation.

This insight created a huge paradigm shift among economists that has resulted in the systematic study of technological innovation and the ways in which it can be improved by government policies like patents and copyrights. It also opens up the refreshing possibility that technological innovation will allow us to enjoy higher living standards without having to constantly increase our use of the earth's resources.

Gary Becker

Gary Becker (b. 1930) has been hugely influential because he has pushed economics into areas that were previously immune to economic thinking.

His first major contribution was to argue that free markets would tend to work *for* equality and *against* racial and gender discrimination. The intuition is that firms that refuse to hire the best qualified workers because of their race or gender put themselves at a competitive disadvantage relative to non-biased firms. Becker backed up this intuition by showing that industries that are more competitive do, in fact, employ more minorities and women.

Another significant contribution Becker made was to model families as economic units in which family members tend to act on the basis of cost–benefit analyses. For instance, as societies became richer and paid employment became more plentiful (and better paying), Becker predicted that more women would choose to work rather than stay at home. He provided an economic explanation for a huge change in the labor force that otherwise would have been explained only in terms of sociological considerations (such as changing gender roles).

Similarly, he was the first to model criminal behavior in terms of how criminals view the potential costs and benefits of committing any given crime. If the expected benefits exceed the expected costs, the criminal will most likely attempt the crime. This theory of criminal behavior is radically different from previous explanations, and it led Becker to propose the very influential idea that the best way to deter crime is to raise the costs relative to the benefits.

Robert Lucas

Robert Lucas (b. 1937) showed that people are sophisticated planners who constantly modify their optimal strategies in response to changes in government policy. If you assume that people only very slowly change their behavior in response to policy changes, you'll overestimate the results of those changes.

In particular, monetary policy loses most of its effectiveness if people rationally plan for policy changes. Suppose the government announces that in three months it's going to double the money supply in an attempt to stimulate increased purchases of goods and services. If store owners keep prices the same despite the fact that more money is on the way, the economy will be stimulated because people will be able to buy a lot more stuff with all that new money.

But if, instead, store owners rationally react to the announcement, they're going to raise their prices in anticipation of all the new money that's going to be spent in their stores. By doing so, they greatly reduce the amount by which sales of goods and services increase when people begin to spend all the new money.

In particular, if the shop owners double their prices in anticipation of the doubling of the money supply, the policy change won't result in any increase in the amount of goods and services sold. With prices twice as high, having twice as much money will only allow customers to buy exactly as much as they did before.

Lucas's idea came be known as *rational expectations,* and it brought with it a new humility about the extent to which government policy — monetary policy in particular — can influence the world.

Chapter 17

Ten Seductive Economic Fallacies

In This Chapter

▶ Avoiding logical fallacies that sucker intelligent people

▶ Steering clear of bad economic reasoning

*I*n this short chapter, I outline the most attractive and compelling incorrect ideas in economics. Some are logical fallacies. A few are myopic opinions that don't take into account the big picture. And others are poorly thought out examples of economic reasoning. All are to be avoided.

The Lump of Labor Fallacy

The argument that there's a fixed amount of work that you can divide up among as many people as you want is often presented as a cure for unemployment. The idea goes that if you convert from a 40-hour work week to a 20-hour work week, firms will have to hire twice as many workers. France, for instance, recently reduced its work week to only 35 hours in the hope that firms would hire more workers and cure France's persistent unemployment problem.

It didn't work; such policies have never worked. One problem is that hiring workers involves many fixed costs, including training costs and health insurance. So two 20-hour-per-week workers cost more to employ than one 40-hour-per-week worker. What's more, two 20-hour-per-week workers don't produce any more output than one 40-hour-per-week worker.

So if laws were passed that forced firms to move from a 40-hour work week to a 20-hour work week, firms wouldn't double the size of their workforces. They'd hire fewer than twice as many workers because costs would go up.

In addition, even if cutting the work week in half actually did double the number of workers used, it would only hide the overall unemployment problem by spreading it around. If 100 percent of workers are working half-time, they are all 50 percent underemployed. That situation is not a significant improvement over having 50 percent of the population employed full-time and 50 percent unemployed.

What you really want is a situation in which every worker who wants a full-time job is able to get one. Shortening the work week doesn't achieve this goal.

The World Is Facing an Overpopulation Problem

Various versions of this myth have been floating around since the late 18th century when Thomas Malthus first asserted it. He argued that living standards couldn't permanently rise because higher living standards would cause people to breed faster. He believed that population growth would outpace our ability to grow more food, so we would be doomed to return to subsistence levels of nutrition and living standards.

Even at the time that Malthus first published this idea, lots of evidence indicated that it was bunk. For generations, living standards had been rising while birth rates had been falling. And because that trend has continued up to the present day, we're not going to breed our way to subsistence.

Indeed, many nations now face an *under*population problem. In most developed countries, birthrates have fallen below the replacement rate necessary to keep the population stable. As a result, their populations will soon start shrinking dramatically. And because birthrates are falling quickly all over the world, the total human population is predicted to max out at around 9 billion people in 2050 before beginning to shrink dramatically.

A related problem is that rapidly falling birth rates are wreaking havoc on government-sponsored retirement systems because there aren't enough young workers to pay all the taxes needed to fund retirees' pensions. In desperation, some countries are going so far as to pay mothers cash bounties for each new child they give birth to.

While many countries with relatively high birth rates do have poverty and malnutrition problems, economists now believe that the high birth rates aren't to blame. Rather, poor government policies are typically the problem. When these policies improve, living standards rise, birth rates fall, and whatever population crisis seemed to exist quickly disappears.

The Fallacy of Confusing Sequence with Causation

Post hoc ergo propter hoc is a Latin phrase that translates roughly as, "Because you see one thing precede another, you think that it causes the other." That is, if A happens before B, you assume that A causes B.

Such a deduction is false because A and B often don't have any relationship. For instance, sometimes it rains in the morning, and I get a headache in the afternoon. That doesn't mean that the rain caused my headache.

Politicians try to pull this logical fallacy all the time when discussing the economy. For instance, suppose that politician A gets elected, and a few months later there's a recession. The two may have nothing to do with each other, but you can be sure that during the next election, an opponent of politician A will claim that the recession was the result of politician A's policies. The only proof offered is that one event happened before the other.

Protectionism Is the Best Solution to Foreign Competition

Trade union members and many politicians often argue in favor of trade barriers and taxes on imports on the grounds that these policies benefit citizens and prevent jobs from being exported. The problem is that their arguments consider only the benefits of protectionism without also considering the costs.

Trade barriers and taxes on imports *do* protect the specific jobs that they're intended to protect. However, other jobs are often sacrificed in the process.

For instance, raising tariffs on foreign coal protects the jobs of domestic miners. But such a policy results in higher energy costs all over the economy. Domestic manufacturers have to pay higher energy costs than they would if they had access to the cheaper foreign coal, so they have to raise the prices of the goods they produce. As a result, demand for these goods decreases, and the manufacturers don't need as many employees.

Another problem with protectionism is that citizens are consumers as well as producers. For instance, if the government prevents the importation of lower cost, higher quality foreign automobiles, it preserves jobs in the domestic auto industry. But costs for domestic consumers rise as a result.

Protecting an unproductive industry that faces foreign competition only allows it to keep using resources that would otherwise be better used by more vibrant industries. Workers who would otherwise move to jobs in innovative, highly productive new industries instead get stuck in an industry so unproductive that it can survive only by having the government rig the economy in its favor.

Granted, the move from a dying industry to an innovative new industry can be rough for an individual worker. But rather than avoid the need for change by protecting unproductive industries, the government can help domestic workers more efficiently by providing retraining programs for employees. (In the case of older workers who have only a few years of employment left, early retirement programs may be more viable than retraining.)

The Fallacy of Composition

Assuming that what's good for one person to do is good for everyone to do all at once is another common fallacy. For instance, if you're at a sold-out sporting event and want to get a better view, standing is a good idea — but only if you're the only one who stands up. If everyone else also stands up, everyone's view is just as bad as when everyone was sitting down (but now everyone's legs are getting tired). Consequently, what was good for you to do alone is actually bad for everyone to do at the same time.

The fallacy of composition is false because some things in life have to do with relative position. For instance, if you start out as the lowest paid employee at your firm but then get a 50 percent raise while nobody else gets a raise, your relative position within the firm improves. However, if everyone gets a 50 percent raise at the same time, you're still the lowest paid person at the firm. If what matters to you is your relative standing within the firm, getting the same raise as everyone else doesn't make you any happier. (On the other hand, if you are more interested in where you stand relative to people who work at other firms, getting a 50 percent raise is good even if everyone else at your firm gets it, too!)

If It's Worth Doing, Do It 100 Percent

We all value safety. But was a famous U.S. politician really being sensible when he said that we should spend whatever money might be necessary to make flying on commercial airlines "as safe as possible"?

Economists would say, "No!" The problem is that making commercial airline travel "as safe as possible" would mean making it prohibitively expensive. Although safety is a good thing, achieving complete safety is not a worthy goal if doing so makes flying so expensive that only the extremely wealthy can afford it.

The politician failed to apply *marginalism* — the idea that the best way to approach a problem is to compare marginal benefits with marginal costs. Applying marginalism to airline safety, you realize that making flying "as safe as possible" is wasteful.

The first few airline safety innovations (such as seatbelts and radar) are sensible to undertake because the extra, or marginal, benefit that each brings is greater than the extra, or marginal, cost required to pay for it. But after the first few safety innovations are implemented, successive innovations become more costly and less effective. At some point, additional innovations bring only small marginal increases in safety while running up high marginal costs.

When the costs for the extra safety innovations exceed their benefits, they *shouldn't* be implemented. You should add safety features only as long as the marginal benefits exceed the marginal costs — which means that you'll usually stop adding safety features long before you get anywhere near making things "as safe as possible."

Free Markets Are Dangerously Unstable

Free markets are volatile because supply and demand often change very quickly, causing rapid changes in equilibrium prices and quantities (which I discuss in Chapter 8). Rapid change isn't a problem, however. The responsiveness of markets is actually one of their great benefits. Unlike a government bureaucracy that can never react quickly to anything, markets can adjust to huge changes in world events in only minutes.

The new equilibrium prices and quantities see to it that resources are allocated to their best uses and that society suffers from neither shortages nor gluts. So don't call markets unstable. Call them *responsive*.

Low Foreign Wages Mean That Rich Countries Can't Compete

You often hear that U.S. firms can't compete with firms based in developing countries because of vast differences in hourly wages. To see the problem with this thinking, let's compare a factory in the United States with a factory in a developing country.

Say the U.S. factory pays its workers $20 per hour while the factory in the developing country pays $4 per hour. People mistakenly jump to the conclusion that because the foreign factory's labor costs are so much lower, it can easily undersell the U.S. factory. But this argument fails to take into account two things:

- What actually matters is labor costs per *unit,* not labor costs per *hour.*
- Differences in productivity typically mean that labor costs per unit are often nearly identical despite huge differences in labor costs per hour.

To see what I mean, compare how productive the two factories are. Because the U.S. factory uses much more advanced technology, one worker in one hour can produce 20 units of output. The U.S. worker gets paid $20 per hour, so the labor cost *per unit of output* is $1. The factory in the developing country is much less productive; a worker there produces only 4 units in one hour. Given the foreign wage of $4 per hour, the labor cost per unit of output in the developing country is also $1.

Obviously, the developing country's lower hourly wage rate *per hour* does not translate into lower labor costs *per unit* — meaning that it won't be able to undersell its U.S. competitor.

People who focus exclusively on the difference in labor costs per hour never mention the productivity differences that typically equalize labor costs per unit. And don't think that my example uses happy-happy numbers. Wage differences across countries really do tend to reflect productivity differences.

Keep in mind that governments can seriously screw up what would otherwise be a near equality of labor costs per unit by fixing artificially low exchange rates. For instance, if at an exchange rate of 8 Chinese yuan to 1 U.S. dollar labor costs per unit are equal, the Chinese government could make labor costs per unit look artificially low to U.S. consumers if it fixes its currency at, for instance, 16 yuan to 1 dollar. In such situations, the inability of U.S. workers to compete with Chinese workers is due to the currency manipulation, not to the lower wage rate per hour found in China.

Tax Rates Don't Affect Work Effort

Some politicians argue for raising income taxes as though the only effect of doing so will be to raise more money. But it's been demonstrated over and over again that beyond a certain point, people respond to higher taxes by working less. And that reduction in labor denies society all the benefits that would have come from the extra work. (Because people work less, the increased tax rate also doesn't bring in nearly as much revenue as expected.)

So if you see a politician arguing for an increase in income taxes, look into the details to make sure that the disincentive effects of the tax hike don't cause more mischief than the benefits that will be derived from spending the money raised by the tax increase.

Forgetting That Policies Have Unintended Consequences, Too

When evaluating a policy, people tend to concentrate on how the policy will fix some particular problem while ignoring or downplaying other effects it may have. Economists often refer to this situation as *The Law of Unintended Consequences*.

For instance, suppose that you impose a tariff on imported steel in order to protect the jobs of domestic steelworkers. If you impose a high enough tariff, their jobs will indeed be protected from competition by foreign steel companies. But an unintended consequence is that the jobs of some autoworkers will be lost to foreign competition. Why? The tariff that protects steelworkers raises the price of the steel that domestic automobile makers need to build their cars. As a result, domestic automobile manufacturers have to raise the prices of their cars, making them relatively less attractive when compared to foreign cars. Raising prices tends to reduce domestic car sales, meaning that some domestic autoworkers lose their jobs.

Unintended consequences are far too common. Be aware of them whenever a politician tries to persuade you to see things his way. Chances are that he's mentioning only the good results of a certain policy; he may not have even thought about its not-so-good side effects.

Chapter 18

Ten Economic Ideas to Hold Dear

In This Chapter

▶ Understanding basic economic principles

▶ Arming yourself against the economic follies of politicians

In this chapter, I list ten economic ideas that all informed people should understand and be ready to use to evaluate the policy proposals that politicians make. Some of these ideas aren't necessarily true in all situations, but because they are usually correct, be wary if some guy wants you to believe that they don't apply to a particular situation. Make him convince you, because chances are that he's wrong.

Society Is Better Off When People Pursue Their Own Interests

This concept is basically Adam Smith's famous invisible hand. If all economic interactions in a society are voluntary on the parts of all parties involved, the only transactions that will take place are those where all parties feel that they are being made better off.

For instance, if I trade my gold for another guy's bread, you can be sure that I'm doing it because I value his bread more than my gold. I trade because trading makes me better off. Meanwhile, you can be sure that the other guy values my gold more than his bread. So trading makes him better off, too. By each pursuing his own self interests, we are both made better off.

This concept of what motivates people doesn't mean that charitable acts are bad for society. Rather, it means that even philanthropy is generated by self-interest. People give because they enjoy helping others. By doing so, both they and the people they help are made better off.

Free Markets Require Regulation

Economists firmly believe that voluntary transactions in free markets tend to work toward the common good. But they also believe that nearly every participant in the marketplace would love to rig the system in his or her own favor. Adam Smith, in particular, was quick to point this out and argue that for markets to work and serve the common good, the government has to fight monopolies, collusion, and any other attempts to prevent a properly functioning market in which firms vigorously compete against each other to give consumers what they want at the lowest possible price.

Economic Growth Depends on Innovation

At any given moment, there is a fixed amount of wealth that could be divided equally among all people, like slicing a pie into equal pieces and giving each person one equal slice. But if living standards are to keep rising, you need a bigger pie to split up. In the short run, you can get a bigger pie by working harder or using up resources faster. But the only way to have sustained growth is to invent more efficient technologies that allow people to produce ever more from the limited supply of labor and physical resources.

Freedom and Democracy Make Us Richer

Very good moral and ethical reasons exist for favoring freedom and democracy. But a more "bottom line" reason is that because freedom and democracy promote the free development and exchange of ideas, free societies have more innovation and, consequently, faster economic growth.

Education Raises Living Standards

Educated people not only produce more as workers — and hence get paid higher salaries — but, more importantly, they produce innovative new technologies. Sustained economic growth and higher living standards are only possible if you educate your citizens well. There are, of course, other good reasons for getting an education, including the ability to appreciate high art and literature. But if all you care about is living in a country that has rising living standards, you should work hard to promote education in the sciences and engineering, sectors where revolutionary technologies are created. (Notice I'm not saying that lots of people should become economists. There's scant evidence that economists can do much more for growth than urge others to become engineers!)

Protecting Intellectual Property Rights Promotes Innovation

People need incentives to encourage them to take risks. One of the biggest risks you can take is to leave a secure job in order to start a new business or work at developing a great new idea. Intellectual property rights, such as patents and copyrights, guarantee that you will be the only one making money off your hard, innovative work. Without this assurance, fewer people would be willing to take the personal risks necessary to provide society with innovative new technologies and products.

Weak Property Rights Cause All Environmental Problems

People always need to do some polluting. After all, even if you don't want gas-guzzling SUVs running around causing lots of pollution, you probably still want ambulances and fire trucks to operate despite the fact that they, too, pollute the environment. The difference is that the overall benefit to society outweighs the cost of the pollution in the case of the emergency vehicles but not in the case of the SUVs.

Seen in this light, society's goal isn't to ban pollution completely, but to make sure that the benefit exceeds the cost for whatever pollution is generated. As I discuss in Chapter 14, strong property rights are key to ensuring that people weigh the complete costs and benefits of pollution. Property rights force people to take into account not only their personal costs of generating pollution, but the costs that their actions impose on others.

For instance, because nobody owns the atmosphere, you don't have to pay anyone for the right to pollute. Polluting the air is, in fact, free — which leads to way too much polluting.

By contrast, I can't just throw my trash anywhere because every bit of land in the world is owned by somebody. If I want to throw my trash on someone's land, I have to either pay that person for permission or risk huge fines (or even jail time) for dumping trash without permission. Also, because I have to pay garbage hauling fees to throw out my trash, I am discouraged from generating wasteful amounts of it.

All environmental problems stem from poorly defined or nonexistent property rights that allow polluters to ignore the costs that they impose on others. Therefore, economists favor the creation and enforcement of property rights systems that force people to take all costs into account.

International Trade Is a Good Thing

Opening your country to international trade means opening your country to new ideas and new innovations. Competition from foreign competitors causes local businesses to innovate to match the best offerings of companies from around the world.

Quite simply, throughout history, the richest and most dynamic societies have been the ones open to international trade. Countries that close themselves off from international trade grow stagnant and are quickly left behind. Of course, what economists have in mind when they think of the benefits of international trade is *free trade,* where companies compete across borders to provide people with the best goods and services at the lowest prices. Economists strongly condemn the many government subsidies and trade restrictions that impede free trade and that try to rig the game in one country's favor.

Free Enterprise Has a Hard Time Providing Public Goods

Private firms can provide goods and services only if they can at least break even doing so. To break even (or make a profit), whatever a firm is selling has to be *excludable,* by which I mean that only those paying for the good or service receive it.

As I explain in Chapter 15, some goods and services are not excludable. For instance, a lighthouse provides warning services to all ships in the vicinity regardless of whether they pay the lighthouse keeper. Because every ship knows that it can get the service without having to pay for it, the private lighthouse quickly goes bankrupt because only a few ships are fair-minded enough to pay for the service.

Goods and services that are not excludable are called *public goods* because they're essentially open to the public and can't be kept private.

Because private firms can't make a profit producing public goods, you typically need governments to provide them. Unlike private firms, governments can force people to pay for public goods. They do this by levying taxes and using the tax revenues to pay for public goods, such as national defense, police departments, lighthouses, public fireworks displays, basic scientific research, and so on.

Economists view the existence of public goods as one of the most important justifications for government intervention in the economy. Although private philanthropy can also provide some public goods, many public goods are so expensive that they can be provided only if the government uses its power of taxation to fund them. Consequently, public goods are typically publicly provided.

Preventing Inflation Is Easy

High rates of inflation are always caused by the government increasing the money supply too rapidly. A growing economy always has a growing demand for money because with more stuff to buy, you need more money with which to buy it. If you want to keep the overall level of prices constant, the correct response is to increase the money supply at the same rate that demand is increasing. If the supply of money increases faster than the demand for money, the value of money falls, creating an inflation. (In other words, it takes more money to buy the same amount of stuff as before, meaning that prices go up.)

The way to prevent an inflation is to make sure that the government increases the money supply at the same rate that the demand for money increases. Modern central banks like the Federal Reserve Bank in the United States can do this quite easily, so there is no excuse for high rates of inflation.

Appendix

Glossary

aggregate demand: The total demand for goods and services in an economy.

aggregate supply: The total supply of goods and services in an economy.

allocatively efficient: A term describing a situation where the limited resources of an economy are allocated to the production of the goods and services that consumers most greatly desire to consume.

antitrust laws: Laws that regulate *monopolies* and *cartels.*

asymmetric information: Situations in which either the buyer or the seller knows more about the quality of the good that they're negotiating over than does the other party.

capital: Machines, factories, and infrastructure used to produce output.

cartel: A group of firms that colludes and acts as a single coordinated whole to restrict output and drive up prices; formerly called trusts.

command economy: An economy in which all economic activity is directed by the government.

comparative advantage: The argument developed by David Ricardo that each country should specialize in the production of the goods and services that it can deliver at lower costs than other countries. Doing so increases total worldwide output and raises living standards.

Consumer Price Index (CPI): The Bureau of Labor Statistics' *market basket* used to measure changes in the prices of goods and services bought by a typical family of four.

consumer surplus: The benefit consumers get when they can buy something for less than the maximum amount that they are willing to pay for it.

deadweight loss: The amount by which *total surplus* is reduced whenever output is less than the *socially optimal output level.*

deflation: When the overall level of prices in the economy is falling.

demand: The whole range of quantities that a person with a given income and preferences will demand at various possible prices.

demand curve: A line on a graph that represents how much of a good or service buyers will consume at various prices.

depreciation: A decrease in the economy's stock of *capital* caused by wear and tear or obsolescence.

diminishing marginal utility: A situation where each additional, or marginal, unit of a good or service that you consume brings less *utility* than the previous unit.

diminishing returns: A situation where each additional amount of a resource used in a production process brings forth successively smaller amounts of output.

economic costs: Total costs, including money spent on production and *opportunity costs.*

economic profits: Any monies collected by a firm above and beyond what is required to keep an entrepreneur owner interested in continuing in business.

economics: The study of how people allocate scarce resources among alternative uses.

externality: A cost or benefit that falls not on the person(s) directly involved in an activity, but on others. Externalities can be positive or negative.

factors of production: Inputs (resources) used to create goods and services, including land, labor, capital, and entrepreneurship.

financial markets: Markets where people either trade the property rights to assets (like real estate or stocks) or where savers lend money to borrowers.

fiscal policy: A government's policy on taxes and spending. Increased government spending and/or lower tax rates help to fight recessions.

fixed costs: Costs that have to be paid even if a firm isn't producing anything.

full-employment output (Y^*): How much output is produced in the economy when there's full employment in the labor market.

gross domestic product (GDP): The value of all goods and services produced in the economy in a given period of time, usually a quarter or a year.

human capital: The knowledge and skills that people use to help them produce output.

hyperinflation: When the inflation rate exceeds 20 or 30 percent per month.

increasing returns: A situation where each additional amount of a resource used in a production process brings forth successively larger amounts of output.

inflation: When the overall level of prices in the economy is rising.

inflation rate: A measure of how the overall level of prices in the economy changes over time. If the inflation rate is positive, prices are rising. If the inflation rate is negative, prices are falling.

interest rate: The price you have to pay to borrow money.

investment: Any increase in the economy's stock of *capital.*

invisible hand: Adam Smith's famous idea that when constrained by competition, each firm's greed causes it to act in a socially optimal way, as if guided to do the right thing by an invisible hand.

Law of Demand: The fact that, for most goods and services, price and quantity demanded have an inverse relationship.

long-run shutdown condition: A situation where a firm's total revenues exceed its *variable costs* but are less than its total costs. The firm will operate until its *fixed cost* contracts expire (in the long run).

macroeconomics: The study of the economy as whole, concentrating on economy-wide factors like interest rates, inflation, and unemployment. It also encompasses the study of economic growth and how governments use monetary and fiscal policy to try to moderate the harm caused by recessions.

marginal cost: How much total costs increase when you produce one more unit of output.

marginal utility: The change in total *utility* that results from consuming the next unit of a good or service. Marginal utility can be positive or negative.

market basket: A bundle of goods and services selected to measure inflation. Economists define a market basket, such as the *Consumer Price Index,* and then track how much money it takes to buy this basket from one period to the next.

market economy: An economy in which almost all economic activity happens in markets, with little or no interference by the government; often referred to as a *laissez faire* ("to leave alone") economic system.

market failures: Situations where markets deliver socially non-optimal outcomes. Two common causes of market failure are *asymmetric information* and *public goods.*

microeconomics: The part of economics that studies individual people and individual businesses. For people, it studies how they behave when faced with decisions about where to spend their money or how to invest their savings. For businesses, it studies how profit-maximizing firms behave individually, as well as when competing against each other in markets.

monetary policy: Using changes in the money supply to change interest rates in order to stimulate or slow down economic activity.

monopolistic competition: A situation in which many firms with slightly different products compete. Production costs are above what could be achieved by perfectly competitive firms, but society benefits from the product differentiation.

monopoly: A firm that has no competitors in its industry. It produces less output, has higher costs, and sells its output for a higher price than it would if constrained by competition. These negative outcomes usually generate government regulation.

natural monopoly: An industry in which one large producer can produce output at a lower cost than many small producers. It undersells its rivals and ends up as the only firm surviving in its industry.

nominal interest rates: Interest rates that measure the returns to a loan in terms of money borrowed and money returned (as opposed to *real interest rates*).

nominal prices: Money prices, which can change over time due to inflation. (See also *real prices.*)

nominal wages: Wages measured in money. (See also *real wages.*)

oligopoly: An industry with only a few firms. If they collude, they form a *cartel* to reduce output and drive up profits the way a *monopoly* does.

opportunity cost: The value of the next best alternative thing you could have done. It measures what you gave up in order to do the best thing.

perfect competition: A situation where numerous small firms producing identical products compete against each other in a given industry. It leads to firms producing the *socially optimal output level* at the minimum possible cost per unit.

price ceiling: A market intervention in which the government ensures that the price of a good or service stays below the free market price.

price floor: A market intervention in which the government keeps the price of a good or service above its free market price.

Prisoner's Dilemma: A situation in which a pair of prisoners (or firms) has to decide whether or not to cooperate. The dilemma is that while the individual incentives favor not cooperating, if both players could figure out a way to cooperate, they'd be better off.

producer surplus: The gain that producers receive when they can sell their output at a price higher than the minimum amount for which they are willing to make it.

Production Possibilities Frontier (PPF): A graph economists use to help them visualize the tradeoffs you make when you efficiently reallocate inputs from producing one thing to producing another; sometimes referred to as the *Production Possibilities Curve.*

productively efficient: A term describing firms that produce goods and services at the lowest possible cost.

public goods: Goods or services that can't be profitably produced by private firms because they are impossible to provide to just one person; if you provide them to one person, you have to provide them to everybody. Because all consumers hope somebody else will pay for public goods so they can get them for free, nobody ends up paying.

quantity demanded: How much of a good or service a consumer will demand at a specific price given his or her income and preferences.

quantity theory of money: The theory that the overall level of prices in the economy is proportional to the quantity of money circulating in the economy.

rational expectations: The theory that people will optimally change their behavior in response to policy changes. Depending on the situation, their behavioral changes can greatly limit the effectiveness of policy changes.

real interest rates: Interest rates that compensate for inflation by measuring the returns to a loan in terms of units of stuff lent and units of stuff returned (as opposed to *nominal interest rates*).

real prices: How much of one kind of thing (such as hours worked) you have to give up to get a good or service, no matter what happens to *nominal prices.*

real wages: Wages measured not in terms of money itself (as *nominal wages* are) but rather in terms of how much output that money can buy.

recessions: Periods of time in a business cycle during which an economy's total output falls.

recoveries: Periods of time in a business cycle during which an economy's total output expands.

scarcity: The fact that we don't have enough resources to satisfy all our wants; the phenomenon that creates the need for *economics.*

short-run shutdown condition: A situation where a firm's total revenues are less than its *variable costs,* and the firm is better off shutting down immediately and losing only its *fixed costs.*

socially optimal output level: The output level that maximizes the benefits that society can get from its limited supply of resources.

sticky prices: Prices that are slow to adjust to shocks. Price stickiness can cause recessions to linger.

supply and demand: An economic model of markets that separates buyers from sellers and then summarizes each group's behavior with a single line on a graph. The buyers' behavior is captured by the *demand curve,* while the sellers' behavior is captured by the *supply curve.* By putting these two curves on the same graph, economists can show how buyers and sellers interact in markets to determine how much of any particular item will be sold, as well as the price at which it will be sold.

supply curve: A line on a graph that represents how much of a good or service sellers will produce at various prices.

total surplus: The sum of *producer surplus* and *consumer surplus*.

Tragedy of the Commons: If a resource is open to public use, it typically becomes rapidly exhausted or ruined because each person's personal incentive is to use it up before anyone else can. This problem is solved by private property rights, which give owners an incentive to conserve the resource and harvest it at sustainable rates.

utility: A measure of happiness that economists suppose people use to compare all possible things that they may experience.

variable costs: Costs that vary with the amount of output produced.

Index

SPORTS, FITNESS, PARENTING, RELIGION & SPIRITUALITY

0-7645-5146-9

0-7645-5418-2

Also available:

- Adoption For Dummies
  0-7645-5488-3
- Basketball For Dummies
  0-7645-5248-1
- The Bible For Dummies
  0-7645-5296-1
- Buddhism For Dummies
  0-7645-5359-3
- Catholicism For Dummies
  0-7645-5391-7
- Hockey For Dummies
  0-7645-5228-7

- Judaism For Dummies
  0-7645-5299-6
- Martial Arts For Dummies
  0-7645-5358-5
- Pilates For Dummies
  0-7645-5397-6
- Religion For Dummies
  0-7645-5264-3
- Teaching Kids to Read For Dummie
  0-7645-4043-2
- Weight Training For Dummies
  0-7645-5168-X
- Yoga For Dummies
  0-7645-5117-5

TRAVEL

0-7645-5438-7

0-7645-5453-0

Also available:

- Alaska For Dummies
  0-7645-1761-9
- Arizona For Dummies
  0-7645-6938-4
- Cancún and the Yucatán For Dummies
  0-7645-2437-2
- Cruise Vacations For Dummies
  0-7645-6941-4
- Europe For Dummies
  0-7645-5456-5
- Ireland For Dummies
  0-7645-5455-7

- Las Vegas For Dummies
  0-7645-5448-4
- London For Dummies
  0-7645-4277-X
- New York City For Dummies
  0-7645-6945-7
- Paris For Dummies
  0-7645-5494-8
- RV Vacations For Dummies
  0-7645-5443-3
- Walt Disney World & Orlando For Dumm
  0-7645-6943-0

GRAPHICS, DESIGN & WEB DEVELOPMENT

0-7645-4345-8

0-7645-5589-8

Also available:

- Adobe Acrobat 6 PDF For Dummies
  0-7645-3760-1
- Building a Web Site For Dummies
  0-7645-7144-3
- Dreamweaver MX 2004 For Dummies
  0-7645-4342-3
- FrontPage 2003 For Dummies
  0-7645-3882-9
- HTML 4 For Dummies
  0-7645-1995-6
- Illustrator CS For Dummies
  0-7645-4084-X

- Macromedia Flash MX 2004 For Dumm
  0-7645-4358-X
- Photoshop 7 All-in-One Desk
  Reference For Dummies
  0-7645-1667-1
- Photoshop CS Timesaving Technique
  For Dummies
  0-7645-6782-9
- PHP 5 For Dummies
  0-7645-4166-8
- PowerPoint 2003 For Dummies
  0-7645-3908-6
- QuarkXPress 6 For Dummies
  0-7645-2593-X

NETWORKING, SECURITY, PROGRAMMING & DATABASES

0-7645-6852-3

0-7645-5784-X

Also available:

- A+ Certification For Dummies
  0-7645-4187-0
- Access 2003 All-in-One Desk
  Reference For Dummies
  0-7645-3988-4
- Beginning Programming For Dummies
  0-7645-4997-9
- C For Dummies
  0-7645-7068-4
- Firewalls For Dummies
  0-7645-4048-3
- Home Networking For Dummies
  0-7645-42796

- Network Security For Dummies
  0-7645-1679-5
- Networking For Dummies
  0-7645-1677-9
- TCP/IP For Dummies
  0-7645-1760-0
- VBA For Dummies
  0-7645-3989-2
- Wireless All In-One Desk Reference
  For Dummies
  0-7645-7496-5
- Wireless Home Networking For Dummi
  0-7645-3910-8

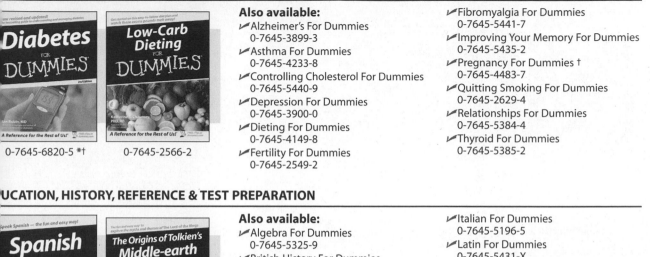

0-7645-6820-5 *†

0-7645-2566-2

Also available:
- Alzheimer's For Dummies
  0-7645-3899-3
- Asthma For Dummies
  0-7645-4233-8
- Controlling Cholesterol For Dummies
  0-7645-5440-9
- Depression For Dummies
  0-7645-3900-0
- Dieting For Dummies
  0-7645-4149-8
- Fertility For Dummies
  0-7645-2549-2

- Fibromyalgia For Dummies
  0-7645-5441-7
- Improving Your Memory For Dummies
  0-7645-5435-2
- Pregnancy For Dummies †
  0-7645-4483-7
- Quitting Smoking For Dummies
  0-7645-2629-4
- Relationships For Dummies
  0-7645-5384-4
- Thyroid For Dummies
  0-7645-5385-2

UCATION, HISTORY, REFERENCE & TEST PREPARATION

0-7645-5194-9

0-7645-4186-2

Also available:
- Algebra For Dummies
  0-7645-5325-9
- British History For Dummies
  0-7645-7021-8
- Calculus For Dummies
  0-7645-2498-4
- English Grammar For Dummies
  0-7645-5322-4
- Forensics For Dummies
  0-7645-5580-4
- The GMAT For Dummies
  0-7645-5251-1
- Inglés Para Dummies
  0-7645-5427-1

- Italian For Dummies
  0-7645-5196-5
- Latin For Dummies
  0-7645-5431-X
- Lewis & Clark For Dummies
  0-7645-2545-X
- Research Papers For Dummies
  0-7645-5426-3
- The SAT I For Dummies
  0-7645-7193-1
- Science Fair Projects For Dummies
  0-7645-5460-3
- U.S. History For Dummies
  0-7645-5249-X

Get smart @ dummies.com®

- **Find a full list of Dummies titles**
- **Look into loads of FREE on-site articles**
- **Sign up for FREE eTips e-mailed to you weekly**
- **See what other products carry the Dummies name**
- **Shop directly from the Dummies bookstore**
- **Enter to win new prizes every month!**